W9-DIZ-298

Crime Statistics in the News

Jairo Lugo-Ocando

Crime Statistics in the News

Journalism, Numbers and Social Deviation

palgrave
macmillan

WLU BRANTFORD CAMPUS
DISCARD

Jairo Lugo-Ocando
School of Media and Communications
University of Leeds
Leeds, United Kingdom

ISBN 978-1-137-39840-6   ISBN 978-1-137-39841-3   (eBook)
DOI 10.1057/978-1-137-39841-3

Library of Congress Control Number: 2017954749

© The Editor(s) (if applicable) and The Author(s) 2017
The author(s) has/have asserted their right(s) to be identified as the author(s) of this work in accordance
with the Copyright, Designs and Patents Act 1988.
This work is subject to copyright. All rights are solely and exclusively licensed by the Publisher, whether
the whole or part of the material is concerned, specifically the rights of translation, reprinting, reuse of
illustrations, recitation, broadcasting, reproduction on microfilms or in any other physical way, and trans-
mission or information storage and retrieval, electronic adaptation, computer software, or by similar or
dissimilar methodology now known or hereafter developed.
The use of general descriptive names, registered names, trademarks, service marks, etc. in this publication
does not imply, even in the absence of a specific statement, that such names are exempt from the relevant
protective laws and regulations and therefore free for general use.
The publisher, the authors and the editors are safe to assume that the advice and information in this book
are believed to be true and accurate at the date of publication. Neither the publisher nor the authors or
the editors give a warranty, express or implied, with respect to the material contained herein or for any
errors or omissions that may have been made. The publisher remains neutral with regard to jurisdictional
claims in published maps and institutional affiliations.

Cover illustration: Getty Images/Jason Stang

Printed on acid-free paper

This Palgrave Macmillan imprint is published by Springer Nature
The registered company is Macmillan Publishers Ltd.
The registered company address is: The Campus, 4 Crinan Street, London, N1 9XW, United Kingdom

DISCARD

In memory of my uncles Lidice Ocando and Aquiles Materan, an extraordinary couple who set me in the intellectual pathway to journalism

Contents

List of Figures

List of Tables

1

Introduction

Back in 1999, in the United Kingdom (UK), the solicitor and mother of two Sally Clark was convicted of murdering her two baby sons. She was initially condemned to serve a life sentence after being found guilty of smothering 11-week-old Christopher in 1996 and shaking eight-week-old Harry to death two years later. Although the conviction was later overturned and she was freed from prison in 2003, after serving several years of the original sentence, the experience caused her to develop serious psychiatric problems and she died in her home in March 2007 from alcohol poisoning.[1] The conviction against her was based mainly on the statistical evidence provided by an "expert" witness used by the Crown Prosecution, Professor Sir Roy Meadow, who argue about the very unlikely statistical chances of two toddlers dying from the same causes. At that time, he suggested that these chances were astronomically small:

> Prof Meadow appeared as an expert witness at the trial, telling the jury the chance of two children in an affluent family suffering cot death was "one in 73 million". He said of the children: "Each death has the characteristic of unnatural causes which is enhanced by the fact that two deaths have occurred at about the same age in one home. The evidence sadly increases the strength with which I feel that the two deaths are not natural."[2]

© The Author(s) 2017
J. Lugo-Ocando, *Crime Statistics in the News*,
DOI 10.1057/978-1-137-39841-3_1

At the time of Sally Clark's initial conviction, the news media headlines regarding her sentence on 27 November 1999 included among others: "Life for killer mother" from newspapers such as *The Daily Mail*. Even less sensational titles such as *The Times* opened with the headline "Life terms for lawyer who killed her babies". Moreover, a few weeks later after being attacked in jail by another inmate, *The Daily Mail* ran a story under the headline "Jail attack on baby-murder mother; Convicted lawyer targeted on first day behind bars".[3] In that piece reporter Adam Powell wrote,

> The attack happened on Clark's first day in the prison where she is awaiting sentence for the murder of baby sons Christopher and Harry. The prisoner who attacked Clark has admitted the assault. Clark, whose husband is convinced of her innocence, was on Tuesday found guilty of murdering her children. She could not cope with her husband's frequent absences from home and the pressures of the babies, despite having a nanny, and became depressed, the trial jury was told. She was also battling a chronic drink problem, it was revealed.

Powell went on to remind readers of her guilt by pointing out the statistical chances of the unlikelihood of her second baby's death being natural:

> She smothered Christopher when he was 11 weeks old in December 1996 and shook eight-week-old Harry to death in January last year at the couple's £250,000 home in Wilmslow, Cheshire. Clark claimed the babies had both been victims of cot death syndrome but experts said the chances of that were 73 million to one.

Although the claim made by the expert witness was disputed at the time by the Royal Statistical Society, which wrote to the Lord Chancellor saying there was "no statistical basis" for that figure, the decision of the jury was upheld and Sally Clark went to jail for a crime she did not commit, condemned by a jury of her peers who largely lacked the numeracy skills to critically assess these claims and vilified by a large segment of the news media whose incompetence led them to believe that statistics were solid "facts". In other words, the jury, the media and a large segment of the public had been convinced by the "improbable" statistical chances of this case not being anything other than a murder.

It was only a second appeal in 2003 that led to reverse the initial decision and award her freedom. The appeal judges said that Professor Roy Meadow's "one in 73 million" figure was "tantamount to saying that without consideration of the rest of the evidence one could be just about sure that this was a case of murder". The court concluded that the figure "grossly overstates the chance of two sudden deaths within the same family from unexplained but natural causes". This second Court of Appeal established that the statistical evidence presented by the Crown Prosecution by means of expert witness was flawed and based on flaky assumptions that many failed to spot and that was only rectified too late when her reputation was tarnished and her life had completely unravelled.

Indeed, on closer examination, some of the mistakes made in this particular case were simply astonishing; all the more so since they were made and not corrected in the full glare of a very public murder trial and subsequent appeal. These were mistakes of the most basic kind, which any person with a limited understanding of probability theory would almost certainly have avoided. One of the main mistakes that emerged was the assumption of independence in the occurrence between the two deaths. According to Professor Roy Meadow, the expert witness for the Crown Prosecution Service, the risk of one Sudden Infant Death Syndrome (SIDS) in a family without any of the three risk factors cited above was 1 in 8543. So, according to him, the probability of two SIDS deaths in a single family without any of these risk factors was simply 1 in 8543 squared, or about 73 million. In other words, just as the probability of throwing a six is 1 in 6, and the probability of throwing a six followed immediately by another six is 1 in 36. In so doing:

> He assumed that the death of Christopher Clark was independent of the death of Harry Clark. However, assuming that the figure of 8543 was correct for one death, it clearly does not follow that 73 million is correct for two deaths. This would only be true if SIDS occurred randomly, without any chance of there being an unknown, hidden cause which might make a particular family more vulnerable to SIDS. Yet, and by its very nature, the

cause (or causes) of SIDS is (or are) unknown. It was simply not possible for anyone to assume that SIDS is caused by random factors, which are wholly independent of one another. Indeed, in a criminal trial, if the prosecution wishes to cite figures of this nature then it must prove—beyond all reasonable doubt—that the two events are entirely independent. This was just not possible in the circumstances. (Scheurer, 2009)

However, as it became more obvious later on, unexplained infant deaths may well have a genetic cause. This means that particular families are more likely to be afflicted by SIDS than the "average" family. Therefore, squaring the probabilities in order to reach the figure of 1 in 73 million was a gross mistake. Nevertheless, once the jury accepted that there was only a 1 in 73 million chance that the deaths occurred due to SIDS, it was a short step for them to conclude that this was the same probability as the probability of any other natural cause of death. In their view, as their verdict showed at the time, this meant a 1 in 73 million chance that she was not guilty of murder. The jury accepted, in other words, that the "innocent" explanation for certain facts is highly improbable, therefore making them deduce that the "guilty" explanation was the correct one (Scheurer, 2009). All in all, Sally Clark was let down by the police, the initial judge, the first Court of Appeal, the jurors and by the last bastion of defence for the innocent, the journalists covering her story, whose lack of understanding of statistical data sealed her personal tragedy.

I want to present this book overall as an apology to her and her family. An apology from all of us, journalists and journalists' educators, who should have known better. We largely failed miserably in our duty to bring accountability and transparency to the delivery of justice and to prevent the innocent from being wrongly accused and sentenced. It is also an apology to the dozens of Sally Clarks out there who never got justice and to the many communities who are often criminalised by the sensational headlines that use crime statistics as a weapon of mass deception (O'Neil, 2016). This book is therefore an admission of guilt to the general public, who for years have been deceived and manipulated thanks to the misunderstanding and/or deliberately misuse of crime statistics. It is, nevertheless, a book that also looks to highlight and recognise the journalists out there who have a clear sense of what statistics are for and who, over the years, have also demonstrated that it is possible to do good reporting using crime statistics. Therefore, it is in addition a piece of gratefulness to the journalists out there who despite all the pressures and all the problems are still strongly committed to bring light to the facts while informing the public.

Where to Begin

So let us start by reminding ourselves that journalistic truth is a process that begins with the professional discipline of assembling and verifying facts (Zelizer, 2004, p. 5). In the case of crime reporting, one of the key elements considered as "facts" are statistics. As problematic as this is, as we will discuss in the book, crime statistics are perceived and treated as "facts" by many journalists on their daily beat. However, as we will also discuss here, these numbers are representations intended to summarise a diversity of phenomenon and which end up underpinning the construction of social reality according to values and ideologies that are prevalent in a particular society. Hence, while statistics claim to convey the "reality" of crime, what they really express is what is consider to be the deviation of a norm in a particular community. For example, 50 years ago, homosexuality was counted still as a crime in the UK, while only 10 years ago people were still being detained and counted as prisoners for smoking marijuana in all of the states of the United States of America (USA). In addition to this, as we will discuss later on the book, the way journalists use statistics reflects not only common approaches but also ideological choices linked to the wider context of journalism as a social practice (Lugo-Ocando & Lawson, 2017).

So, it is important firstly to define what crime statistics are. In this sense, statistics have been described in a variety of ways by researchers and institutions with different backgrounds. For instance, Young and Veldman (1972, p. 2) defined statistics as "a set of techniques for describing groups of data, and for making decisions in the absence of complete information". In addition, as Mallows (2006, p. 322) points out, "statistics concerns the relation of quantitative data to a real-world problem, often in the presence of variability and uncertainty. It attempts to make precise and explicit what the data has to say about the problem of interest". In general, statistics can be understood both as a "quantitative data" (Mallows, 2006, p. 322) or a "set of techniques" (Young & Veldman, 1972, p. 2) that facilitate the understanding of reality, and thus allow effective decision making (Mallows, 2006, p. 322; Young & Veldman, 1972, p. 2).

In this sense, official crime statistics can be understood as based on recorded offences by official law enforcement agencies such as the police and courts. These recording summarise and in part explain the contextual picture on crime. However, it is important to note that some crime statistics are also drawn from criminological research studies and in particular from surveys. Indeed, one method for collecting crime data is based on looking at law enforcement reports, which reflect crimes that are reported, recorded and not subsequently cancelled. The other is based on victimisation statistical surveys, which rely on individual accounts and perceptions. Most experts agree that for crimes such as intentional homicide and armed robbery, reported incidences are generally more reliable. Though, other more frequents crimes such as pickpocketing, assault and even rape tend to suffer from under-recording. Criminal statistics were first produced in France around 1827 and regularly for England and Wales since 1837. Since then crime statistics have become a key source of information that have allowed a more contextualised understanding of individual crimes for policy makers and the media at large.

From Then to Now

From then to now, crime statistics used today have evolved into a series of categories and concepts that help define social deviation in terms that can be operasionalised and that are measurable. By this I mean, that the numbers allow experts to summarise and express the particular conduct of individuals and groups who deviate from particular norms, which are inscribed under the law as expected behaviour. In this sense, statistics allow us to count the number of people and times that this norm or expected behaviour is not complied with. In some cases these are internationally accepted categories such as "homicide"—defined as an unlawful death purposefully inflicted on a person by another person—"assault"—which refers to physical attack against the body of another person resulting in serious bodily injury—and "robbery—defined for the purpose of this article as the theft of property from a person, overcoming resistance by force or threat of force—among many other concepts. It is because of this feature that allows us to both define and measure, that crime statistics are used by journalists to conceptualise, define and measure reality in terms that are—in the view of journalists and news editors/producers—objective and factually based.

All things considered, however, journalists face important challenges when they deal with crime statistics as they are far from being the assumed factual objects. As this book discusses later on, these challenges can be summarised in omission, validity, reliability and interpretation. By omission, we mean the lack of statistics or when we confront the omission of particularly relevant statistics that for one reason or other are not incorporated into the news story. For example, back in 2007 the then US Republican presidential hopeful and former Mayor of New York, Rudy Giuliani, in a visit to London, criticised the record of the National Health Service (NHS) by saying that he would have been less likely to have survived had he been treated in the UK:

> Healthcare right now in America—and I think it has been true of your experience of socialised medicine in England—is not only very expensive, it's increasingly less effective. I had prostate cancer seven years. My chance of survival in the US is 82%; my chance of survival if I was here in England is below 50%. Breast cancer is very similar. I think there's something to the idea that there are many more private options driving the system that create altogether better results. (BBC, 2007)

What the journalists failed to incorporate when reporting Giuliani's visit is the fact that overall prostate cancer in the USA is widely overdiagnosed. In fact, as Cancer Research UK has pointed out, just comparing the USA and the UK, and saying that the bigger number is "better", misses a deeper truth as the USA uses the PSA blood test far more widely than the UK does—despite questions over how effective it is at spotting cancers that would actually kill, as opposed to those that cause no symptoms:

> As a result, the USA has one of the highest recorded rates of prostate cancer in the world. So although it's undoubtedly 'better' at spotting prostate cancers, it's also fair to say that some of these Americans will never die from their disease. This 'overdiagnosis' inflates the survival statistics, at the expense of 'overtreating' men—which is expensive and can cause long-term side effects (which can need further treatment). So you might just as well argue that the '91 per cent' survival figure could be due to a system that overdiagnoses and overtreats prostate cancer, as opposed to saying our 51 per cent stat is due to poor healthcare in the UK. [Moreover] if you look at UK survival rates for early stage prostate cancer, a different picture emerges—men in the UK have a 98.6 per cent five-year survival rate. (Scowcroft, 2009)

In other cases, there are numerous news stories in which journalists suggest or explicitly make assumptions that statistically speaking are baseless. In these cases we are faced with the challenges of "validity" and "reliability" which are two issues that we will pay attention to in this book as they encompass the most important analytical strategies for journalists dealing with crime numbers. On the one hand, statistical validity should be interpreted as accuracy in the realm of journalism as it deals with the relevance of the statistics in relation to what the news story wants to convey. On the other, statistical "reliability" also needs to be translated into journalism jargon, but in this case in terms of "rigour" as it looks at the procedure used to reach that number and the level of confidence that we should have that is a solid and sound summary of the phenomenon in question. In this sense, Maier (2005) suggests that there is a lack of compatibility in terms of media focused on methodological inconsistencies and attendant problems of validity and reliability in accuracy research. Overall, his work has pointed out serious problems of accuracy in the news media in general, and not only in relation to the use of crime statistics. Finally, the next challenge is that of interpretation of the numbers beyond what official accounts make of them. This is an aspect that we also emphasis here and which of course raises important issues and dilemmas. Some of them arise because of the lack of knowledge and skills of journalists to carry out these interpretation (Nguyen & Lugo-Ocando, 2015) and others are the result of the pressures generated by declining resources in the newsroom and the increasing role of "spin" and public relations (PR) in filling the information deficit. The message is clear: journalists need far more capabilities in order to perform critical thinking around crime statistics.

Other important challenges worth highlighting come from the way in which journalists think with regard to statistics. In this sense, John Allen Paulos (2013 [1995]) highlights two kind of side-effects in relation to how we tend to deal with statistics. One is the "halo effect" and the other is what he refers to the "anchoring effect". These effects relate to the availability error, which is the tendency for people to make judgements or evaluations in light of the first thing that comes to mind. In other words, when people seek information related to one theory, they are resistant to seeking information with respect to another theory at the same time. Because of this, people test theories one at time, or sequentially. Secondly, as people seek information with which to test their theories, they tend to use a theory-confirming strategy, something that Thomas Kuhn also observed in natural science (Kuhn & Hawkins, 1963; Kunh, 1962). For instance, a reporter who has theorised that there is a crime wave against the elderly may unconsciously seek out sources that confirm this theory; the potential and actual elderly victims in a bad part of town, the head of a crime prevention programme for the elderly, etc. In addition, the reporter may ask questions of these sources (about increases in reported crimes, efforts to reduce crimes, etc.) that tend to confirm the pre-conceived theory, without asking probing questions that might disprove the hypothesis (Stocking & Gross, 1989a, 1989b). The idea that journalists go to the scene of the news with a completely open and natural mind is baseless and naïve as most studies in news gathering have demonstrated over the years.

Beyond Statistics

Consequently, any examination of the way crime statistics are reported in the news media needs to happen in the context of wider conceptual debates around the role of journalism in relation to the "construction of social reality" (Berger & Luckmann, 1991; Searle, 1995). This is, in my view, the only way in which we can offer a useful explanatory theoretical framework of the subject approached. It is also the only manner in which we can make this discussion relevant for journalists reporting these issues and the society at large. By doing that, we can then start to understand why it is so important to examine the role of statistics in the reporting of crime and assess the real impact of these numbers on the way the public sees law and order, and subsequently on the way political leaders and policy makers react to their presence in the media.

This is increasingly important as statistics in general are prominently featured in most major newspapers on a daily or weekly basis, yet most citizens, and even many reporters, do not have the knowledge required to read them critically (Utts, 2003, p. 74). The result is that the public is often ill informed and the democratic participation of the citizenry in the process of policy making is subject to flawed public reasoning.

In the case of crime reporting, furthermore, the coverage of statistics seemed to have promoted, in particular circumstances, the fear of crime (Schlesinger & Tumber, 1994) therefore creating a state of moral panic that pushes the public and elected leaders into decisions that are unsound at best. Crime statistics are in fact often misused and abused by those setting the political agenda to mobilise the public towards a particular position, as we saw in the 2016 US election when the then presidential candidate, Donald Trump, misrepresented crime statistics to gain advantage over his rival Hillary Clinton by trashing President Barak Obama's record on crime. In other places, such as the UK and Australia, crime statistics referring to immigration and violent crime are commonly misused to create moral panic, something that we will discuss later on this book. Needless to say, however, that the issue of managing and using crime statistics in the news became so concerning that in 2006 it was brought to public attention by the then UK Statistics Commission, which made a national call to improve the use of statistics by the media and politicians. This translated into the creation of the UK National Statistics Authority, which—as we will discuss later—has had a very positive impact in the UK.

However, this is not only an institutional problem, it is also an individual one. In truth, journalists who learn to read statistics and are able to establish their importance, validity and reliability are at a significant advantage to those who cannot, particularly in relation to producing "quality" stories (Martinisi, 2017). These journalists recognise that many stories have statistical elements and that if incorporated and interpreted skilfully, statistics can bring about the best stories possible. This was certainly the case for Mark Fazlollah, Craig R. McCoy, Michael Matza and Clea Benson, when they presented an investigative series for *The Philadelphia Inquirer* in the USA revealing how the police department of that city had routinely minimised sexual assault claims, many of which had not been investigated. Analysing statistical evidence from previous years, the reporters were able to detect inconsistencies in the number of rapes recorded by Philadelphia police (Brockway & Beshkin, 2000).

Following the publication of the series, the then Police Commissioner John F. Timoney not only acknowledged that the police rape squad had manipulated the data but also had to recognise that they had done so "for years and years". In doing so, the police was able to keep some sexual assault cases out of the city's crime statistics, which meant in practice that they curtailed proper police investigations. The series led to a reform in the mode of crime reporting and their work was shortlisted for the Pulitzer Prize in the year 2000. This ground breaking story was produced mainly thanks to a team of journalists who were keen to work with numbers and able to draw from them the implications in the figures that other reporters who also had equal access to these numbers did not.

Other examples of how statistics can help define social trends and contextualise individual stories include that of Brad Knickerbocker from *The Christian Science Monitor* who on 29 April 1999 published a piece titled "Young and male in America: It's hard being a boy". In this work, Knickerbocker wrote about how boys in the USA tend to be more prone to drop out of school and are four times more likely to commit suicide than girls. He also highlighted that they get into twice as many fights as girls and, by adulthood, tend to murder 10 times more frequently while also being 15 times more likely to become the victim of a crime. Knickerbocker went on to underline that boys were less likely than girls to go to college, because they haven't done as well in high school and are labelled "slow learners". What the journalist did in this case was not only to describe the distribution of a series of data, including what he thought were the most significant frequencies, but also use this data to contextualise and highlight a broader issue in society, turning a personal tragedy into a political issue that needed to be widely debated.

Despite the prevalence of many stories like these and other similar ones, there are few scholarly works that examine the gathering and dissemination of crime statistics by journalists in the wider media (Feilzer, 2007, p. 290) and the potential that the practice of using crime statistics has in providing genuine public service journalism. Let us contrast this with, for example, the research that has been carried out on the use of statistics in health reporting, which is by far more prolific in academic research (Dentzer, 2009; Gigerenzer, Gaissmaier, Kurz-Milcke, Schwartz, & Woloshin, 2007). Instead, there is still a shortage of systematic and comprehensive scholarly works on the use of crime statistics by journalists and this is precisely one of the gaps that this book intends to highlight. This book does not, however, aspire to fill that gap. This is a task that will need additional years of research and work. What it does, nevertheless, is to try to bring into the discussion a series of works that have looked at these issues while promoting a necessary debate around the relationship between journalism and crime statistics.

To deliver this objective, the book has been structured around thematic chapters. Each one of these chapters reflects a particular subject that I thought it was important to address. In Chap. 2 we explore and examine crime reporting and provide a framework for what the rest of the book will be discussing. This chapter deals with issues such as how news cultures have defined the discourses and narratives that emanate from the news media when covering crime. It is a more general chapter that gives the reader a general background and context in relation to crime reporting. Chapter 3 provides a historical account of how crime statistics became part of the daily news by looking at archives and the evolution of the news reporting of crime statistics. In so doing, it examines the history of crime statistics in the news and explains how these numbers were pivotal in the changing landscape of modern crime reporting. Chapter 4 then discusses how the news media frames crime statistics and how this framing consequently defines the media representations of overall crime. Chapter 5, which I co-wrote with Renata Faria Brandão, at King's College London, looks specifically at the way knife crime statistics are reported, based on a particular case study, in order to highlight some of the fundamental issues raised in this book. In this chapter we look at knife crime as it is one that has had a major effect on public perceptions of crime in the UK. Chapter 6 assesses the relationship between the news reporting of crime statistics and the way this feeds and affects public policy. Chapter 7 discusses the ethical and moral dilemmas that journalists face in reporting crime statistics, particularly in relation to the increasing presence of spin and PR influence upon the newsrooms. In so doing it explores the ethical and moral dilemmas that journalists confront due to the corporate nature that crime reporting has acquired over the years. This not only means the introduction of private companies to outsource tasks traditionally carried out by the state but also, fundamentally, how the increasing corporate character of the professional communications of the police enforcement bodies themselves have affected the way crime statistics are reported to the public. Chapter 8 examines the visualisation of statistics in the context of crime reporting. It does so by asking how this process of visualisation has contributed towards a better public understanding of data. In so doing, the chapter then discusses issues around the visualisation of data in relation to the initial promises regarding accessibility and the original claims that somehow it would bring greater participatory and interactive capabilities to both journalists and the general public. Chapter 9 addresses the very important issue of audiences and how the reporting of crime statistics affects public perceptions around crime. Although the relationship between news audiences and crime statistics goes beyond this book, as it would certainly need a whole monograph of its own, I felt it was important to include a preliminary discussion as to where a research agenda on this topic might go. Finally, in the conclusion (Chap. 10) I have attempted to offer more than a critical summary of the book. Instead, I have tried to offer a space for future dialogues that can bring about better practices from both journalists and those who implement public policy.

Big Thanks

As with any book like this one, it is never totally an individual effort. Therefore, I want to thank some particular friends and colleagues who gave me ideas and inspiration when preparing the original manuscript. Firstly, I want to thank An Nguyen at Bournemouth University and Eddy Borges Rey at the University of Stirling for their criticism, guidance and support which have proven to be invaluable over the years. Our joint collaboration, which now expands over a decade, has been exceptionally productive and intellectually enriching. Moreover, I should highlight that despite all the pressures and all the tensions that collaborative scholarly work entails, they remain very close and dear friends; which is lot to say in the academic world. Secondly, I also want to thank current and former Ph.D. researchers whom I have had the privilege to work with in the past few years in this particular area of statistics and journalism. They are Renata Faria Brandão, Alessandro Martinisi, Fisal Alaqil, Abdullah Alhuntushi and Brendan Lawson who all came into this subject accepting the challenges posed by an under-researched area. They are pioneers and will hopefully greatly help improve journalism education and research in this area. Thirdly, I want to thank Professor Tim Hope at the University of Salford whose own work on how crime statistics have been misused has been so inspirational for all of us and with whom I had some initial conversations that encouraged me to go into this topic. To my colleagues and friends at the School of Media and Communication at the University of Leeds I owe a lot, particularly for offering such a stimulating environment to work in. In addition, I am deeply grateful to Palgrave for their patience and support without which this book would not have seen the light of day. Finally, I would want to thank my former colleagues José (Cheo) Nava and Gustavo Bauer Griman who during my journalistic career became mentors and close friends when we cover the crime beat together. They are two of the most exceptional and talented photojournalists who over the years reported crime in my hometown city of Maracaibo. From the three of us, however, only Cheo has managed to stomach for over three decades enough resilience to continue in a country where violence is such a daily occurrence. During all that time, he has treated crime with respect so, as he says, 'never allow death to have the last word'. I learnt from them that each victim and each perpetrator is a human being, with a family, a past and sometimes even a future. Through their lenses, they always saw—and showed me and to the rest of the world—that people are people not just numbers. It is in their images, paradoxically, that I found the inspiration to write about numbers and crime.

Notes

1. Shaikh, Thair (2007). Sally Clark, mother wrongly convicted of killing her sons, found dead at home. *The Guardian*. https://www.theguardian. com/society/2007/mar/17/childrensservices.uknews [Accessed on 20 March 2016].
2. Misery of four mothers who faced "expert" professor. *The Daily Mail*. http://www.dailymail.co.uk/news/article-355939/Misery-mothers-faced-expert-professor.html#ixzz4bJXnwL5m [Accessed on 10 January 2017].
3. Powell, Adam (12 November 1999). Jail attack on baby-murder mother; Convicted lawyer targeted on first day behind bars. *The Daily Mail*. Page 5.

References

BBC. (2007). Giuliani's warning over UK's NHS. Retrieved March 2, 2017, from http://news.bbc.co.uk/1/hi/uk_politics/7003286.stm

Berger, P. L., & Luckmann, T. (1991). *The social construction of reality: A treatise in the sociology of knowledge*. London: Penguin.

Brockway, K., & Beshkin, A. (2000). Winners of Pulitzer prizes in journalism, letters, drama and music, announced April 10th at the journalism school. Retrieved February 2, 2017, from http://www.columbia.edu/cu/news/00/04/pulitzer/pulitzer.html

Dentzer, S. (2009). Communicating medical news—Pitfalls of health care journalism. *New England Journal of Medicine, 360*(1), 1–3.

Feilzer, M. (2007). Criminologists making news? Providing factual information on crime and criminal justice through a weekly newspaper column. *Crime, Media, Culture, 3*(3), 285–304.

Gigerenzer, G., Gaissmaier, W., Kurz-Milcke, E., Schwartz, L. M., & Woloshin, S. (2007). Helping doctors and patients make sense of health statistics. *Psychological Science in the Public Interest, 8*(2), 53–96.

Kuhn, T. S., & Hawkins, D. (1963). The structure of scientific revolutions. *American Journal of Physics, 31*(7), 554–555.

Kunh, T. (1962). *The structure of scientific revolutions*. Chicago: The University of Chicago Press.

Lugo-Ocando, J., & Lawson, B. (2017). Poor numbers, poor news: The ideology of poverty statistics in the media. In A. Nguyen (Ed.), *News, numbers and public opinion in a data-driven world*. London: Bloomsbury.

Maier, S. R. (2005). Accuracy matters: A cross-market assessment of newspaper error and credibility. *Journalism & Mass Communication Quarterly, 82*(3), 533–551.

Mallows, C. (2006). Tukey's paper after 40 years. *Technometrics, 48*(3), 319–325.

Martinisi, A. (2017). Understanding quality of statistics in news stories: A theoretical approach from the audience's perspective. In *Handbook of research on driving STEM learning with educational technologies* (pp. 485–505). Hershey, PA: IGI Global.

Nguyen, A., & Lugo-Ocando, J. (2015). Introduction: The state of statistics in journalism and journalism education—Issues and debates. *Journalism, 17*(1), 3–17.

O'Neil, C. (2016). *Weapons of math destruction. How big data increases inequality and threatens democracy*. New York: Crown.

Paulos, J. A. (2013 [1995]). *A mathematician reads the newspaper*. New York: Basic Books.

Scheurer, V. (2009). Convicted on statistics? Retrieved March 2, 2017, from https://understandinguncertainty.org/node/545#notes

Schlesinger, P., & Tumber, H. (1994). *Reporting crime. The media politics of criminal justice*. Oxford: Oxford University Press.

Scowcroft, H. (2009). We need to be careful when comparing US and UK cancer care. Retrieved March 21, 2017, from http://scienceblog.cancerresearchuk.org/2009/08/17/we-need-to-be-careful-when-comparing-us-and-uk-cancer-care/

Searle, J. R. (1995). *The construction of social reality*. New York: Simon and Schuster.

Stocking, S. H., & Gross, P. H. (1989a). *How do journalists think? A proposal for the study of cognitive bias in newsmaking*. Bloomington: ERIC Clearinghouse on Reading and Communication Skills, Smith Research Center, Indiana University.

Stocking, S. H., & Gross, P. H. (1989b). Understanding errors, biases that can affect journalists. *The Journalism Educator, 44*(1), 4–11.

Utts, J. (2003). What educated citizens should know about statistics and probability. *The American Statistician, 57*(2), 74–79.

Young, R. K., & Veldman, D. J. (1972). *Introductory statistics for the behavioral sciences* (2nd ed.). New York: Holt, Rinehart, Winston.

Zelizer, B. (2004). *Taking journalism seriously: News and the academy*. London: Sage.

2

Crime in the News

Despite the fact that since the post-war era the amount of crime news published and broadcasted has been rising constantly along with some significant changes (Reiner, Livingstone, & Allen, 2003, p. 17), crime reporting itself is no longer what it used to be. Gruesome pictures of horrible crimes in the front pages, which in the past sold hundreds of thousands if not millions of copies of newspapers are nowadays no longer morally tolerated by news people or the general public in most countries in the West. Neither is criminal life presented in the same manner, such as the way that the news media used to romanticise gangsters' lives and acts in the past (Davies, 2007; Fields, 2004). Today, crime reporting is more pragmatic and based more on a combination of mathematical skills, looking at the big picture by means of statistics and storytelling in which victims, more than perpetrators, tend to receive the attention of the reporters' work. This is mainly as a result of a shift of writing style from feature reporting to more hard news and beat reportage when it comes to crime. In our content analysis of four newspapers in England, *The Guardian*, *The Times*, *The Daily Mail* and *The Mirror*, we found that between 2013 and 2015 most crime stories with statistical content were written in hard news style, with more than 70% of the news stories being

© The Author(s) 2017
J. Lugo-Ocando, *Crime Statistics in the News*,
DOI 10.1057/978-1-137-39841-3_2

written in that journalistic genre (Lugo-Ocando & Faria Brandão, 2015). These changes in the news coverage of crime can also be observed in the quantity of coverage this news beat has received. We found that only 10% of the total amount of articles with statistical content in the four newspapers in the three year period falls into the categories of Crime, Law Enforcement and Corrections, with *The Guardian* at the top of the list with slightly more than 12% and *The Daily Mail* at the bottom, with less than 8%. Overall, there is evidence to suggest that in today's crime reporting the fundamental journalism genre used is that of hard news but that nevertheless this is overall far less predominant than in previous decades.

From a historical perspective, the largest and most consequential of the media's crime sprees occurred after the 1960s, triggered by some very high profile cases. In the United States of America (USA), for example, these running stories spawned a larger issue that refers to the breakdown of law and order. Gang fights, drugs busts, and other manifestations of a disorderly and dangerous society filled the headlines. This 1960s spree did not go with the end of the decade and in fact many big crime stories took place after that. Take the example of the Yorkshire Ripper. This case has been considered the biggest story of all time in twentieth century England (Hollway, 1981; Soothill, Peelo, Pearson, & Francis, 2004). For years after the case came to the spotlight in 1975, it has occupied the first pages of local and national newspapers and bewitched the public's attention even after it was solved in 1981.

Then during the eighties news reporting on crime declined, but later crime news tripled in the 1992–1994 period, overshadowing every other issue in the news (Patterson, 2013, p. 22). During the 1990s, law and order became not only a central issue of the news agenda but it also became closely associated with central ideas such as those of moral panics, anti-immigration and what was perceived to be the "breakdown" of society. After that period, in places such as the UK and the USA, crime reporting became closely associated with attacks against more liberal governments—Tony Blair's and Bill Clinton's—which then had to responded by showing themselves as "tough on crime" (Beckett, 1999; Greer & McLaughlin, 2011; Marion, 1997).

Although since the 1990s crime reporting has changed overall (Reiner et al., 2003) and in some ways was subdued, it nevertheless continues to be one of the most influential journalistic beats (Romer, Jamieson, & Aday, 2003, p. 88). This is because despite important societal changes, crime reporting remains one of the few areas, together with sports and celebrities, which is still able to attract the attention of large segments of the audiences (Wood, 2016, p. 310). As a news beat, crime reporting still allows mainstream traditional media to increase ratings and sales in a declining and increasingly fragmented media market. Consequently, crime reporting's position in accessing large audiences is still very relevant as it permits news people to reach the largest segments of the public and appeal to them in ways in which other news beats do not (Weitzer & Kubrin, 2004). This need to draw audiences while reporting sensitive issues in society highlights the very important tensions and dilemmas between aspirational and normative principles associated with news values and the empirical reality of having to compete in the marketplace in order to access commodified audiences.

This dichotomy between informing the public and storytelling, as we discuss here, is a central issue in this book. Indeed, many professional journalists claim that crime reporting is there to "inform" the public about deviance as a social issue, as in the case of the Yorkshire Ripper, and to question public policy in relation to policing, justice and security in general (Neavling, 2014). Those journalists who practise crime reporting tend to perceive themselves as inquirers of truth in the name of justice (Cavender & Miller, 2013; Ettema & Glasser, 1998; Schlesinger, Tumber, & Murdock, 1991) they assume that their work is pivotal in helping to set or have an impact upon public policy (Harper, 2014; Mawby, 2014).

Their role brings accountability to the public's concerns regarding personal security and transparency to the intervention of the state as the legitimate actor upon which the rest of society has placed the responsibility to monopolise, administrate and use, when necessary, violence and justice in order to safeguard law and order (Chan & Chan, 2012; Connolly, 2014). On the other hand, crime reporting is very efficient at increasing the size of media audiences (Lipschultz & Hilt, 2014; Romer et al., 2003). In this sense, Rod McKenzie (2008), former editor and a presenter of BBC's *Newsbeat*, made an important point when he said that:

> Like it or not—viewers and listeners are interested in crime stories. They may make them worry—they may appeal to the heart—or they may make them wonder if the authorities could do more to halt the perceived march of knife crime. There's nothing new about crime interest and viewers, listeners and readers—it's an even older phenomenon than Jack the Ripper, after all. So why do news organisations—especially those who are audience driven or influenced—give such prominence to crime, when as authorities point out, violent crime is falling—and you are very unlikely to be a victim? (…) Is the audience interested in the story in the first place? Our evidence is that they are—and that whatever we say—they are very worried about violent crime.

In countries such as Canada, to give an example, crime stories constitute the fourth largest category of stories for newspapers and television after sports, general interest and business, which is an over-representation of the actual amount of crime occurring in that society (Landau, 2014, p. 20). There are some indications that these numbers are similar across the Western world, where there is a constant appetite for crime stories. In the United Kingdom (UK), "murder as entertainment" is deeply rooted in the history of the country and it is no surprise that readers' appetites for it do not decrease. Generally speaking, this could be explained by inner psychological implications that define us as human beings. According to Harold Schechter (2003) the appetite for tales of real-life murder, the more horrific the better, has been a permanent feature of human society.

In most cases, the media is most likely to focus on stories that highlight the sensational nature of certain crimes. For example, homicides committed by young offenders are often front page news and may cause people to believe that youth violence is at significant levels, despite being incredibly rare nowadays. The reason why these stories are so newsworthy however is precisely because they are so rare and therefore shocking to the audiences. They are unique and because of that, they tend to dominate headlines for days and weeks, thereby giving the public a distorted view of how frequent these crimes actually are (CRCVC, 2015).

This way of highlighting the sensational also draws the attention of large sections of the audiences. As mentioned above, crime reporting is also about entertainment and storytelling (Jewkes, 2004, p. 41). Scholars such as Daya Kishan Thussu (2008) have called this "infotainment" while others refer to the "tabloidization" of news (Esser, 1999; McLachlan & Golding, 2000; Winston, 2002). In any case, the distinction between "hard" (current affairs, societal issues, etc.) and "soft" (sports, celebrity stories, etc.) news has blurred over the past decades (Reinemann, Stanyer, Scherr, & Legnante, 2012, p. 221). In this regard, crime news is nowadays perhaps far less gruesome that it was in the past, but in terms of narrative it is undeniably storytelling as ever.

These are, in fact, the two very distinctive functions of crime reporting. Both reflecting the dichotomy between what journalism aspires to be and what it actually does, particularly in the sphere of mainstream journalism. As a consequence, crime reporting aspires to be an "interpretative community" of individuals (Berkowitz & TerKeurst, 1999; Zelizer, 1993a) whose work brings about social justice thanks to their ability to deliver accountability and force transparency onto power by means of scrutinising public policy. As the former editor of *The Times*, Harold Evans (2013), wrote a few years ago:

> Every editor is duty-bound to scrutinise the use of power—responsibly but fearlessly—however personally unappealing a leaker may be. Conflict between the conceptions of duty is inevitable, indeed healthy. Reporting often exposes an ill that government has not recognised or been willing to acknowledge. The state is not omniscient. Nor is it unknown for government to conceal its own mistakes.

This "Watchdog" aspiration is a core value of the journalistic profession, at least in most Western countries. It encompasses the explicitly articulated ethical view that journalism is there to serve as a "Fourth Estate" (Hampton, 2010; Schultz, 1998); one that has the moral responsibility of overseeing and guaranteeing accountability to the actions of those at the top of the political pyramid by providing citizens with the necessary information to make sound political decisions as a whole.

On the other side of the coin is that mainstream journalism continues to be a commercial enterprise still largely based on a political economy model that demands increasing audiences. As such, it provides news, information and entertainment in order to capture our attention. This prevalent model demands turning audiences into commodities, which later can be exchanged in the marketplace for money, power or both (Boyd-Barrett, 1995; Napoli, 2011). This is the very case of those journalists who operate within traditional commercial mainstream media outlets as well as of those working for public services broadcasters. This logic of commodification of audiences for political or market purposes remains the cornerstone of the current model of news production despite its current crisis and the important changes taking place across the industry (Doyle, 2013; Napoli, 2012).

This dichotomy between ethical commitments towards public services and commercial purposes and prerogatives, as well as aspirational principles and empirical reality, results in tensions that stem from occupational practices and indeed cognitive dynamics. The result is a kind of tension that happens between the deontological aspirations of journalists and the backdrop of their collective behaviour within the mainstream news organisations and news cultures. Consequently, in most news pieces about crime, one can observe the struggle between reporters trying to provide a factual account of the crime together with an accurate picture of law and order against the constant emphasis on storytelling that the commercial pressures place upon them. This struggle is stretched to the degree of altering, on occasions, the meaning in order to appease commercial imperatives; something that is evermore present given declining revenues, audience fragmentation and competition from other media outlets (Davies, 2008; Underwood, 1993).

Therefore, in order to explain why crime statistics are used in the news media in the way they are, we need to understand first this dichotomy between the deontological aspirations and the practical prerogatives set by the political economy of the media. This means contextualising crime statistics within the news in the wider context of media discourses and, more specifically, locating it within the context of the tensions between normative claims of public policy accountability, often referred to as the Fourth Estate, and the need to use crime reporting to create commodities able to sustain the political economy of the media industry that produces these stories.

Over the years, there has been an extensive and comprehensive amount of literature regarding the way news media represents crimes (Chibnall, 1977; Ericson, Baranek, & Chan, 1987; Hall, 1975; Sparks, 1992) and how crime is constructed in the journalistic narratives as a news item (Schlesinger & Tumber, 1994; Schlesinger et al., 1991). Most of this literature tends to underline the tensions mentioned above, while specifically exploring issues like the mediatisation of crime and moral panics among others. This includes elements such as the different dynamics that take place in the newsroom, the prevalent news and organisational cultures that define the work, the output of journalists and the political economy and technological elements underpinning the news media landscape as a whole.

By examining some of the key scholarly works in this field, it is possible to provide a critical and lucid overview. To do so, we need to discuss issues such as crime reporting and media representations of crime, among other important issues that academic scholars have addressed in the past. Therefore, the aim is to examine key ideas and theories regarding the reporting of crime and the use of statistics which will include concepts such as Mediatisation of Crime, Moral Panics, Media Securitisation and Agenda Setting, among others; all of which will be examined in details in the context of a wider discussion about crime reporting, politics and democracy.

Accordingly, this chapter aims to introduce the reader to the most relevant aspects of journalism and media studies theory regarding crime reporting. It proposes doing this by looking at what past and recent research says about how journalists and news editors gather, produce and disseminate crime news and the numerical figures. Moreover, this chapter will try to highlight how journalism, as profession practised in the mainstream media, relates to crime in the workflow management of news to stimulate the public imagination and, lastly, to cast some light on the role of crime news in the construction of social reality.

Crime News

To start with, it is important to highlight that crime reporting tends to be practised within the context of very specific news cultures (Curran, Salovaara-Moring, Coen, & Iyengar, 2010; Dowler, Fleming, & Muzzatti, 2006). Hence, it follows similar procedures and practices to those in other news beats while broadly adhering to similar organisational dynamics and professional imperatives. In this respect, accuracy and rigour are both normative and ethical values widely accepted and embraced by journalists. However, these values are often in sharp tension against the need to produce storytelling entertainment. Over the years, far from easing, these tensions have become instead ever-more present in a time of digital, interactive and mobile technology and increasing audience fragmentation. The need to commodify publics in a time of fragmented audiences has underpinned these tensions between commercialisation and public service in a manners that has re-shaped the way content is presented and delivered.

However, while crime reporters do compete against each other they also collaborate in order to get the next great story that will attract the attention of large segments of the public. All this, while attempting to perform what they consider to be a public service: that is to report facts and information from which individuals and communities can make sound decisions in tune with the rules of a democracy. In fact, crime reporting is not only about scoops—getting the news story that no one else has—but it is also about routines and dealing with daily reporting where journalists covering the crime news beat have to make the ordinary appear as extraordinary on slow days—those days when there are not many news stories. Because of this, and due to decreasing resources in the newsroom, they have become particularly dependent upon public relations (PR) to fill the content gap left by the downsizing of newsrooms (Davies, 2008; Lewis, Williams, & Franklin, 2008). In the context of crime reporting, these cuts create a situation in which the relationship between the police and journalists continues to be asymmetric in favour of the police (Mawby, 2010, p. 124), which has at its disposal a large amount of resources and access to the expertise of armies of professional communication practitioners which include former journalists and PR people.

Nowadays crime and justice as news beats are starved of resources and many national and local newspapers and broadcast stations have stop sending their reporters to court altogether. For example, many newspapers and local broadcasters have reduced or stopped completely the coverage of local courts and their beat is now reduced to asking the local police for an update (Davies, 2008; Davis & Taras, 2017) or the local court clerk for the transcripts. This follows a more general trend where:

> Journalists are relying less on their readers for news, and that stories of little consequence are being elevated to significant positions, or are filling news pages at the expense of more important stories. Additionally, the reliance on a single source means that alternative views and perspectives relevant to the readership are being overlooked. Journalists are becoming more passive, mere processors of one-sided information or bland copy dictated by sources. These trends indicate poor journalistic standards and may be exacerbating declining local newspaper sales. (O'Neill & O'Connor, 2008, p. 487)

In the case of reporting local courts, not only are there are less journalists attending hearings and spending enough time on specific court cases that merit a second look, but whole areas such as follow-up court reporting and sentencing have disappeared from the news beat in many media outlets. The end result is a type of journalism that is even more dependent upon what press bulletins from the authorities state.

Mediatisation of Crime

This increasing dependency upon PR is taking place at the same time as political institutions and leaders have become even more adapted to the media's dynamics and logic. Some scholars have called this the process of mediatisation of politics (Hjarvard, 2013; Schulz, 2004; Strömbäck, 2008). It is a concept that describes the complex linkages between media and political institutions in a context of increasing media influence in politics. By this, these authors mean how political institutions are adapting their processes and dynamics to those of the media; i.e.

adapting to the news cycle and re-configuring their own organisations to meet the needs of the media. In so doing, the interaction with the media ends up shaping and framing the processes of political communication between the organisations and institutions and society. This process is not only constrained to Western democracies but has also happened in illiberal and authoritarian systems, in which governments have also adapted to the media's logic (Cottle, 2006; Jinfeng, 1997; Motschall & Cao, 2002).

Law enforcement agencies and courts worldwide are no exception to this process. Not surprisingly, the mediatisation of the police enforcement agencies' relations with the public occurred almost in parallel with the increase in crime reporting in the 1960s and the increasing acceptance of political correctness among wider society. Indeed, as some scholars have already observed, by the early 1960s there was a profound shift in power as a consequence of the increasing role played by political reporters in Washington DC (Cater, 1964; Cornwell, 1965). This shift, they claimed, went to the heart of policy formulation, turning the news media into "the facto quasi-official fourth branch of government" (Cater, 1964, p. 11). The mediatization of politics, a "process whereby a political system to a high degree is influenced by and adjusted to the demands of the mass media in their coverage of politics" (Asp, 1986, p. 359), extended to most areas of society. Stig Hjarvard explains this in more detail, when he points out that:

> By the mediatization of culture and society we understand the process whereby culture and society to an increasing degree become dependent on the media and their logic. This process is characterized by a duality, in that the media have become integrated into the operations of other social institutions and cultural spheres, while also acquiring the status of social institutions in their own right. (Hjarvard, 2013, p. 17)

This "mechanism of institutionalisation of media logic in other societal subsystems" (Schrott, 2009, p. 42) was concurrent with modernity (Thompson, 1995). It meant that those in power not only constantly sought public support and legitimation (Esser, 2013; Marcinkowski &

Steiner, 2014) but also used the media to pursue governance (Crozier, 2007; Strömbäck & Esser, 2014; Thompson, 1995).

In the case of the police as a societal institution, this meant embracing areas such as PR, marketing communication and political communication as professional disciplines (Mawby, 2014; Mawby & Worthington, 2002; Motschall & Cao, 2002). Today, in countries such as Australia, the UK and the USA it is almost inconceivable to have a police department big or small without at least a press officer attached to it. This is because, over the years, the relationship with the media in general and journalists in particular have become increasingly "bureaucratised" around the media's logic. Consequently, police routines and dynamics have, over the years, adapted to the media's own routines and dynamics, something that would have been unthinkable a few decades ago.

This process, as one might expect, has also included the reporting of crime statistics, which has become ever more important in the process of constructing "social reality" (Quinney, 1970; Searle, 1995). Indeed, the process of gathering, producing and presenting crime statistics is heavily determined by the mediatisation of law and order. In this context, the reporting of crime statistics has become the quintessential element that allows law enforcement agencies not only to communicate with the public but also to mobilise that same public against crime or in favour of more allocation of resources towards policing by creating pressure on governments.

In this context, and given their association with justice and therefore the need to present themselves as impartial, the use of crime numbers allows the authorities to articulate reality according to specific political narratives. As a result, increases and decreases of figures in crime statistics either convey a message of success or failure, or shape perceptions around the so-called "social fear" and the exercise of power that are often interrelated. This is one of the fundamental reasons why the professionalisation and bureaucratisation of police communication has become such a central activity, particularly in relation to managing "social fear" and its immediate outcome: "moral panic".

Moral Panic and Crime News

Moral panic is traditionally understood as the process of arousing social concern over an issue, especially in the light of news media framing of these issues (Cohen, 1972 [2002]; Goode & Ben-Yehuda, 2010). It is a wider phenomenon historically connected to "fear" of particular groups of people or ideas (Bourke, 2005) and which is contextualised within the emergence of both modernity (Plamper & Lazier, 2010) and the "society of risk" (Beck, 1992; Luhmann, 1993). Although only labelled as such relatively recently, moral panic has been among us for a long time. It is said, for example, that the popularity of Johann Wolfgang von Goethe's novel, *The Sorrows of Young Werther* (1787), was blamed for a spate of suicides as it turned overnight into a media sensation. Indeed:

> The scale of the reaction to Werther perturbed authorities throughout Europe. Many officials and critics perceived the vivid and sympathetic manner with which Goethe described Werther's descent into self-destruction as legitimating the act of suicide. They condemned the novel as a danger to the public, particularly to impressionable young readers. The novel was blamed for the unleashing of an epidemic of copycat suicides throughout Europe among young, emotionally disturbed and broken-hearted readers. The numerous initiatives to ban the novel indicated that the authorities took these claims very seriously. In 1775 the theological faculty of the University of Leipzig petitioned officials to ban Werther on the grounds that its circulation would lead to the promotion of suicide. The city council of Leipzig agreed and cited the increased frequency of suicides as justification for banning both the novel and the wearing of Werther's costume. The ban, which was introduced in 1775, was not lifted until 1825. The novel was also banned in Italy and Denmark. (Furedi, 2015)

In politics, moral panic was also particularly present in the early twentieth century after the Soviet Revolution of 1917 and its impact around the world. This was subsequently used by governments in the USA and Europe to impose draconian measures against left-wing movements, political parties, unions and journalists, all justified by the need to "re-establish order", bring about political stability and stop the spread of Soviet communism (Murray, 1955; Nielsen, 2001).

This phenomenon can also be traced back to World War I, when the wartime government in the UK used the news media to portray the Germans in a certain manner. In those times, mass media consumption and sowing propaganda were almost incomprehensible by many, therefore becoming in many ways a Pandora box for future generations (Taylor, 1999, p. 8). Moral panic as a political phenomenon has had practical effects and was, for example, decisive in convincing the US public of the need to inter US citizens of Japanese descent during World War II and was also detrimental in setting attitudes against US Chinese descendants during the Cold War by dismissing them with the racist term "Internal Yellow Peril" (Kawai, 2005; Lee, 2007).

Yet in scholarly works, moral panic is often linked to issues of crime, law and order. This is because it is historically seen as a means of fomenting social anxiety over specific issues, especially when the news media frame these types of issues. Generally speaking, "moral panic" describes the reaction, and the over-reaction, of the public towards particular type of crimes. In relation to the subject of this book, we can say that it has a tendency to emphasise statistics that allow us to implant a "folk-devil", in sociological terms, in the public imagination. The central assertion is that the hostile reaction to some activities is out of all proportion to the actual threat posed, while other more serious events are ignored, neglected or minimised (Carrabine, 2008, p. 161).

In recent years, moral panic has covered a wide-ranging number of topics including health issues (such as epidemics), computer viruses (such as the Millennium Bug) and immigration. However, we should highlight that moral panic is still foremost associated with crime, which the public still perceives as a direct threat, although some studies reveal declining levels of deviance in many countries (Waddington, 1986; Welch, Fenwick, & Roberts, 1997). Therefore, it is mostly related to the media and the role that it plays in creating moral panic among the public (Chiricos, Eschholz, & Gertz, 1997; Hunt, 1997).

The concept is still very useful as a theoretical framework to understand and contextualise the role of statistics in the construction of crime news precisely because the persuasive power of numbers can help to underpin or dissuade those fears. Pragmatic questions such as "Why does the media ignore the statistics in some stories and over-emphasise them in others?", can only be answered if we take into consideration the role of "folk-devils" and "moral panic" (Cohen, 2002) in the explanatory theoretical framework of our analysis. These concepts are also extremely useful in helping us understand the role of statistics in the articulation of crime news, because the media are most likely to focus not only on events that have occurred multiple times, for example a number of assaults or break-ins that are centred in a small geographical area, but also on those that have the potential to affect the greatest number of people but are nevertheless very rare.

The reason might lie in the fact that moral panic research continues to invert the traditional focus away from the deficiencies of the deviant, and attends more to the definers of "deviance". In other terms, to the labellers rather than to those labelled by paying particular attention to the interplay between the "deviants", the agents of social control, the media and the general public. In this sense, moral panic has encroached onto the centre stage of politics, particularly as it tends to foster the type of "politics of anxiety" that has propelled populists movements in Europe and the USA (Hier, 2011; Ungar, 2001). It is because of this last aspect particularly, that we can place the use of crime statistics in creating moral panic as a central issue to be debated.

Media Securitization

Another very important and interconnected concept is that of the "securitization" of public life, which has become particularly relevant in the wake of 9/11 and the series of terrorist attacks across the West in recent years. The concept itself has been applied to international relations in which elites within a state have classified a variety of matters as issues of national "security", which has enabled "extraordinary means to be used in the name of security" (Buzan, Wæver, & De Wilde, 1998). Thanks to having been "securitized" some issues which were not necessarily that important in the public agenda have suddenly become an existential threat to society as a whole. However, precisely because of this, securitized subjects receive a disproportionate amount of attention and resources compared to non-securitized subjects causing not only a deviation of resource allocation but, most importantly, a distortion of societal priorities.

The "securitization" of societal issues is exacerbated by the mediatization of politics, particularly in the face of televisual communication (Williams, 2003, p. 511). This is particularly the case of crime given, not only the blurring of the global and local in the face of international terrorism networks, but also the conceptual connections between terrorism and crimes articulated in prevalent narratives. In fact, a large proportion of the news beat of crime has been effectively securitized thanks to the perceived terrorist threat and consequently receives an excessive amount of attention compared to other factors that are perhaps more important. This makes this concept increasingly relevant to the analysis of the relationship between media and crime.

Over the years, a variety of areas within deviance have been both "criminalised" and consequently "securitized" in the political and media discourses. To the securitization of topics such as organised crime (Emmers, 2002; Schuilenburg, 2015) we now need to add the criminalisation and securitization of other areas such as immigration (Ceyhan & Tsoukala, 2002; Huysmans, 2000) which became a defining issue, for example, in both the primary and general US presidential elections of 2016. The fact that news topics such as immigration, prostitution and drug trafficking have been securitized in the public discourses means that they tend to be at the centre of media attention and resources. For example, immigration in the UK is one of the areas of legislation about which the UK parliament has issued more laws, on which the media tends to over-focus and which is mostly highly ranked by public opinion as a problem, a lever that played a crucial role in convincing people to leave the European Union in the Brexit vote of 2016.

Another very interesting example is that of the "War on Drugs" and how this has been securitized over the years. Securitization can help explain how and why the drugs, originally viewed and approached as a crime issue, became over time an existential threat discourse that was capable of wielding a significant amount of power. In this sense, some research shows that:

> Speech acts such as the UN Single Convention on Narcotic Drugs, the UN Convention Against Illicit Traffic in Narcotic Drugs and Psychotropic Substances and Russia's 'Rainbow-2 Plan' clearly illustrate the development

of the 'drugs as an existential threat' discourse at a global level with particular reference to mankind, the State and global peace and security, respectively. Analysis of these speech acts also shows how the power of the security narrative means that the global drug prohibition regime continues to remain pre-eminent despite the wealth of unintended consequences that it causes. (Crick, 2012, p. 407)

Because of this, some scholars have already pointed out the need to better understand the process of securitization in terms of its ability to mobilise resources and audiences towards a specific political agenda (Léonard & Kaunert, 2010, p. 57). In this context, statistics have either been used to try to debunk assertions or have become "weaponised" by those looking to profit from public fear. Consequently, thanks to the securitisantion of crime, the use of statistics can help to either set or re-shape the agenda that both the public and the media are supposed to follow.

Agenda Setting

In their seminal work, McCombs and Shaw (1972) concluded that the mass media exerted a significant influence on what voters considered to be the major issues of an electoral campaign. According to them, in choosing and displaying news, editors, newsroom staff, and broadcasters played an important part in shaping political reality. Audiences therefore not only learn about a given issue, but also the media was central in shaping public attitudes towards how much importance to attach to that issue from the amount of information in a news story and its position. In reflecting what it is said during an electoral campaign, the mass media was able to determine the important issues to be debated and talk about.

Bernard Cohen (1967 [1963]) is reputed to have been the firt to highlight that the news media (which he referred to as the press) might not be good at telling people what to think but that it is extremely efficient in telling them what to think about. In his time, Cohen was referring to the ability of reporting international affairs, numbers and foreign policy to place a particular story at the forefront of attention for an extended period at the expense of other issues that necessarily were cast in the shade (1967 [1963], p. 98). But Cohen was not saying that it was by any means a unidirectional process in which the media had almost absolute power to dictate the agenda. On the contrary, he pointed out that:

> Correspondent hover around the major foreign policy story like moths around the brightest light; and. Like moths, they drift away when the light fades or is surpassed by another. A discerning official with many years of foreign policy experience in Washington observed that reporters "don't bother you unless there is something urgent going on". To follow "the big story" is to "stick with the news that comes to the top". (1967 [1963], p. 99)

Therefore, the power to set in the public imagination what is "urgent" and what is not, is not exclusively held by journalists or even the sources they use to articulate the news stories. Over the years, those working in professional communication (i.e. PR practitioners, spin-doctors, electoral strategists) have exercised an important influence in the process of agenda setting (Esrock & Leichty, 1998; Manheim & Albritton, 1983; Protess & McCombs, 2016). In recent times, we have witnessed other voices such as activist groups, non-governmental organisations and a variety of actors gaining increasing influence in their ability to shape the news agenda (Joachim, 2007; Jordan & Van Tuijl, 2000).

In this context, those controlling the media are not the only ones deciding what stories get that kind of attention, and what stories do not, but have to negotiate with other actors and with a variety of organisations, institutions and individuals who are all competing for the public's attention in order to secure the prioritisation of their own agenda of issues. In the field of crime reporting, for example, the murder of a homeless man is not likely to get as much media attention as the murder of a teenage girl from a white middle-class family. This might not only be because the girl's killing creates more empathy and in many cases is rarer in wealthier societies, but also because the latter plays more to specific political agendas (such as the securitisation of crime) or because it fits into the prevalent discursive regime.

An example of this was the distinctive news treatment received by the assassination of two clergy figures in 2016. The first was the assassination of 84-year-old Catholic priest, Father Jacques Hamel while he said mass in his own church. He was killed and four other people taken hostage by two armed men who stormed his church in a suburb of Rouen in northern France on July 2016. The two attackers, who said they were from the so-called Islamic State (IS), slit Fr Jacques' throat during a morning Mass (Worley, 2016). The event received ample news coverage from all over the world and hours of footage both from the events and his funeral service was broadcasted by the key media outlets throughout the world. This particular event was treated as a terrorist act from the start and the word "terrorism" appears in every single news report.

Now, let us contrast this with the killing of Imam Maulama Akonjee, 55, and his assistant Thara Uddin, 64, who were gunned down execution-style in broad daylight by Oscar Morel, 35, of Hispanic origin. This happened almost exactly a month later in New York, USA as both the Iman and his assistant walked home in their traditional robes after prayers at a Queens mosque. Not only was this event barely covered by the news media outlets outside the USA, but news agencies such as Associate Press treated the whole thing as "a hate crime" (McGibney, Roberts, Celona, & Pagones, 2016). In none of the reports of that day or of the subsequent days was the word "terrorism" mentioned, despite 9/11 been mentioned several times in the story around Morel being charged with the killing. In the media narratives instead, the explanation given for the killing was that the man charged with the crime, Oscar Morel, was said to hold "hatred" toward Muslims (Celona, Moore, & Cohen, 2016).

One must ask why one story was treated as a terrorist act and the other not, even though only one person was killed in France against two in the USA. Why was one event articulated in the news media as an issue of mental health from the start while the other securitised in the public discourses almost immediately? Why did one become a news priority and the other did not? These are important questions that help us explore and discuss the very complex relationship between the media and crime in the context of news values and journalistic dynamics that defines what is important and what is not by overcoming what we might call "the objectivity of the senses" (Alessandro Martinisi & Lugo-Ocando, 2015). In asking these questions, we can also explore why the media can focus on a particular story, thereby making it headline news, and ignore a different story altogether, while the public remains ill-informed or is kept completely in the dark about the issues at stake.

The concept referred to as "agenda setting" plays a vital role in the definition of the topics and issues that both the news agenda and the public at large discuss or about which they remain silent (Althaus & Tewksbury, 2002, p. 180). In the specific context of crime reporting, this means the difference between considering crime as a whole, as an important issue, or not. In fact, public perceptions of crime as the most important problem (MIP) facing countries such as the USA grew exponentially over the years despite the fact that crime rates were actually decreasing. Growing crime perception rates instead had far more correlation with television news variables, which alone accounted for almost four times more variance. In other words, it was not the facts on the ground but the way broadcast news was presenting crime that was partially responsible for people's views (Lowry, Nio, & Leitner, 2003, p. 61).

In other countries such as Australia, Canada and the UK, the news media has also demonstrated a pivotal factor in defining what people speak about in relation to crime (Althaus & Tewksbury, 2002; Soroka, 2002). This happens not only at times of electoral campaigns but also during non-campaign periods. One example of this is the way immigration is covered. Not only because it is constantly brought into the spotlight as a theme of discussion but also because of the way is mostly framed in negative terms (Lugo-Ocando, 2011, p. 95). Furthermore, great parst of the London-based press tend to frame immigration in terms of crime (Lugo, 2007; Philo, Briant, & Donald, 2013).

The concept of framing is intertwined with that of agenda setting; looking at the nature of the issues being reported around particular topics. According to this notion, the media focuses attention on certain events and then contextualises the events being covered in a set of symbolic elements, narratives and language, which ends up placing these events within a specific field of meaning. Hence, news reports about terrorist attacks from around the world would be framed as "barbaric" and "irrational" by associating them with religion and fanaticism through words, images and discourses.

People, topics and issues are represented to the audience with certain characteristics and elements that influence the choices that people make about how to process the given information. For example, news images used to illustrate journalists' works on global poverty are overwhelmingly those of black African children and women despite the fact that it is Asia that is the continent with the largest proportion of poverty on the planet (Lugo-Ocando, 2014; Parvez, 2011). This makes a great majority of the audiences in the Western world see poverty as mainly a black and African problem. This is because these frames are abstractions that allow audiences to organise and structure the meaning of the messages in terms of the cultural and symbolic references that they have been given (Abraham & Appiah, 2006; Goffman, 1986).

Framing influences the perception of the news by the audience. In this way it is a form of second-level agenda setting, telling the audience what to think about (agenda setting theory) and also "how" to think about the issues being reported. In this context, we need to acknowledge that journalists constantly decide which facts to include or emphasise, who to use as sources and what is really "at issue" when in reporting a story:

> These choices combine to create a frame that both supports the story (like the frame of a house) and defines what belongs inside (like a picture frame), and thereby signals what news consumers should find important. Broadly speaking, news frames can be classified as predominantly "episodic" or "thematic" (Iyengar & Simon, 1993, p. 369). Episodic frames focus on the immediate event or incident and give little or no context about underlying issues or context. Thematic frames focus on the big picture, for instance, by providing statistics, expert analysis or other information to help the public view the event in a broader context. This fact sheet reviews current scholarship and studies on how trauma-related news is framed. (Tiegreen & Newman, 2008)

Statistics, as will be discussed later on in the book, play a crucial role in both helping the news media to set the agenda and influencing people about "how" to think about certain topics and issues in society. They have the power to frame news stories and, as such, numbers in the news headlines have, in the recent past, triggered financial stampedes when people en mass withdraw their money from banks, and have helped mobilise millions to vote in favour or against a policy or a candidate.

These numbers can legitimise and underpin both agenda setting and framing and therefore we need to examine the power and influence they award to those who use them.

General Framework

In order to understand and contextualise the use of statistics by journalists and examine how numbers underpin crime news, we also need to understand the cultural, professional and organisational context in which all news is produced. In this sense, we need to start by reminding ourselves that the deontological aspirations of journalism see the work of journalists as a mirror of reality, where objectivity is considered as a key value to be observed. In opposition to this view, scholars such as Gaye Tuchman (1978) claim instead that news does not mirror reality. For her, news rather helps construct reality as a shared social phenomenon, since the process of defining an event and defining the news gives way to the event itself. That is, the story is constantly defining and re-defining, constituting and reconstituting, social phenomena.

So if news is not reality, what exactly is it? To answer this question without entering the realm of philosophy, we need to focus on two different definitions. First, news is often defined by practitioners as reporting something that is new, that is currently happening. It is the reporting of recent events or pristine unknown information that makes it into the news media. It is the process of transforming raw information into a news item. For most journalists, news is foremost information that is of broad interest to the intended audience. A variety of studies shows that they select the news items and issues by following a series of "news values" that set the criteria for determining what is newsworthy and what is not (Cohen, 1967 [1963]; Galtung & Ruge, 1965; Harcup & O'Neill, 2001). The method of news gathering, news selection and news dissemination are shaped by the collective values of journalists who perform their work as part of an interpretative community (Berkowitz & TerKeurst, 1999; Zelizer, 1993b), that is a community of professionals that broadly speaking share similar ethical values and world views (Martin Conboy,

2004; Eldridge, 2014) and which operate within specific "news cultures" (Allan, 2004; Deuze, 2002) that define the dynamics and interactions around which news is produced.

The second way of understanding news is by defining it as a social practice that links equally to both journalists and their audiences. This social practice that calls us to see the world outside, reflects "our need to know about contemporary events as they occur" (Harrison, 2006, p. 1). By this, it is meant that news cannot be seen simply as a product or an object, but as an interactive process that lives from the ability to exchange timely and opportune information that is somehow made relevant and interesting to those who participate in the exchange. In contemporary times, news has been treated as a commodity (Langer, 1998; McManus, 1992; McNair, 2009), one that is a "sequence of socially manufactured messages, which carry many of the culturally dominant assumptions of our society" (GlasgowMediaGroup, 1976, p. 1) and which is exchanged in the marketplace.

Initially, what we would nowadays call mainstream news was inaccessible to most except to the elites of the time. Timely access to mainstream news such as stories about wars, earthquakes, revolutions and other major events only started to be popularised in the West from the sixteenth century onwards (Briggs & Burke, 2009, p. 71; Pettegree, 2014, p. 5). Interestingly, for this book, the first type of modern manifestation of commercial news was dedicated to disseminate what by all accounts could today be described as statistical data (Martin Conboy, 2004; Pettegree, 2014) and many international news agencies such as Reuters were originally funded to disseminate statistical data (Boyd-Barrett, 1980; Read, 1999). However, news media content rapidly evolved into its present, more human-driven, stories (many about gruesome crimes) that were able to capture the hearts and minds of readers or, let us say, the imagination and the gut-feeling of the public. It was upon this type of news content that the news media expanded in the twentieth century, but only to revert in more recent times to focus again on data, statistics and, even more recently, on infographics and interactive visualizations. This discussion is in part an opportunity to explore this transition and to see how statistics and crime are represented in the news media through the intervention and agency of journalists and editors.

References

Abraham, L., & Appiah, O. (2006). Framing news stories: The role of visual imagery in priming racial stereotypes. *The Howard Journal of Communications, 17*(3), 183–203.

Allan, S. (2004). *News culture*. Cambridge: Cambridge University Press.

Althaus, S. L., & Tewksbury, D. (2002). Agenda setting and the "new" news patterns of issue importance among readers of the paper and online versions of the New York Times. *Communication Research, 29*(2), 180–207.

Asp, K. (1986). *Mäktiga massmedier: Studier i politisk opinionsbildning* [Powerful mass media: Studies in political opinion-formation]. Stockholm: Akademilitteratur.

Beck, U. (1992). *Risk society: Towards a new modernity*. London: Sage.

Beckett, K. (1999). *Making crime pay: Law and order in contemporary American politics*. Oxford: Oxford University Press.

Berkowitz, D., & TerKeurst, J. V. (1999). Community as interpretive community: Rethinking the journalist-source relationship. *Journal of Communication, 49*(3), 125–136.

Bourke, J. (2005). *Fear: A cultural history*. Berkeley, CA: Counterpoint Press.

Boyd-Barrett, O. (1980). *The international news agencies* (Vol. 13). London: Constable Limited.

Boyd-Barrett, O. (1995). The political economy approach. In O. Boyd-Barrett & C. Newbold (Eds.), *Approaches to media: A reader* (pp. 186–192). London: Arnold.

Briggs, A., & Burke, P. (2009). *A social history of the media: From Gutenberg to the Internet*. Cambridge: Polity.

Buzan, B., Wæver, O., & De Wilde, J. (1998). *Security: A new framework for analysis*. Boulder, CO: Lynne Rienner Publishers.

Carrabine, E. (2008). *Crime, culture and the media*. Cambridge: Polity.

Cater, D. (1964). *Power in Washington: A critical look at today's struggle to govern in the nation's capital* (Vol. 290). London: Collins.

Cavender, G., & Miller, K. W. (2013). Corporate crime as trouble: Reporting on the corporate scandals of 2002. *Deviant Behavior, 34*(11), 916–931.

Celona, L., Moore, T., & Cohen, S. (2016). Man charged in murder of imam, assistant felt 'hatred' toward Muslims. Retrieved August 17, 2016, from http://nypost.com/2016/08/15/man-charged-with-murder-for-executing-imam-assistant/

Ceyhan, A., & Tsoukala, A. (2002). The securitization of migration in Western societies: Ambivalent discourses and policies. *Alternatives: Global, Local, Political, 27*(1), S21–S21.

Chan, A. K. P., & Chan, V. M. S. (2012). *Public perception of crime and attitudes toward police: Examining the effects of media news.* Run Run Shaw Library, City University of Hong Kong.

Chibnall, S. (1977). *Law-and-order news. An analysis of crime reporting in the British press.* London: Tavistock Publications.

Chiricos, T., Eschholz, S., & Gertz, M. (1997). Crime, news and fear of crime: Toward an identification of audience effects. *Social Problems, 44*(3), 342–357.

Cohen, B. (1967 [1963]). *The press and foreign policy.* Princeton, NJ: Princeton University Press.

Cohen, S. (1972 [2002]). *Folk devils and moral panics: The creation of the mods and rockers.* New York: Psychology Press.

Conboy, M. (2004). *Journalism: A critical history.* London: Sage.

Connolly, E. S. (2014). Crime journalism: Barriers in Ireland. *Journal of Applied Journalism & Media Studies, 3*(1), 59–69.

Cornwell, E. E. (1965). *Presidential leadership of public opinion.* Bloomington: Indiana University Press.

Cottle, S. (2006). *Mediatized conflict: Understanding media and conflicts in the contemporary world.* London: McGraw-Hill Education.

CRCVC. (2015). Understanding how the media reports crime. Retrieved August 11, 2016, from https://crcvc.ca/publications/media-guide/understanding/#fn3

Crick, E. (2012). Drugs as an existential threat: An analysis of the international securitization of drugs. *International Journal of Drug Policy, 23*(5), 407–414.

Crozier, M. (2007). Recursive governance: Contemporary political communication and public policy. *Political Communication, 24*(1), 1–18.

Curran, J., Salovaara-Moring, I., Coen, S., & Iyengar, S. (2010). Crime, foreigners and hard news: A cross-national comparison of reporting and public perception. *Journalism, 11*(1), 3–19.

Davies, A. (2007). The Scottish Chicago? From 'hooligans' to 'gangsters' in inter-war Glasgow. *Cultural and Social History, 4*(4), 511–527.

Davies, N. (2008). *Flat earth news: An award-winning reporter exposes falsehood, distortion and propaganda in the global media.* London: Random House.

Davis, R., & Taras, D. (2017). *Justices and journalists: The global perspective.* Cambridge: Cambridge University Press.

Deuze, M. (2002). National news cultures: A comparison of Dutch, German, British, Australian, and US journalists. *Journalism & Mass Communication Quarterly, 79*(1), 134–149.

Dowler, K., Fleming, T., & Muzzatti, S. L. (2006). Constructing crime: Media, crime, and popular culture. *Canadian Journal of Criminology and Criminal Justice, 48*(6), 837–850.

Doyle, G. (2013). *Understanding media economics*. London: SAGE Publications Limited.

Eldridge, S. A. (2014). Boundary maintenance and interloper media reaction: Differentiating between journalism's discursive enforcement processes. *Journalism Studies, 15*(1), 1–16.

Emmers, R. (2002). *The securitization of transnational crime in ASEAN*. Singapore: Institute of Defence and Strategic Studies, Nanyang Technological University.

Ericson, R., Baranek, O., & Chan, J. (1987). *Visualising deviance*. Buckingham: Open University Press.

Esrock, S. L., & Leichty, G. B. (1998). Social responsibility and corporate web pages: Self-presentation or agenda-setting? *Public Relations Review, 24*(3), 305–319.

Esser, F. (1999). Tabloidization' of news a comparative analysis of Anglo-American and German Press Journalism. *European Journal of Communication, 14*(3), 291–324.

Esser, F. (2013). Mediatization as a challenge: Media logic versus political logic. In H. Kriesi (Ed.), *Democracy in the age of globalization and mediatization* (pp. 155–176). Basingstoke: Palgrave Macmillan.

Ettema, J., & Glasser, T. (1998). *Custodians of conscience: Investigative journalism and public virtue*. New York: Columbia University Press.

Evans, H. (2013). The media has a duty to scrutinise the use of power. Retrieved June 10, 2016, from https://www.theguardian.com/commentisfree/2013/oct/20/media-duty-scrutinise-use-of-power

Fields, I. W. (2004). Family values and feudal codes: The social politics of America's twenty-first century gangster. *The Journal of Popular Culture, 37*(4), 611–633.

Furedi, F. (2015). The media's first moral panic. *History Today, 65*.

Galtung, J., & Ruge, M. H. (1965). The structure of foreign news the presentation of the Congo, Cuba and Cyprus Crises in four Norwegian newspapers. *Journal of Peace Research, 2*(1), 64–90.

GlasgowMediaGroup. (1976). *Bad news*. London: Routledge.

Goethe, J. (1787). *The sorrows of young werther*. Leipzig: Weygand'sche Buchhandlung.

Goffman, E. (1986). *Frame analysis. An essay on the organization of expierence*. Boston: Northeastern University Press.

Goode, E., & Ben-Yehuda, N. (2010). *Moral panics: The social construction of deviance*. New York: John Wiley & Sons.

Greer, C., & McLaughlin, E. (2011). Trial by media': Policing, the 24-7 news mediasphere and the 'politics of outrage. *Theoretical Criminology, 15*(1), 23–46.

Hall, S. (1975). *Newsmaking and crime*. Birmigham: Centre for Contemporary Cultural Studies.

Hampton, M. (2010). The Fourth Estate ideal in journalism history. In S. Allan (Ed.), *The Routledge companion to news and journalism* (pp. 3–12). London: Routledge.

Harcup, T., & O'Neill, D. (2001). What is news? Galtung and Ruge revisited. *Journalism Studies, 2*(2), 261–280.

Harper, S. (2014). Framing the Philpotts: Anti-Welfarism and the British newspaper reporting of the Derby house fire verdict. *International Journal of Media & Cultural Politics, 10*(1), 83–98.

Harrison, J. (2006). *News*. Abingdon, OX: Routledge.

Hier, S. P. (2011). *Moral panic and the politics of anxiety*. Abingdon, OX: Routledge.

Hjarvard, S. (2013). *The mediatization of culture and society*. London: Routledge.

Hollway, W. (1981). I just wanted to kill a woman.' Why? The ripper and male sexuality. *Feminist Review, 9*, 33–40.

Hunt, A. (1997). 'Moral panic' and moral language in the media. *British Journal of Sociology*, 629–648.

Huysmans, J. (2000). The European Union and the securitization of migration. *JCMS: Journal of Common Market Studies, 38*(5), 751–777.

Iyengar, S., & Simon, A. (1993). News coverage of the Gulf crisis and public opinion: A study of agenda-setting, priming, and framing. *Communication Research, 20*(3), 365–383.

Jewkes, Y. (2004). The construction of crime news. In Y. Jewkes (Ed.), *Media and crime* (pp. 35–62). Los Angeles: Sage.

Jinfeng, D. (1997). Police-public relations—A Chinese view. *Australian & New Zealand Journal of Criminology, 30*(1), 87–94.

Joachim, J. M. (2007). *Agenda setting, the UN, and NGOs: Gender violence and reproductive rights*. Washington, DC: Georgetown University Press.

Jordan, L., & Van Tuijl, P. (2000). Political responsibility in transnational NGO advocacy. *World Development, 28*(12), 2051–2065.

Kawai, Y. (2005). Stereotyping Asian Americans: The dialectic of the model minority and the yellow peril. *The Howard Journal of Communications, 16*(2), 109–130.

Landau, T. C. (2014). *Challenging notions: Critical victimology in Canada*. Toronto: Canadian Scholars' Press.

Langer, J. (1998). *Tabloid television: Popular journalism and the "other news".* New York: Psychology Press.

Lee, E. (2007). The "Yellow Peril" and Asian exclusion in the Americas. *Pacific Historical Review, 76*(4), 537–562.

Léonard, S., & Kaunert, C. (2010). Reconceptualizing the audience in securitization theory. In T. Balzacq (Ed.), *Securitization theory: How security problems emerge and dissolve* (pp. 57–76). Abingdon, OX: Routledge.

Lewis, J., Williams, A., & Franklin, B. (2008). A compromised fourth estate? UK news journalism, public relations and news sources. *Journalism Studies, 9*(1), 1–20.

Lipschultz, J. H., & Hilt, M. L. (2014). *Crime and local television news: Dramatic, breaking, and live from the scene.* Abingdon, OX: Routledge.

Lowry, D. T., Nio, T. C. J., & Leitner, D. W. (2003). Setting the public fear agenda: A longitudinal analysis of network TV crime reporting, public perceptions of crime, and FBI crime statistics. *Journal of Communication, 53*(1), 61–73.

Lugo, J. (2007). A tale of donkeys, swans and racism: London tabloids, Scottish independence and refugees. *Communication and Social Change, 1*(1), 22–37.

Lugo-Ocando, J. (2011). Media campaigns and asylum seekers in Scotland. In M. Alleyne (Ed.), *Anti-racism & Multi-culturalism: Studies in international communication* (pp. 95–128). New Brunswick, NJ: Transaction Publishers.

Lugo-Ocando, J. (2014). *Blaming the victim: How global journalism fails those in poverty.* London: Pluto Press.

Lugo-Ocando, J., & Faria Brandão, R. (2015). STABBING NEWS: Articulating crime statistics in the newsroom. *Journalism Practice, 10*(6), 715–729. doi:10.1080/17512786.2015.1058179.

Luhmann, N. (1993). *Communication and social order: Risk: A sociological theory.* Piscataway, NJ: Transaction Publishers.

Manheim, J. B., & Albritton, R. B. (1983). Changing national images: International public relations and media agenda setting. *American Political Science Review, 78*(03), 641–657.

Marcinkowski, F., & Steiner, A. (2014). Mediatization and political autonomy: A systems approach. In H. Kriesi (Ed.), *Mediatization of politics: Understanding the transformation of western democracies* (pp. 74–89). Basingstoke: Palgrave Macmillan.

Marion, N. E. (1997). Symbolic policies in Clinton's crime control agenda. *Buffalo Criminal Law Review, 1*(1), 67–108.

Martinisi, A., & Lugo-Ocando, J. (2015). Overcoming the objectivity of the senses: Enhancing journalism practice through Eastern philosophies. *International Communication Gazette, 77*(5), 439–455.

Mawby, R. C. (2010). Police corporate communications, crime reporting and the shaping of policing news. *Policing & Society, 20*(1), 124–139.

Mawby, R. C. (2014). The presentation of police in everyday life: Police–press relations, impression management and the Leveson Inquiry. *Crime, Media, Culture, 10*(3), 239–257.

Mawby, R. C., & Worthington, S. (2002). Marketing the police—From a force to a service. *Journal of Marketing Management, 18*(9-10), 857–876.

McCombs, M. E., & Shaw, D. L. (1972). The agenda-setting function of mass media. *Public Opinion Quarterly, 36*(2), 176–187.

McGibney, M., Roberts, G., Celona, L., & Pagones, S. (2016). Queens imam and his assistant executed in broad daylight. Retrieved August 17, 2016, from http://nypost.com/2016/08/13/2-wounded-in-queens-shooting/

McKenzie, R. (2008). Crime interest. Retrieved August 13, 2016, from http://www.bbc.co.uk/blogs/theeditors/2008/06/crime_interest.html

McLachlan, S., & Golding, P. (2000). Tabloidization in the British press: A quantitative investigation into changes in. In C. Sparks & J. Tulloch (Eds.), *Tabloid tales: Global debates over media standards* (pp. 75–90). Oxford: Rowman and Littlefield.

McManus, J. H. (1992). What kind of commodity is news. *Communication Research, 19*(6), 787–805.

McNair, B. (2009). *News and journalism in the UK*. London: Routledge.

Motschall, M., & Cao, L. (2002). An analysis of the public relations role of the police public information officer. *Police Quarterly, 5*(2), 152–180.

Murray, R. K. (1955). *Red scare: A study in National Hysteria, 1919–1920*. Minneapolis: University of Minnesota Press.

Napoli, P. M. (2011). *Audience evolution: New technologies and the transformation of media audiences*. New York: Columbia University Press.

Napoli, P. M. (2012). *Audience economics: Media institutions and the audience marketplace*. New York: Columbia University Press.

Neavling, S. (2014). Stabbings? Shootings? Detroit police stop reporting violent crimes to media, public. Retrieved February 1, 2016, from http://motorcity-muckraker.com/2014/04/03/stabbings-shootings-detroit-police-stop-reporting-violent-crimes-to-media-public/

Nielsen, K. E. (2001). *Un-American womanhood: Antiradicalism, Antifeminism, and the first red scare*. Columbus: Ohio State University Press.

O'Neill, D., & O'Connor, C. (2008). The passive journalist: How sources dominate local news. *Journalism Practice, 2*(3), 487–500.

Parvez, N. (2011). Visual representations of poverty: The case of Kroo Bay, Freetown. *City, 15*(6), 686–695.

Patterson, T. E. (2013). *Informing the news*. New York: Vintage.

Pettegree, A. (2014). *The invention of news: How the world came to know about itself*. New Heaven, CT: Yale University Press.

Philo, G., Briant, E., & Donald, P. (2013). *Bad news for refugees*. London: Pluto.

Plamper, J., & Lazier, B. (2010). Introduction: The phobic regimes of modernity. *Representations, 110*(1), 58–65. doi:10.1525/rep.2010.110.1.58.

Protess, D., & McCombs, M. E. (2016). *Agenda setting: Readings on media, public opinion, and policymaking*. Abingdon, OX: Routledge.

Quinney, R. (1970). *The social reality of crime*. Piscataway, NJ: Transaction Publishers.

Read, D. (1999). *The power of news: The history of reuters*. Oxford: Oxford University Press.

Reinemann, C., Stanyer, J., Scherr, S., & Legnante, G. (2012). Hard and soft news: A review of concepts, operationalizations and key findings. *Journalism, 13*(2), 221–239.

Reiner, R., Livingstone, S., & Allen, J. (2003). From law and order to lynch mobs: Crime news since the Second World War. In P. Mason (Ed.), *Criminal visions* (pp. 13–32). London: Routledge.

Romer, D., Jamieson, K. H., & Aday, S. (2003). Television news and the cultivation of fear of crime. *Journal of Communication, 53*(1), 88–104.

Schechter, H. (2003). *The serial killer files: The who, what, where, how, and why of the world's most terrifying murderers*. New York: Ballantine Books.

Schlesinger, P., & Tumber, H. (1994). *Reporting crime. The media politics of criminal justice*. Oxford: Oxford University Press.

Schlesinger, P., Tumber, H., & Murdock, G. (1991). The media politics of crime and criminal justice. *British Journal of Sociology, 42*(3), 397–420.

Schrott, A. (2009). Dimensions: Catch-all label or technical term. In K. Lundby (Ed.), *Mediatization: Concept, changes, consequences* (pp. 41–61). Bern: Peter Lang Publishing Inc..

Schuilenburg, M. (2015). *The securitization of society: Crime, risk, and social order*. New York: NYU Press.

Schultz, J. (1998). *Reviving the fourth estate: Democracy, accountability and the media*. Cambridge: Cambridge University Press.

Schulz, W. (2004). Reconstructing mediatization as an analytical concept. *European journal of communication, 19*(1), 87–101.

Searle, J. R. (1995). *The construction of social reality*. New York: Simon and Schuster.

Soothill, K., Peelo, M., Pearson, J., & Francis, B. (2004). The reporting trajectories of top homicide cases in the media: A case study of The Times. *Howard Journal of Criminal Justice, 43*(1), 1–14.

Soroka, S. N. (2002). Issue attributes and agenda-setting by media, the public, and policymakers in Canada. *International Journal of Public Opinion Research, 14*(3), 264–285.

Sparks, R. (1992). *Television and the Drama of Crime.* Buckingham: Open University Press.

Strömbäck, J. (2008). Four phases of mediatization: An analysis of the mediatization of politics. *The International Journal of Press/Politics, 13*(3), 228–246.

Strömbäck, J., & Esser, F. (2014). Mediatization of politics: Towards a theoretical framework. In *Mediatization of politics: Understanding the transformation of western democracies* (pp. 3–27). London: Palgrave Macmillan.

Taylor, P. M. (1999). *British propaganda in the 20th century: Selling democracy.* Edinburgh: Edinburgh University Press.

Thompson, J. B. (1995). *The media and modernity: A social theory of the media.* Cambridge: Polity Press.

Thussu, D. K. (2008). *News as entertainment: The rise of global infotainment.* London: Sage.

Tiegreen, S., & Newman, E. (2008). How News is "Framed". Retrieved March 27, 2017, from https://dartcenter.org/content/how-news-is-framed

Tuchman, G. (1978). *Making news: A study in the construction of reality.* New York: Free Press.

Underwood, D. (1993). *When MBAs rule the newsroom: How markets and managers are shaping today's media.* New York: Columbia University Press.

Ungar, S. (2001). Moral panic versus the risk society: The implications of the changing sites of social anxiety. *The British Journal of Sociology, 52*(2), 271–291.

Waddington, P. (1986). Mugging as a moral panic: A question of proportion. *British Journal of Sociology, 37,* 245–259.

Weitzer, R., & Kubrin, C. E. (2004). Breaking news: How local TV news and real-world conditions affect fear of crime. *Justice Quarterly, 21*(3), 497–520.

Welch, M., Fenwick, M., & Roberts, M. (1997). Primary definitions of crime and moral panic: A content analysis of experts' quotes in feature newspaper articles on crime. *Journal of Research in Crime and Delinquency, 34*(4), 474–494.

Williams, M. C. (2003). Words, images, enemies: Securitization and international politics. *International studies quarterly, 47*(4), 511–531.

Winston, B. (2002). Towards tabloidization? Glasgow revisited, 1975–2001. *Journalism Studies, 3*(1), 5–20.

Wood, J. C. (2016). Crime news and the press. In P. Knepper & A. Johansen (Eds.), *The Oxford Handbook of the history of crime and criminal justice* (pp. 301–319). Oxford: Oxford University Press.

Worley, W. (2016). Normandy church attack: France fears religious war after symbolic killing of Catholic priest. Retrieved August 17, 2016, from http://www.independent.co.uk/news/world/europe/france-cchurch-attack-normandy-latest-news-religion-jacques-hamel-adel-kermiche-isis-a7157556.html

Zelizer, B. (1993a). Has communication explained journalism? *Journal of Communication, 43*(4), 80–88.

Zelizer, B. (1993b). Journalists as interpretive communities. *Critical Studies in Media Communication, 10*(3), 219–237.

3

How Crime Statistics Became News

There are records dating back to 1587 showing that news on crime has been present in the press since the early pamphlet-based witchcraft reports of the mid-sixteenth (Surette, 1998, p. 53). These reports suggest an acute interest in crime content alongside moral exhortations which used the sentences handed down by the courts as salutary lessons in the dangers of immorality. In these early manifestations of crime news reporting, it was already possible to see key themes emerging, such as the use of news sources within the justice system and how these sources influenced content. Moreover, Andrew Pettegree shows how the emergence of a news market in the early sixteenth century allowed the "news-books"—an incipient version of what later became newspapers—to incorporate notorious crimes in its pages. He points out that although these crime stories were not particularly common in the pamphlet literature, they became increasingly present in the ballad sheets and illustrated broadsheets, which were the genres of news sensation. The title-page of such pulications took pains to emphasise that these reports came "from authentic sources" (Pettegree, 2014, p. 74).

Equally, it is important to mention that the incipient news media, in the form of periodicals, was already publishing data from the fifteenth

© The Author(s) 2017
J. Lugo-Ocando, *Crime Statistics in the News*,
DOI 10.1057/978-1-137-39841-3_3

century onwards (Brownlees, 2011; Griffiths, 1992). This consisted of commodity prices, information about imports and exports, and other types of data that resembled early forms of statistics. However, the first recorded national crime statistics published in the media dates to 1827 in France. Since then, these numbers have become a regular feature of the news. By 1830, the statistical works of Louis Reybaund and Louis-René Villermé started to be referred to by the press to explain criminal behaviour (Rosanvallon, 2012, p. 111) in that country, and became a key feature of journalists' narratives.

Indeed, contrary to what one might assume, the incorporation of statistics in crime reporting is nothing new. During the Victorian era, for example, British journalist Henry Mayhew (1812–1887) used police statistics to produce stories about the effects of poverty upon crime. Together with Bracebridge Hemyng, John Binny and Andrew Halliday, Mayhew wrote *London Labour and the London Poor* (2009 [1851]) in three volumes in 1851, and in 1861 produced a fourth volume on the lives of prostitutes, thieves and beggars in London (Gallagher, 1986; Humpherys, 1977). Moreover, in *The Criminal Prisons of London: And Scenes of Prison Life* (1862), Henry Mayhew and John Binny produced a lengthy investigation into all aspects of the criminal justice system in Britain with detailed statistics on arrests and convictions, descriptions of disciplinary methods in prisons, and how criminals were classified in order to be sent into a particular form of custody. They complemented these statistics with the use of oral testimony from prisoners, guards and wardens to offer a more analytical focus than in their earlier work.

Their work received wide attention from politicians and the general public and it had an important influence on prison policy and reform from then onwards (Garland, 1985; Mair & Burke, 2013; Pratt, 2002) as it was seen as offering a scientific view of the subject matter. The use of statistics by journalists can be linked to important societal discourses such as the "mathematisation" of society, scientific objectivity and the Victorian "detachment", all of which had an important influence upon the shaping of modern news reporting.

Nevertheless, from studying and comparing the use of crime statistics in the different periods one must conclude that its evolution shows anything but a straight line. Moreover, at some periods of time, the way both politicians used crime statistics and journalists failed to report these abuses critically highlights the fact that at times crime statistics in the news went several steps backwards even in those periods in which it seems to have jumped into prominence in public debates, as the more recent history in 1990s New York City showed.

From Then to Now

Let us start by reminding ourselves how, in the face of the recent deaths of a number of Afro-American young men at the hands of the police in the USA and the reaction against this police abuse that included a series of protests across the USA, the former Mayor of New York City, Rudy Giuliani, came out in defence of the police saying that black people had a 99% chance of killing each other:

> If I were a black father and I was concerned about the safety of my child— really concerned about it and not in a politically activist sense—I would say, 'Be very respectful to the police, most of them are good, some can be very bad and just be very careful', Mr Giuliani said. I'd also say, 'Be very careful of those kids in the neighborhoods, don't get involved with them because son, there's a 99 per cent chance they're going to kill you, not the police'. (Garcia, 2016)

He made his comments after a week of massive protests against police brutality and given his image as a law enforcer his words were widely echoed by the news media all over the world. Indeed, according to the US Federal Bureau of Investigation (FBI), 90% of black people murdered in that country in 2014 were killed by other black people. However, Giuliani failed to mention that the same data also shows that some 82% of white people murdered in 2014 were killed by other white people. He also failed to remind people that under his two tenures as a Mayor (1994 and 2001), the New York Police Department (NYPD) killed 160 suspects, with the deadliest year being 1996, when police killed 30 people.

Giuliani is one of those politicians who have learned how to use statistics to advance their own agenda. His "zero-tolerance policy", credited with bringing back law and order to New York and one of the landmarks in US political narratives since then, was entirely underpinned by statistics. This happened despite reservations and controversies about both the anti-crime policy and the validity and reliability of the statistics used by Giuliani (Anderson, 1997; Kelling & Bratton, 1998; Zimring, 2006). Nor was he the first or last politician to have used crime statistics to advance his own career. Indeed, the use of statistics to articulate, justify and legitimise public policy has in fact been a central feature of the political scene for many years. Consequently, for a very long time, journalists have also reflected these political narratives, incorporating the use of statistics in the reporting of crime.

Indeed, there has always been a need for statistics to be incorporated into the reporting of crime both in order to substantiate as well as to legitimise the stories' claims. This is because as part of the prevalent news cultures, the news crime beat follows the key news values in contemporary journalism. That includes aspiring to be objective by being accurate and balanced when reporting and overall allowing the "facts" to speak for themselves (Hackett, 1984; Maras, 2013; Schiller, 1981). Statistics offered precisely that—the opportunity to underpin specific agendas by substantiating them with data. These numbers are arguably considered as significant legitimising elements in social reality constructions (Dorling & Simpson, 1999), even in the articulation of the news and the consequent legitimisation of the news story itself (Lugo-Ocando & Faria Brandão, 2015, p. 6). Because objectivity is still seen as a key notion in newsrooms and has been an aspirational normative referent in the journalistic vocabulary since the early part of the twentieth century (Hampton, 2008, p. 477; Mindich, 1998, p. 1), statistics in this context should be therefore understood as a powerful narrative (Alessandro Martinisi & Lugo-Ocando, 2015, p. 13), which is part of the wider positivist discourse that dominates the profession (Durham, 1998).

Statistics create a sense of legitimacy and objectivity, which news reporters constantly aspire to achieve. This comes from the assumption that the collection and analysis of data and statistics is grounded in the scientific method, society's model of objectivity and neutrality (Lugo-Ocando & Faria Brandão, 2015, p. 5). Because these numbers are considered as "unbiased" and "neutral", there is a tendency to forget that they just represent a convention through groups (Lorenzo Fioramonti, 2014, p. 33).

Thanks to this, nowadays they stand as the ultimate reference in the reporting of crime. If statistics say so, then governments and particularly politicians are seen to be succeeding or failing. This is the power of numbers in crime news.

Having said that, for a great part of the twentieth century crime statistics were not at the centre of crime news nor were they assigned as much influence or power. Two main reasons can be given to explain this. Firstly, because social deviance was not approached as a problem of public policy in the news. Instead, crime was seen as an individual issue that should be addressed by policing. Secondly, but closely related, because storytelling was far more important in the context of crime reporting. Hence, there was far less need to provide context or to link it to public policy. In fact, until a few decades ago, police and politicians were judged on their ability to assess a particular case that had gain notoriety rather than on the broader achievements of their policy and actions.

The triumph of law enforcement officers such as Eliot Ness (1903–1957) who became famous for his efforts to enforce Prohibition in Chicago in the USA and was the leader of a famous team of law enforcement agents nicknamed "The Untouchables"—later immortalised by Hollywood— was not in fact that somehow he managed to reduce alcohol consumption or eliminated organised crime around it, but that he was able to facilitate the imprisonment of the well-known gangster Al Capone in a highly publicised case (Perry, 2014). Ironically, the media left out the fact that Ness did outstanding work as Director of Public Safety in Cleveland in the mid-1930s, when he was able to effectively address crime and municipal government corruption. Ness, had a Master's degree in Criminology from the University of Chicago and was able to apply the latest techniques in police training, combat methods, surveillance, forensic science and neighbourhood patrols, and he started records of crime statistics, many of which he pioneered and improved. This was seldom reported in the press at the time, which instead treated him as a maverick fighter who seemed to use force rather than brains; something that we will revisit in this book in a later chapter.

Over the first half of the twentieth century and way up to the 1980s, the mainstream news media in many Western countries focused mainly on storytelling when reporting crime news (Barnhurst & Mutz, 1997,

p. 27). Hence, statistics were rarely the centre of these stories except in those cases in which they were used to carry out investigative reporting or which served to reinforce a particular sensationalist angle in the story. One of the cases worth mentioning is that of the work of twice Pulitzer-prize awarded investigative reporter at WBBM-TV in Chicago, Pam Zekman, on explaining the recurrent rapes in buildings owned and managed by the Chicago Housing Authority (CHA) at the beginning of the 1980s. By collecting data and cross referencing these sets of data with interviews she managed to expose a systematic failure of the CHA in maintaining minimum security and deep embedded corruption among contractors, all of which had led to the rapes in the first place (Ettema & Glasser, 1998, p. 2). However, in these stories it was not crime data but data related to corruption that was the centre of the stories. The big breakthrough of statistics being at the centre of the news on crime would come a few years later when Rudy Giuliani was New York City's Mayor: then both politicians and news people came to realise the power of crime numbers to convey their messages.

Zero Tolerance for Numbers

During his tenure, Rudy Giuliani appointed William Joseph "Bill" Bratton as New York City Police Commissioner. In 1994, Bratton set up the COMPuter STATistics (CompStat) program, a comparative statistical approach to mapping crime geographically in order to identify emerging criminal patterns and chart officer performance by quantifying apprehensions. This program allowed precinct commanders in New York to take decisions based on local data and determine what tactics to use to reduce crime. These statistics sought to increase the accountability of both commanders and officers, who could then respond better to specific targets and goals set by the Commissioner, while being constantly evaluated. While it is considered by some that the CompStat paradigm has revolutionised the way policing is carried out, its problems are less recognised. These include due process considerations, community relations, leadership issues and inadequate problem solving. Nevertheless, many police agencies throughout the world have tried to emulated the

CompStat program as its recorded achievements have been widely publicized and include dramatic reductions in crime, the accountability of key staff members, and coordination of various units within an agency (Eterno & Silverman, 2006, p. 218).

Indeed, the use of statistics during Giuliani's tenure attracted the attention of both politicians and journalists as this was an appealing narrative based on a hard "common sense" approach that combined both "tough on crime" and "quick fix" to society's problems, rapidly becoming a darling program among conservative voices. The news media then wnt on to report these numbers as "objective" facts, simplifying a far more complex story into one of the "goodies" against the "baddies". Thanks to this simplification, Giuliani was presented as an extremely competent politician who could solve problems; although the subsequent public confrontations with his own police commissioner put this last attribute in doubt. However, for the news media it was the perfect setting as these numbers allowed it to fulfil its duty as a "Watchdog" or "Fourth State", by providing what was seen as unbiased scrutiny of public policy. For the NYPD and Giuliani, on the other hand, it was a perfect opportunity to boost citizens' confidence in law and order and bring about a sense of increased security.

As some scholars have pointed out, though, Rudy Giuliani has been unable to replicate the alleged results of the New York City strategy in places such as Mexico City. Indeed, while as New York Mayor, Giuliani was able to capitalise on residents' fear and insecurity, in Mexico he could not deliver the same sense of stability and security that he promised. These researchers argue that:

> Giuliani's ideas garner high popularity not because of their success on the ground, but due to their currency in public discourses where they produced a 'cult of personality' that masks the very real failures of neoliberalism in everyday life. As such, Giuliani's policies in Mexico City constituted a performance: policing in drag, a dressing up of policies cloaked in the language of control, and alternatively marketed with Giuliani's masculinity and reputation as a 'tough guy.' This performance is part of the 'making up' of neoliberal policy to mask as effective, comforting, logical, and inevitable a set of policy prescriptions that has led to more insecurity, not less. (Mountz & Curran, 2009, p. 1033)

Moreover, if the striking reduction in homicide in New York City between 1991 and 1997 has been claimed as a great success for a new policing tactic dubbed "zero tolerance", based upon the aggressive enforcement of minor offences, some researchers have argued nevertheless that the "New York story" has been over-simplified and over-sold. Moreover, they point out that the term "zero tolerance" was inappropriately used to described a variety of circumstances, police policy and practices that were more over-reaching in explaining levels of crime reduction (Bowling, 1999, p. 531). These researchers have reminded us that "zero tolerance" was originally more to do with collaborative work with the communities and less with "toughness" on crime.

In this context, it is important to highlight that the most recent history of crime statistics in the news has not been one of pause and subtle analysis, but instead it has been a story in which these numbers have been regularly used for scaremongering while underpinning policy that is said to be "tough on crime" but that still has to demonstrate its effectiveness (Fagan & Davies, 2000, p. 457). Yet, this statistical narrative helped to set the agenda during the 1990s, one which would be adopted not only by rightwing politicians but also by those who claim to be progressive and liberal.

Tough on Causes?

The end of the Regan-Thatcher era did not mark the end of the "tough" approach and the arrival to power of Bill Clinton in the USA and Tony Blair in the UK did very little to reverse the political view of crime. The 1990s were in fact a period of ideological confusion in relation to crime policy, where the boundaries between progressive and conservative views became blurred and were constantly crossed by both sectors. The result was a very narrow set of options in relation to crime policy, which mostly centred on punishment and crime control (Poveda, 1994, p. 73). The media reflected this narrowness, and not only political debate and media accountability in relation to crime policy was limited, but this set the conventions and axiomatic assumptions that would mark the boundaries of the political discussion in the years to follow.

In fact, both Bill Clinton and later on Tony Blair would embrace the notion of evidence-based policy in the area of crime and justice and would use this data to justify some of the most draconian pieces of legislation seen in modern time (Vanlandingham & Drake, 2012; Welsh & Farrington, 2004); legislation and policy that overall tended to disproportionally hit the poorest and most excluded groups in society. In 1994, the then President of the USA, Bill Clinton, signed into law an omnibus piece of legislation —the Violent Crime Control and Law Enforcement Act—which among other things established mandatory life sentences for criminals convicted of a violent felony after two or more prior convictions, including drug crimes. The mandatory life sentences became publicly known as the "three-strikes" provision. Even though in reality crime in the USA is an issue that is devolved to the state, and the Federal government had little room for intervention in terms of policy and caution, the policy sent shockwaves across the political spectrum allowing the most right-wing voices to start driving the justice system into further draconian terrain. This is why that law is considered by some to be part of the "symbolic policies in Clinton's Crime Control Agenda":

> [These types of] symbolic policies are legislative acts that do not provide any tangible change, but serve to evoke a particular response from the public. Many symbolic policies make voters "feel good" by given the appearance that something is been done about the problem when, in fact this may not be true. Since crime cannot be significantly through legislation, politicians must rely on symbolic policies to convey the message that they are doing something to solve the problem. (Marion, 1997, p. 67)

There is wide evidence that these symbolic responses have been ineffective in controlling crime and despite being widely supported by the public, the media and many politicians, the "tough on crime" policy approach has proven to be both "costly and unjust" (Mauer, 1999b, p. 9). Nevertheless, numbers have helped in the past to underpin and justify the massive expansion of incarceration both in the USA and in the

UK. The policy was in fact ineffective, but nonetheless easy to justify by politicians such as Michael Howard, who as Home Secretary addressed the Conservative party conference on 6 October 1993 to say:

> Prison works. It ensures that we are protected from murderers, muggers and rapists—and it makes many who are tempted to commit crime think twice…This may mean that more people will go to prison. I do not flinch from that. We shall no longer judge the success of our system of justice by a fall in our prison population. (Nicholls & Katz, 2004)

Years later, using selected statistics and despite ample evidence that the whole approach was wrong, Howard went on again to defend the "tough on crime" policy. In a public lecture in London on 10 January 2003 he was quoted as saying: "An increase in the number of criminals in prison leads to a large fall in crime." In fact, what Howard tried to do was to link the fall in crime with the levels of imprisonment so as to establish a causation factor, where there was none.

Once Tony Blair became Prime Minister of the UK in 1997 under the banner of New Labour he was compelled to follow in the footsteps of Conservative predecessors in order to appease the strident voices on the right and particularly that of the tabloid newspapers. His first Home Secretary was Jack Straw and the motto of their tenure was "tough on crime, tough on the causes of crime" (Brownlee, 1998; Mauer, 1999), which broadly reflected the fact that they had not departed from the prevalent views on crime policy. Nevertheless, in discursive terms Blair's administration was characterised by the use of statistics to justify crime policy. This was not in the same sense the Giuliani had use the crime numbers to attack crime while promoting himself, but more in the sense of using numbers to justify policy that was in reality deeply rooted in ideology rather than reality.

Professor Tim Hope (2008) from the University of Salford, who at some point advised the Blair administration (and later resigned), confronted the government in relation to the use of data. He suggested how "evidence" was loosely used by the Blair government to justify its own policy while advancing an ideologically-driven agenda. He highlights how serious research had originally been expected to inform initiatives such as the Crime Reduction Programme (CRP), the then flagship proposal of New Labour. One of the key problems arose from Home Office officials trying to put their own spin on the data (2008, p. 49). As Hope explains:

> [Problems arise] when responsibility for validating policy—that is, for establishing 'what works'—is placed in the hands of (social) science, but the evidence produced is not, apparently, congenial to the particular 'network of governance' that is responsible for the policy. The outcome for evidence-based policy making in these circumstances is that scientific discourse and method itself falls victim to policy pressures and values. (2004, p. 287)

The experience of that era left an indelible mark; that any policy and government approach can be more or less justified with statistics, as long as they convey the "right" story. In the case of New Labour this was one in which it seems that the fall in the levels of crime were the result of the policy approach, despite ample evidence that they were not connected and that crime levels had been falling for years. Nevertheless, New Labour had learnt from Giuliani the true lesson of spin, as he too had come into power as Mayor of New York when crime levels had already begun to significantly fall under his predecessor. In fact, David Dinkins, who served as the 106th Mayor of New York City, from 1990 to 1993, is said to have contributed to this by increasing the size of the New York Police Department and implementing a series of public expenditure programmes that included housing and urban regeneration initiatives across the city in the context of falling unemployment levels.

The lesson for New Labour, however, was not only in relation to traditional spin, as was the case of Giuliani. In the case of the UK's new government it also had to do with the attempt to make New Labour appear more rational and less ideological in government. Indeed, Norman Fairclough (2000), at Lancaster University, has highlighted that the whole approach of "tough on crime, tough on the causes of crime" was an intrinsic part of the "authoritative" style upon which New Labour articulated its discourses and which was a central feature of Tony Blair's style (2000, p. 106). Consequently, this authoritative style had to appear rational and based on

scientific criteria as New Labour wanted to distance itself from the traditional Labour party image if being ideologically driven. Press releases,
press conferences and all types of presentations to the media, therefore,
would carry statistics and data to support policies and statements. It was a
period characterised by "spin-doctors" dominating British politics (Jones,
1999; McNair, 2004) and a media dynamic that would vacuum in the use
of statistics and cause a storm of constant manipulation. This phenomenon was not only limited to the use of traditional crime statistics, but also
meant incorporating an increasing barrage of new numbers which were
created just for the purpose of measuring achievement and performance,
such as self-imposed targets and so on. This end result was an explosive
combination of quasi-authoritarian managerialism based on target-driven
policy intervention (Barber, 2007; Cutler & Waine, 2000) that led to
irrational assumptions and flawed policies, most of which remained largely
unaccounted for by the mainstream media which never really got hold of
what these numbers actually meant.

Post Tough Period

Some years later, after the New Labour experience, it is possible to say
that the media reporting of crime seems to have overcome the frenzy-
driven statistics news agenda. After all, crime is still very low and it seems
that many politicians have come to realise the absurdity of trying to set so
many targets. Specific areas, such as the incarceration policy both in the
USA and the UK, no longer cite falling crime statistics to justify high
levels of imprisonment and, on the contrary, even very conservative voices
are now advocating prison reform and a substantial reduction of the
prison population—although cynics point out that increasing costs to
the tax payer is the reason for their change of mind. In the USA:

> Conservative support has given criminal justice reform a powerful biparti-
> san boost. Since 2010, 13 states have revised sentencing laws, including
> traditionally red states Arkansas, Kentucky, South Carolina, Louisiana and
> Georgia. Texas began diverting drug offenders from prisons in 2007
> through drug courts, probation and treatment and has cut its incarceration
> rate 11%. (Moore, 2014)

Today, paradoxically, we see the same voices that use to quote statistics to justify mass incarceration using similar statistics to justify exactly the contrary (Lynch, 2000). In a way, we have gone full circle, back to the times of Winston Churchill, who when arguing against over-sentencing and in favour of prison reform said that the mood and temper of the public with regard to the treatment of crime and criminals is one of the most unfailing tests of the civilization of any country (Bailey, 1997; Baxendale, 2010). This change of political mood has also brought about a change in the way crime in general and crime statistics in particular are reported in the news.

In the past few years, in fact, we have seen a more subtle and nuance use of crime statistics in the news media. However, one must ask if this means that the era of statistics-driven crime news is over after the initial 1990s hype. Not at all, would be the answer. On the contrary, as we will discuss later in this book, the fundamental shift from a greater focus on storytelling crime stories to one that seems to be more interested in public policy scrutiny through statistics seems to have become entrenched. This is not to say, however, that storytelling is still not very important, which it is, but to highlight the fact that even in the most mundane crime news report we expect nowadays to see crime statistics being used increasingly more as we enter into an age of big data. This is, after all, the latest stage in a long history of the relationship between the media and crime numbers.

References

Anderson, D. C. (1997). The mystery of the falling crime rate. *American Prospect, 32,* 49–55.

Bailey, V. (1997). English prisons, penal culture, and the abatement of imprisonment, 1895–1922. *The Journal of British Studies, 36*(03), 285–324.

Barber, M. (2007). *Instruction to deliver: Tony Blair, public services and the challenge of achieving targets.* London: Politico.

Barnhurst, K. G., & Mutz, D. (1997). American journalism and the decline in event-centered reporting. *Journal of Communication, 47*(4), 27–53.

Baxendale, A. S. (2010). *Winston Leonard Spencer-Churchill: Penal reformer.* Oxford: Peter Lang.

Bowling, B. (1999). The rise and fall of New York murder: Zero tolerance or crack's decline? *British Journal of Criminology, 39*(4), 531–554.

Brownlee, I. (1998). New labour—New penology? Punitive rhetoric and the limits of managerialism in criminal justice policy. *Journal of Law and Society, 25*(3), 313–335.

Brownlees, N. (2011). *The language of periodical news in seventeenth-century England.* Newcastle upon Tyne: Cambridge Scholars Publishing.

Cutler, T., & Waine, B. (2000). Managerialism reformed? New Labour and public sector management. *Social Policy & Administration, 34*(3), 318–332.

Dorling, D., & Simpson, S. (1999). *Statistics in society: The arithmetic of politics.* London: Arnold.

Durham, M. G. (1998). On the relevance of standpoint epistemology to the practice of journalism: The case for "strong objectivity". *Communication Theory, 8*(2), 117–140.

Eterno, J. A., & Silverman, E. B. (2006). The New York City police department's Compstat: Dream or nightmare? *International Journal of Police Science & Management, 8*(3), 218–231.

Ettema, J., & Glasser, T. (1998). *Custodians of conscience: Investigative journalism and public virtue.* New York: Columbia University Press.

Fagan, J., & Davies, G. (2000). Street stops and broken windows: Terry, race and disorder in New York City. *Fordham Urban Law Journal, 28*, 457–504.

Fairclough, N. (2000). *New labour, new language?* London: Routledge.

Fioramonti, L. (2014). *How numbers role the world. The use and abuse of statistics in global politics.* London: Zed Books.

Gallagher, C. (1986). The body versus the social body in the works of Thomas Malthus and Henry Mayhew. *Representations, 14*, 83–106.

Garcia, F. (2016). Rudy Giuliani says black people have a 99% chance of killing each other. Retrieved August 22, 2016, from http://www.independent.co.uk/news/world/americas/rudy-giuliani-black-people-kill-each-other-99-percent-nyc-mayor-black-lives-matter-a7129926.html

Garland, D. (1985). *Punishment and welfare: A history of penal strategies.* Farnham, Surrey: Gower Aldershot.

Griffiths, D. (1992). *The Encyclopedia of the British press, 1422–1992.* London: Macmillan.

Hackett, R. A. (1984). Decline of a paradigm? Bias and objectivity in news media studies. *Critical Studies in Media Communication, 1*(3), 229–259.

Hampton, M. (2008). The "objectivity" ideal and its limitations in 20th-century British journalism. *Journalism Studies, 9*(4), 477–493.

Hope, T. (2004). Pretend it works evidence and governance in the evaluation of the reducing burglary initiative. *Criminal Justice, 4*(3), 287–308.

Hope, T. (2008). The first casualty: Evidence and governance in a war against crime. In P. Carlen (Ed.), *Imaginary Penalities* (pp. 45–63). London: Routledge.

Humpherys, A. (1977). *Travels into the poor man's country: The work of Henry Mayhew.* Atlanta: University of Georgia Press.

Jones, N. (1999). *Sultans of spin.* London: Gollancz.

Kelling, G. L., & Bratton, W. J. (1998). Declining crime rates: Insiders' views of the New York City story. *The Journal of Criminal Law and Criminology (1973–), 88*(4), 1217–1232.

Lugo-Ocando, J., & Faria Brandão, R. (2015). STABBING NEWS: Articulating crime statistics in the newsroom. *Journalism Practice, 10*(6), 1–15.

Lynch, T. (2000). Population bomb behind bars. Retrieved March 21, 2017, from https://www.cato.org/publications/commentary/population-bomb-behind-bars

Mair, G., & Burke, L. (2013). *Redemption, rehabilitation and risk management: A history of probation.* London: Routledge.

Maras, S. (2013). *Objectivity in journalism.* Hoboken, NJ: John Wiley & Sons.

Marion, N. E. (1997). Symbolic policies in Clinton's crime control agenda. *Buffalo Criminal Law Review, 1*(1), 67–108.

Martinisi, A., & Lugo-Ocando, J. (2015). Overcoming the objectivity of the senses: Enhancing journalism practice through Eastern philosophies. *International Communication Gazette, 77*(5), 439–455.

Mauer, M. (1999). Why are tough on crime policies so popular. *Stanford Law & Policy Review, 11*(1), 9.

Mayhew, H. (2009 [1851]). *London labour and the London poor: A cyclopædia of the condition and earnings of those that will work, those that cannot work, and those that will not.* Lodnon: Cosimo, Inc..

Mayhew, H., & Binny, J. (1862). *The criminal prisons of London: And scenes of prison life.* London: Griffin, Bohn, and Company.

McNair, B. (2004). PR must die: Spin, anti-spin and political public relations in the UK, 1997–2004. *Journalism Studies, 5*(3), 325–338.

Mindich, D. T. Z. (1998). *Just facts: How objectivity came to define American journalism.* New York: University Press.

Moore, M. (2014). Conservatives, liberals unite to cut prison population. Retrieved August 29, 2016, from http://www.usatoday.com/story/news/politics/2014/03/16/conservatives-sentencing-reform/6396537/

Mountz, A., & Curran, W. (2009). Policing in drag: Giuliani goes global with the illusion of control. *Geoforum, 40*(6), 1033–1040.

Nicholls, M., & Katz, L. (2004). Michael Howard: A life in quotes. Retrieved July 2, 2016, from http://www.theguardian.com/politics/2004/aug/26/conservatives.uk

Perry, D. (2014). *Eliot Ness: The rise and fall of an American hero*. London: Penguin.

Pettegree, A. (2014). *The invention of news: How the world came to know about itself*. New Heaven, CT: Yale University Press.

Poveda, T. G. (1994). Clinton, Crime, and the Justice Department. *Social Justice, 21*(57), 73–84.

Pratt, J. (2002). *Punishment and civilization: Penal tolerance and intolerance in modern society*. London: Sage.

Rosanvallon, P. (2012). *La Sociedad de los Iguales*. Barcelona: RBA Libros.

Schiller, D. (1981). *Objectivity and the news: The public and the rise of commercial journalism*. Philadelphia: University of Pennsylvania Press.

Surette, R. (1998). *Media, Crime and Criminal Justice: Images and Realities*. Belmont, CA: West/Wadsworth.

Vanlandingham, G. R., & Drake, E. K. (2012). Results first: Using evidence-based policy models in state policymaking. *Public Performance & Management Review, 35*(3), 550–563.

Welsh, B. C., & Farrington, D. P. (2004). Surveillance for crime prevention in public space: Results and policy choices in Britain and America. *Criminology & Public Policy, 3*(3), 497–526.

Zimring, F. (2006). *The great American crime decline*. Oxford: Oxford University Press.

4

Media Representations of Crime Statistics

In order to understand the basics of crime statistics representations in the news media, we first need to reiterate that journalists treat statistics both as a "news source" and as "facts" (Lugo-Ocando & Faria Brandão, 2015, p. 716). Because of this, journalists quote statistics as if they were "subjects" providing information, which can then underpin the central narrative in their news stories. Consequently, we often find news items in which one can read or hear phrases pointing out such things as: "according these statistics, young women under 20 are more likely to be victims of domestic abuse". In many of such stories, journalists using statistics seem to leave "agency" out of the news account. The news media is full of references to statistics as a news source and in terms of daily practice, journalists award these numbers similar credibility and status as they give to "experts sources" in other news beats such as science (Conrad, 1999; Kruvand, 2012) and place them in their narratives as authoritative voices. In this sense, statistics in crime reporting become "primary definers" (Hall, Critcher, Jefferson, Clarke, & Roberts, 1978) in the articulation of news, underpinning meaning and providing legitimacy to what is said.

Paradoxically, most journalists also perceive and treat statistics as "objective facts". That is, they see statistics as objects that exist independently of perception or of individual conceptions and values. They use

© The Author(s) 2017
J. Lugo-Ocando, *Crime Statistics in the News*,
DOI 10.1057/978-1-137-39841-3_4

these numbers as "solid" evidence to support their narratives and to substantiate the arguments being made. This dual conceptualisation of statistics, as we have seen in the previous chapters, is a result of historical developments, which placed numbers at the centre of the notion of objectivity. Statistics are especially potent when they give a sense of solid reality (usually false) to something people vaguely apprehend and when they prove or document what people already feel or want to believe (Kamisar, 1972, p. 239).

Because of this, crime statistics play a fundamental role in underpinning the core arguments made by journalists while legitimising their narratives; this regardless of how much or how little truth there is in these narratives. In an Aristotelean sense, crime statistics in the news play the function of "logos" as they support the argument, providing the logic and a rational explanation by means of "demonstrable evidence". As mentioned above, statistics are used and presented in the news as factual evidence, which can corroborate or refute what it is said by some. These "facts" are then seen and treated in ways that uncritically assume that they are "natural" as it is anticipated that they represent factual reality. When journalists report that the number of crimes is rising or decreasing, they do so as a "factual reality" without considering that these numbers might aggregate very dissimilar realities or in fact represent just a particular or partial interpretation of those designing the statistics. For example, while the overall numbers of crimes reported in the news is said to have increased, this might be because new categories have been introduced that did not exist before—such as hate crimes and cyber-crime—or just because some crimes are just being reported more often (such as rape or fraud). For example, on April 2017 the media reported in its headlines that homicide and knife crime rates were "up in England and Wales" (BBC, 2017) in what was the final set of crime statistics to be released before the general election. This despite the fact that the Office for National Statistics (ONS) warned, in relation to this specific set of data, that this increase was "thought to reflect changes in recording processes and practices rather than crime". In other cases, it is because traditional social and cultural practices have been criminalised (such as free speech under new anti-terrorism laws or female genital mutilation) or decriminalised (such as the use of certain drugs for recreational purposes). Hence, considering this, one might argue that the original statistically-based picture portrayed by the news media might not be as "factual" as original thought.

Moreover, if —normatively speaking—the public purpose of the use of statistics in news media reports is to provide an accurate and true description of society, then in reality journalists tend to use—intentionally or not—statistics to reinforce particular worldviews about social problems. "Numbers are created and repeated because they supply ammunition for political struggles, and this political purpose is often hidden behind assertions that numbers, simply because they are numbers, must be correct" (Best, 2012, p. 13). Consequently, one must conclude that these numbers play an important role within the interpretative function of journalism as a social practice.

Indeed, as some scholars have pointed out, journalists as a professional body can be seen to be members of an "interpretive community", one that it is united by its shared discourse and collective interpretations of key public events. In this sense, journalists tend to generate collective interpretations and provide a shared meaning of these news events (Zelizer, 1993, p. 219). This shared meaning develops through on-going social interaction and it is mostly "shaped by the preferred meanings of a community's interpretive groups, including journalists and their news organisations" (Berkowitz & TerKeurst, 1999, p. 125). This shared meaning creates "conventions", which become the default axiomatic referent for journalists when producing news.

These conventions are determined by a variety of "logics", "dynamics" and "rationales" that are set by the relationship between the journalists and their communities, which are fostered in the context of the news organisation for which they work and their "news cultures" (Allan, 2004; Deuze, 2002; Preston, 2008). These conventions also define the "discursive regimes" (Gee, 2014) within which news stories are articulated and make sense. It is because of this that the way the news media represents crime statistics needs to be understood within the notion of these conventions. This is because they set the explanatory framework for how statistics are read and interpreted and then inserted into the journalistic narratives. Moreover, these conventions are rarely questioned by journalists and they are instead taken as axiomatic assumptions which end up shaping their news stories.

This explain why, for example, journalists, on many occasions, tend to interpret the "facts" presumably conveyed by crime statistics in ways that do not necessarily reflect the subtleness and complexity of a particular situation or event but rather through the lens of broad agreements common to the interpretative community to which they belong. Consequently, to give an example, the number of random assaults and abuses against people with a disability are rarely interpreted as hate crimes as that category of crime is reserved to ethnicity and religion in the prevalent convention. In this sense, this chapter examines the way in which crime statistics are presented to the public and are articulated in the news while assessing how crime statistics are used by journalists when producing news stories. In so doing, it discusses how crime statistics are used by journalists to produce, contextualise and substantiate their stories while explaining also their role as "objective" facts in the news stories.

Statistics as Source and Fact

Let us start here by re-emphasising that statistics is perhaps one of the most important legitimising elements in the construction of social reality in modern society. This because as society becomes more and more mathematised, it increasingly also becomes dependent on measuring things to provide meaning to ideas and objects that surrounds us. This mathematisation of society, and particularly of its governance and understanding, underpins the process of bureaucratisation that is increasingly overtaking the public and private spheres (Bennett, 2006). Thanks to the "axiological neutrality" (Bourdieu, 2000; Wacquant, 2011) that mathematics offers, the analysis and process of decision making tends to reflect a positivist influence. The social theories that are developed and used by policy makers and academics to explain and govern society are then mathematically formulated and have the objective of developing a collection of models that can offer predictability and support to bureaucratic planning. For journalists, on the other hand, the process of mathematisation offers the possibility of bringing about "objective" accountability while providing a sense of transparency. This because, if all processes and dynamics in society can be quantified, then it is arguably possible to provide an accurate and objective account of them.

In historical terms, some foresaw how this process of "mathematisation" would affect the way the news media would report societal issues in the future. Such was the case of the French sociologist and criminologist Gabriel Tarde, who predicted in the nineteenth century that:

> The public journals will become socially what our sense organs are vitally. Every printing office will become a mere central station for different bureaus of statistics just as the ear-drum is a bundle of acoustic nerves, or as the retina is a bundle of special nerves each of which registers its characteristic impression on the brain. At present statistics is a kind of embryonic eye, like that of the lower animals which see just enough to recognise the approach of foe or prey. (Tarde, 2005 [1890], p. 136)

In fact, statistics have been an intrinsic part of the positivist discourse upon which the conceptualisation of modern journalism is based (Pahre, 1995, 1996). Moreover, the journalistic concept of objectivity in various theoretical schools can be found in that positivistic tradition (Wien, 2005, p. 3). Indeed, journalistic practices in the West have a most important foundation in the philosophical system that recognises that truth can only be based on facts that can be scientifically verified, particularly those which are capable of logical or mathematical proof (Martinisi, 2017; Martinisi & Lugo-Ocando, 2015). Statistics provide precisely the opportunity to verify or challenge the different accounts and narratives by making "reality" measurable.

Consequently, these numbers are valued by journalists and news editors/producers as an objective source of information precisely because statistics, as the ultimate expression of positivist thinking, are an intrinsic part of the construction of what is truth. In this sense, the power of statistics to legitimise news resides in their external appreciation as an objective and scientific source of information, which creates consensus among the audiences while setting the parameters for conventions among those publicly debating policy and issues.

Indeed, these numbers underpin the acceptable "conventions" in order to act for the collective view and against the subjective perceptions of the individual (Ian Parker, 1999, p. 86). The ability of statistics to underpin socially constructed reality is such, at least among journalists working with the mainstream news media, that one is perhaps inclined to set statistics apart from any other news source as they tend to confer legitimacy and strength to news stories that deal with public policy. This because, as I mentioned before, statistics are articulated in the news within the wider conceptual notion of objectivity as a news source. In this regard, they help journalists to fulfil the aspiration to perform the "strategic ritual" of objectivity (Tuchman, 1972, p. 661) by providing the "factual evidence" in their narratives. As news sources, these numbers are a key element in deciding content and credibility of the news, while determining how audiences interpret news. Moreover, these statistics as news sources are also a vital aspect of the news manufacturing process as they confer additional legitimacy to what journalists report.

If, traditionally speaking, news sources have been defined as "actors whom journalism observe and interview", including interviewees who appear on air or who are quoted in the news reports or provide background information for the stories (Gans, 1980, p. 80), in reality it is far more complex than that and journalists approach "sources" in a variety of ways, which include considering the use of "inanimate objects" as the key reference for the story. Such was the case of a story on tax evasion in the Panama newspapers where, in some cases, not one single person was quoted. Hence, for many journalists, news sources are also those "elements" that can provide information that can generate, substantiate and/or legitimise news stories. In these cases, official documents or access to a data set is also considered by many practitioners as a "news source". It is into this last category that we can place statistics as a news source, which in terms of articulating news can become a legitimate way to account for the events and issues being reported.

However, this creates problems regarding rigour and fact checking; two of the most important practices around verifying every news story. This is because, contrary to what occurs with other news sources, these numbers are seldom crossed-referenced in order to be verified. Therefore, journalists and news editors tend to take the information presumably conveyed by the statistics at its face value without sufficiently assessing critically what these numbers really mean, their nature or the way they were created. Moreover, due to what some authors describe as "increasing pressures and limited resources" in the newsroom (Davies, 2008; Lewis, Williams, & Franklin, 2008), these news editors/producers and journalists also have to accept the interpretations and explanatory framework provided by those who produce these statistics and take for granted the angle and focus that spin-doctors and PR people add to them; something that we will explore in more depth in a later chapter. However, it is sufficient to say for now that this directly affects the level of credibility and trust that news audiences have about what is being reported.

Journalists award credibility to a news source because they see it as possessing an expertise relevant to the topic or issues about which they are reporting. Therefore they need to be considered trustful and accurate when confirming facts and events, communicating a message or supporting a particular opinion or view. For journalists, there are objective sources that are seen to be independent from corporate or government interests in order to produce a fair and balanced account in the stories (Franklin & Carlson, 2011, p. 104). To be that, the news source needs to be characterised by trustworthiness, expertise, respect for privacy, honesty and neutrality. This is something that tends to happens mostly in science news but thanks to statistical journalists it is also expected to happen in crime reporting.

Indeed, crime statistics seem to comply with all these characteristics. News editors and journalists, as well as large segments of the audiences, trust statistics despite the saying attributed to Benjamin Disraeli: "There are three kinds of lies: lies, damned lies, and statistics." This happens primarily among journalists because these numbers are produced by official bodies, making them an "official source". Consequently, they are perceived as providing "expert" evidence that can be corroborated. This because statistics included in information packs that go into the newsrooms are normally accompanied by a technical explanation of how they were gathered and processed. Therefore, most journalists assume that they are scientific and transparent, hence they are a politically "neutral" element/facts from which they can draw their own "honest" conclusions.

More importantly, statistics represent general populations and from them trends rather than individual behaviours are inferrred. Consequently, they underpin universal conventions by means of representing these general trends in the public imagination. In so doing, statistics provide the basis for discursive regimes that frame all political discussions and debate, creating and reinforcing the borders of axiomatic truth. In saying, for example, that the majority of people do not commit crimes, statistics then reinforce the idea that crime is an unacceptable deviation from the norm. This despite the fact that it is those in power who define what crime is and that crime itself is a social category. This is not only the case with broad areas such as murder, manslaughter or armed robbery (where the conventions that dictate that these crimes are much stronger and more generalised), but also— depending on the society and time of history—of types of behaviour where there is less consensus about what is and what is not crime, such as free speech, religious tolerance, dress codes, homosexuality, trade union militancy and political protest, to cite a few.

To explain the importance of this further, it is necessary to point out that journalists tend, at least in theory, to stick to widely accepted conventions. These conventions relate to well-accepted frameworks when reporting news. Journalists are expected to make at least some basic distinctions between "criminals" and "the general public" and between "crime" and "normal behaviour", even though these are in themselves socially constructed categories which are mostly defined by the politics of each era and place. A few years ago, for example, one would not imagine that wearing a burkini publicly on the beaches of Marseille would be counted as a crime, but today it is a growing statistic in France. By allowing journalists to summarise and simplify crime through statistics, these numbers facilitate communicating prevalent worldviews and conventions. This is what journalists need to bear in mind.

Media Portrayal

Firstly, let us underline one of the key aspects in relation to media representations of crime statistics. This is the fact that many crime news stories do not explicitly contain or make direct reference to statistics. However, the overwhelmingly number that do so present these stories in the format of "hard news stories" (Lugo-Ocando & Faria Brandão, 2015, p. 727). Hard news is the most prevalent genre in news. It is based on the inverted pyramid style, which demands that one places the most important elements of the story at the start, then go on to the explanatory passages, leaving the less relevant facts to the end in a declining order of importance. Accordingly, journalists allocate in the first couple of sentences of a news story the most newsworthy elements. That is often referred to as "the lead", which includes the 5W's—Who? What? When? Where? Why?—and How? By doing so, journalists can summarise a story in the first two or three paragraphs of a written piece (in the case of print and online media outlets) or in the opening of a broadcast story.

The other important fact to highlight is that in many cases where news stories include statistics, these are not the core of the stories. Instead, they tend to be mostly used to contextualise or substantiate the stories. Only in some cases do statistics become the key element of a particular news item. In those cases in which statistics are the centre of a hard news story, these numbers would had been made available or released to journalists on the day they were producing their news stories. Accordingly, journalists feel the need to report statistics immediately, otherwise they assume that the statistics will lose their "newsworthiness" and become a "cold" story with little or no interest for the editors and the public.

This need to immediately communicate statistics has two main consequences. First, crime statistics tend to be communicated in news stories with little analysis beyond what is attached to them by the officials and spin-doctors who make them available to the media. Journalists fail to process them appropriately and tend to concentrate on the key numbers such as overall trends in crime or specific areas such as violent crime. This leaves very little opportunity for journalists to produce more in-depth and interpretative works based on these numbers. Secondly, and equally important to mention, is that journalists seem to have little time to fact-check these numbers or contrast them against other sources. So if the official statistics point towards a decrease on the overall rate of crime, journalists would seldom be able to challenge that assertion.

This is fundamentally important as what makes crime statistics such a "hot" political topic is that they are often used as a measurement of the degree of success of a government in terms of justice and crime policy. They are used by politicians in office and by those in opposition to assert their own respective narratives of success and failure. The news media, on the other hand, has to cover the statistics in this way as the release of the data happens in an orchestrated and ritualistic manner that turn the whole thing into a "media event" (Couldry, Hepp, & Krotz, 2009; Katz & Dayan, 1992), one which escapes from the control of journalists and news editors. In other words, in most cases, the agenda on crime statistics is set by those who provide the statistics in the first place rather than by the journalists or news media on their own accord. We should not underestimate the importance of this fact as it turns what should be a process of reflective social analysis, derived from the mathematical processing of numerical data, into a descriptive reporting exercise that tends to reproduce the assumptions made and worldviews held by those in power. Moreover, on only a few occasions do journalists provide in-depth analysis of the data released by officials in the same way they do, for example, with electoral polls.

This would not be such a problem if it was an accurate depiction of crime. However, that is not the case and on many occasions the news media plays an important role in creating a sense of violence and danger on our streets because violence makes good news (Battersby, 2010, p. 11). In this sense, it is important to acknowledge that the media tends to cherry-pick elements of statistics involving knife crime in order to gain readership and fulfil its own agenda, therefore failing to bring a sense of proportion to controversial subjects such as drug misuse, to give an example (Silverman, 2010, p. 31).

Some scholarly literature has already highlighted that there are important discrepancies between what the media says regarding crime and what actually statistical data informs (Ditton & Duffy, 1983; Schlesinger & Tumber, 1994; Williams & Dickinson, 1993). Because of these discrepancies, violent crime and street crime in general tends to be historically the most over-reported area in newspapers (O'Keefe & Reid-Nash, 1987, p. 149). This is despite the fact that crime statistics indicate that most crime is non-violent, yet media reports suggest the opposite (Sacco, 1995, p. 143). There is in fact, as some authors have suggested, a "disproportional emphasis on crime violence within crime news [which] is, at one level, easily explained by the fact that sensational stories about violent crime sell newspapers" (Barlow, Barlow, & Chiricos, 1995, p. 10). It is because of this that the reporting of crime statistics tends to focus on violent crime while downplaying other forms of crime that nevertheless tend to have far more societal consequences; such as the so-called "white-collar crime" which refers to financially motivated non-violent crime committed by business and government professionals (Levi, 2006; Taibbi, 2014). In terms of why the news media makes so much of violent crime statistics and so little of corporate and white-collar crime, one can say that overall "the media favours disturbing statistics about big problems because they are more interesting, compelling news" (Best, 2012, p. 57). Statistics about violence are, therefore, more appealing for the news editors and journalists although not always as important for society as statistics relating to more elitists crime, as sadly the 2008 financial crisis demonstrated. In Western industrialised countries it is precisely the rarity of violent crime occurring which makes it so appealing for the news.

Although, many news reports on crime do not include statistics it is these numbers that frame the news as part of the political debate. Numbers in the news give context and a sense of how well or bad policy makers and authorities are dealing with crime. They are, intrinsically, at the core of socially constructed reality around crime. However, let us not forget, that these statistics are not necessarily facts or the truth. They are part of that reality that we construct on a daily basis with our values and worldviews. It is enough to remind ourselves that many crimes from the past, which we counted with accuracy and rigour, no longer exist. Meanwhile others, which we do not even imagine happening yet or that could not exist a few decades ago—such as those related to cybercrime—are already making the headlines of tomorrow. After all, crime statistics not only reflect reality, they are part of the many tools that we use to create social reality and present it as truth.

Indeed, the media "use statistics to support their point of view, to bring others around to their way of thinking" (Best, 2012, p. 18) because it is part of its rhetorical strategy to assure that what is being reported is understood by all as truth. While there is an almost statutory duty in democratic society—given the normative claims of the news media of being the Fourth Estate—to report these statistics, present them to the public and analyse them critically, this is done in a way that seems instead to reinforce prevalent discourses of power around crime. Because of this, as we will see in the next chapter, the understanding of crime by the

general public is complicated and the ability of many people to participate in and engage with serious debates around law and order have
become, over the years, seriously compromised.

References

Allan, S. (2004). *News culture*. Cambridge: Cambridge University Press.

Barlow, M., Barlow, D., & Chiricos, T. (1995). Economic conditions and ideologies of crime in the media: A content analysis of crime news. *Crime &
Delinquency, 41*(1), 3–19.

Battersby, M. (2010). *Is that a Fact?* Peterborough, ON: Broadview Press.

BBC. (2017). Homicide and knife crime rates 'up in England and Wales'.
Retrieved March 28, 2017, from http://www.bbc.co.uk/news/uk-39729601

Bennett, J. (2006). Modernity and its critics. In J. S. Dryzek, B. Honig, &
A. Phillips (Eds.), *The Oxford Handbook of political theory* (pp. 211–224).
Oxford: Oxford University Press.

Berkowitz, D., & TerKeurst, J. V. (1999). Community as interpretive community: Rethinking the journalist-source relationship. *Journal of Communication,
49*(3), 125–136.

Best, J. (2012). *Damned lies and statistics: Untangling numbers from the media,
politicians, and activists*. Berkeley: University of California Press.

Bourdieu, P. (2000). For a scholarship with commitment. *Profession*, 40–45.

Conrad, P. (1999). Uses of expertise: Sources, quotes, and voice in the reporting
of genetics in the news. *Public Understanding of Science, 8*(4), 285–302.

Couldry, N., Hepp, A., & Krotz, F. (2009). *Media events in a global age*. London:
Routledge.

Davies, N. (2008). *Flat earth news: An award-winning reporter exposes falsehood,
distortion and propaganda in the global media*. London: Random House.

Deuze, M. (2002). National news cultures: A comparison of Dutch, German,
British, Australian, and US journalists. *Journalism & Mass Communication
Quarterly, 79*(1), 134–149.

Ditton, J., & Duffy, J. (1983). Bias in the newspaper reporting of crime news.
*The British Journal of Criminology: An International Review of Crime and
Society, 23*(2), 159–165.

Franklin, B., & Carlson, M. (2011). Sources, credibility and the continuing
crisis of UK journalism. *Journalists, Sources and Credibility: New Perspectives*,
90–106.

Gans, H. J. (1980). *Deciding what's news NBC. A study of CBS Evening News Nightly News, Newsweek, and Time.* New York: Vintage Books.

Gee, J. P. (2014). *An introduction to discourse analysis: Theory and method.* Abingdon-on-Thames, OX: Routledge.

Hall, S., Critcher, C., Jefferson, T., Clarke, J., & Roberts, B. (1978). The social production of news. In S. Hall (Ed.), *Policing the crisis; Mugging, the state and law and order* (pp. 53–60). London: Macmillan.

Kamisar, Y. (1972). How to use, abuse -and fight back with- crime statistics. *Oklahoma Law Review, 25,* 239–258.

Katz, E., & Dayan, D. (1992). *Media events: The live broadcasting of history.* Cambridge, MA: Harvard University Press.

Kruvand, M. (2012). "Dr. Soundbite" the making of an expert source in science and medical stories. *Science Communication, 34*(5), 566–591.

Levi, M. (2006). The media construction of financial white-collar crimes. *British Journal of Criminology, 46*(6), 1037–1057.

Lewis, J., Williams, A., & Franklin, B. (2008). A compromised fourth estate? UK news journalism, public relations and news sources. *Journalism Studies, 9*(1), 1–20.

Lugo-Ocando, J., & Faria Brandão, R. (2015). STABBING NEWS: Articulating crime statistics in the newsroom. *Journalism Practice, 10*(6), 715–729. doi:1 0.1080/17512786.2015.1058179.

Martinisi, A. (2017). Understanding quality of statistics in news stories: A theoretical approach from the audience's perspective. In *Handbook of research on driving STEM learning with educational technologies* (pp. 485–505). Hershey, PA: IGI Global.

Martinisi, A., & Lugo-Ocando, J. (2015). Overcoming the objectivity of the senses: Enhancing journalism practice through Eastern philosophies. *International Communication Gazette, 77*(5), 409–412.

O'Keefe, G., & Reid-Nash, K. (1987). Crime news and real-world blues the effects of the media on social reality. *Communication Research, 14*(2), 147–163.

ONS. (2017). Crime in England and Wales: Year ending Mar 2017. *Office for National Statistics.* Retrieved June 12, 2017, from https://www.ons.gov.uk/peoplepopulationandcommunity/crimeandjustice/bulletins/crimeinenglandandwales/yearendingmar2017

Pahre, R. (1995). Positivist discourse and social scientific communities: Towards an epistemological sociology of science. *Social Epistemology, 9*(3), 233–255.

Pahre, R. (1996). Mathematical discourse and cross-disciplinary communities: The case of political economy. *Social Epistemology, 10*(1), 55–73.

Parker, I. (1999). Qualitative data and the subjectivity of 'objective' facts. Research fails unless it engages with subjectivity. In D. Dorling & L. Simpson (Eds.), *Statistics in society. The arithmetic of politics* (pp. 83–88). London: Arnold.

Preston, P. (2008). *Making the news: Journalism and news cultures in Europe.* Abingdon-on-Thames, OX: Routledge.

Sacco, V. (1995). Media constructions of crime. *The Annals of the American Academy of Political and Social Science,* 141–154.

Schlesinger, P., & Tumber, H. (1994). *Reporting crime. The media politics of criminal justice.* Oxford: Oxford University Press.

Silverman, J. (2010). Addicted to getting drugs wrong. *British Journalism Review, 21*(4), 31–36.

Taibbi, M. (2014). *The divide: American injustice in the age of the wealth gap.* New York: Spiegel & Grau.

Tarde, G. (2005 [1890]). *The laws of imitation.* New York: Holt.

Tuchman, G. (1972). Objectivity as strategic ritual: An examination of newsmen's notions of objectivity. *American Journal of sociology, 77*(4), 660–679.

Wacquant, L. (2011). From 'public criminology' to the reflexive sociology of criminological production and consumption a review of public criminology? by Ian Loader and Richard Sparks (London: Routledge, 2010). *British Journal of Criminology, 51*(2), 438–448.

Wien, C. (2005). Defining objectivity within journalism. *Nordicom Review, 26*(2), 3–15.

Williams, P., & Dickinson, J. (1993). Fear of crime: Read all about it? The relationship between newspaper crime reporting and fear of crime. *British Journal of Criminology, 33*(1), 33–56.

Zelizer, B. (1993). Journalists as interpretive communities. *Critical Studies in Media Communication, 10*(3), 219–237.

5

Stabbing News: What Knife Crime Tells Us About Crime Statistics in the News Room

Statistical data has an important role in facilitating public understanding of social issues (Dorling & Simpson, 1999; Theodore Porter, 1996). Understandably, an accurate and critical dissemination and representation of quantitative data by the media is paramount for both the public in general as well as policy makers in particular (Jaffe & Spirer, 1987; Utts, 2003). In light of this, as some authors have pointed out, there is a urgent need to present quantitative data in a simpler and more accessible form to the public (Hough & Roberts, 2005; Thomas & Durant, 1987), one that nevertheless incorporates a more comprehensive and critical understanding of the theories behind the data and how they relate to their research methodologies (Zuberi, 2001). This, it is argued here, is the case of the reporting of crime statistics, which has had over the years a profound influence on both public attitudes and public policy towards law and order (Dowler, 2003).

Overall, there is a comprehensive body of scholarly work regarding the way in which the media represents crime (Chibnall, 1977; Ericson, Baranek, & Chan, 1987; Hall, 1975; Jewkes & Yar, 2010; Sparks, 1992)

This chapter is broadly based on an article by Jario Lugo-Ocando and Renata Faria Brandão (2016): "STABBING NEWS: Articulating crime statistics in the newsroom".

© The Author(s) 2017
J. Lugo-Ocando, *Crime Statistics in the News*,
DOI 10.1057/978-1-137-39841-3_5

and how it is constructed as a news narrative (Rowbotham, Stevenson, & Pegg, 2013; Schlesinger & Tumber, 1994; Sparks, 1992). Some of these scholars have gone on to suggest, for example, that public anxieties in relation to crime levels are often not justified by actual data (Ditton & Duffy, 1983; Williams & Dickinson, 1993), which undermines and distorts policy formulation and implementation.

One part of this body of work has looked at how the media disseminates crime statistics (Feilzer, 2007; Gomes de Melo, 2010) and has indicated important limitations in the access, use and reporting of crime statistics among journalists and news editors (Martin, 2010; Utts, 2010; Wilby, 2007). One well-studied cause of these limitations concerns the moment data is gathered and transformed into statistical information (Koch, 1990; Zuberi, 2001). This because it is a process that remains largely opaque to many journalists, who have little knowledge about the methodologies that underpin statistical gathering and analysis in relation to "reliability" and "validity" of the data that they use in their own stories. This is further problematised by the fact that these journalists find that "quantitative data can be overwhelming, both due to their nature and their proliferation" (Lindgren, 2008, p. 93).

This chapter aims to provide additional insights into the way quantitative data on crime is gathered and processed by journalists, while helping us assess statistics-related methodologies and approaches used when producing stories related to crime. We believe that in so doing we can help elucidate the essential criteria and characteristics of news gathering and dissemination not only in this but also in other news beats, as well as highlighting the key issues that need to be addressed. It uses the reporting of knife crime statistics as a case study given its role in shaping public perceptions (Hohl, Stanko, & Newburn, 2012; Levi & Jones, 1985) and influencing the construction of social reality in general (O'Keefe & Reid-Nash, 1987). We also believe that this is an appropriate case study to show how news is constructed with reference to these statistics while allowing us to highlight more general problems and limitations regarding the management of quantitative data in the newsroom.

Methodology and Approaches

This study triangulates qualitative and quantitative research strategies. In so doing, it incorporates content analysis of news items produced by journalists in UK newspapers. To delimit the scope, this analysis looked only at news on knife crimes in the UK and reported by the British press. This sample contained material from *The Guardian, The Times, The Daily Mail, The Independent* and *The Scotsman* from 2007 to 2014 (including their Sunday editions such as *The Observer*) as they are representative of the "quality press" in the UK (Conboy, 2001). Following this, we investigated news articles that mentioned or made reference to statistics on knife crime in the lead paragraph of the news item and we looked at the nature of the sources used by the journalist(s) writing the story. This gave a total of 501 articles that focused on knife crime statistics, allowing us to do a longitudinal analysis.

Content analysis was used in order to examine the way statistical data had been reported by journalists. This means of measuring allows for the inference of knowledge regarding "the production/reception conditions (inferred variables) of these messages" (Bardin, 1977, p. 44) and because it is an empirically grounded method, "exploratory in process and inferential in intent" (Krippendorff, 2013, p. 1). Following methodological conventions, we used coding to group different elements contained in the news articles and turned this into quantitative data that showed the most relevant characteristics in relation to practice. We used unique codes, mostly to highlight frequency, and these were: (1) year of publication, (2) newspaper, (3) by-line, (4) type of news, (5) total number of sources quoted, (6) number of primary sources quoted, (7) number of secondary sources quoted, (8) nature of the main source, (9) nature of the source that provided the statistics, (10) main emphasis in the headline, (11) main emphasis in the article, (12) whether it included statistics, (13) nature of the statistical source, (14) who presented the statistics, (15) nature of the statistics provided, (16) nature of the statistics, (17) presentation of the statistics, (18) type of test performed, (19) what the statistics were used for and (20) time scale of the statistics used. The idea was to use content analysis to scrutinise the association between statistics and methodologies used by journalists when reporting crime and how this is reflected in the final output.

Following the content analysis we also performed a close, mindful and disciplined reading of a stratified sample of 186 articles from the total universe in order to understand the deeper meaning of the object of study (Brummett, 2010, p. 28). This close reading follows a more literary tradition that gives relevance to narrative, genre and persona in relation to the management of social and political issues. We used this technique as it has allowed, in the past, other researchers to produce a critical understanding of what the media says in terms of intentionality while enabling scholars to deconstruct news media output in a diversity of ways (Rubin, 1987).

This technique was complemented with semi-structured interviews carried out with a small group of journalists in London and Edinburgh to achieve an in-depth understanding of practices and methodologies used in the newsrooms to deal with data. These interviews followed standard practices to explore the context for the practice based on the individual's experiences (Josselson, 2013, p. 169). To do so, we posed a series of standard questions to all participants to provide information about areas such as common practices, while allowing them free range in other areas such as to clarify particular problems and limitations. We gave discretion to the interviewees to present their views in an anonymise manner or not. We interviewed a total of four journalists, which we considered sufficient to examine the issue more qualitatively.

This multi-layered analysis was carry out to take account of actors and other aspects that serve as sources of information and which consequently affect the media representation of crime statistics. This due to the fact that portrayals of social problems, such as knife crime, in the media are unavoidably dependent on the inclinations and opinions of those who produce and shape information as well as their sources (Schlesinger & Tumber, 1994). Hence, the deconstruction of journalistic discourse must take into account precisely these two discursive interventions: (1) the sources' interventions and (2) the journalists' interventions (Carvalho, 2008, p. 164).

The main question explored in this research was: how do non-specialist journalists in newsrooms access and manage quantitative data when producing news stories that relate to crime? Our research question is relevant in the current context whereby the process of public policy design and implementation seems to be influenced by public opinion and media representations (Banks, 2005, p. 184; Kidd-Hewitt & Osborne, 1995, p. 12) more so than in the past (Manning, 2006, p. 62) and since the reporting of crime statistics seems to feed the process of policy making (Hope, 2004, p. 287).

Moreover, when constructing itself as a "mirror of reality", the media has developed a powerful tool to mobilise public opinion (Kaplan, 2009; Mindich, 1998) using this phenomenon as a way of attracting and then commodifying audiences. By analysing the relationship between news coverage, interpretation and the meaning of statistical-based and statistical-related crime news, we were able to examine agencies and inter-actions of individuals in the articulation of news stories and their impact on policy.

Theory and Background

One of the aspects we have established in this book is that statistics confer power to shape our understanding of the world (Boyle, 2000; Devlin, 1998; Fioramonti, 2014; Karabell, 2014; Porter, 1997). In this sense, "cold statistics" and purportedly "value-neutral" numbers seem to lead to moral issues in policy (Eberstadt, 1995, p. 26). Therefore, the notion that one must "travel mathematical roads in order to arrive at objectivity in the real world" (Davis & Hersh, 1986, p. 276) is essential in understand-ing the important role statistics play in the production of news.

Actually, journalistic over-dependency on official sources in general and acceptance at face value of the statistical data in particular is intrinsically linked to the doctrine of objectivity (Manning, 2001; Tuchman, 1972). In this context, numbers are seen as "neutral" and "unbiased" and most of the public tends to forget, at times, that they just represent a convention or agreement among groups (Fioramonti, 2014, p. 33). In point of fact, "numbers, pure and precise in abstract, lose precision in the real world". That is because, if a number "has been counted, it has been defined, and that will almost always have meant using force to squeeze reality into boxes that don't fit" (Blastland & Dilnot 2008, p. 15): something that journalists tend to forget too often when using them to articulate their stories.

Numbers saturate the news and for good or ill, they are today's pre-eminent public language (Randall, 2000)—and those who speak it rule the world of "facts". In the case of journalism, numbers give us a "revealing albeit oblique, slant on the traditional who, what, where, when, why and how of journalists craft" (Paulos, 1996). Indeed, for a long time, many have come to believe that "good journalism should entail the practice of the highest scientific virtue" (Lippmann, 1922, p. 49) for which "comment is free, but facts are sacred", as C.P. Scott, the then editor of *The Guardian*, wrote in 1921.

Accordingly, statistics need to be understood as a powerful narrative which is part of a wider positivist discourse that dominates the profession (Durham, 1998; Martinisi & and Lugo-Ocando, 2015). Indeed, "objectivity" is perhaps one of the most enduring notions shaping liberal journalism (Schudson, 2001, p. 149) and therefore often referred to as a "universal norm" (Maras, 2013, p. 226). Objectivity has been the key concept in journalistic vocabulary and newsroom guidelines since the beginning of the twentieth century. This is a worldview that infers that news should be produced so as to present facts and events independently of biases, subjective methods and personal views.

It is this notion of objective reality, based on the appreciation of facts over opinions, that allows journalists to play the role of mediator of sense and meaning. They do so by using what some authors have defined as "the web of facticity" (Tuchman, 1980, p. 82). That is, by claiming to be scientifically driven in their approach, therefore able to speak "truth" to the public. This "truth" is considered one of the fundamental elements of journalism as it confers its power derived from public trust. Concurrently, most journalists have, as an objective of their own work, the clarification and exposition of factual "truth" to the public at large.

The appetite for "facts", as we explained in an earlier chapter, is characterised by positivist thinking, and underpins journalists' need to favour certain types of news sources that confer credibility to their work (Franklin, 2011; Manning, 2001; Tuchman, 1980), and statistics, by all accounts, make the case for this. Regarding this point, it is important to remember that statistical facts "are inscribed in routinized practices" (Desrosieres, 1993, p. 1), which provide a commonly accepted language that helps ratify the verisimilitude of the picture depicted.

This explains why statistics are almost revered by journalists and editors as a "neutral" source of information that brings closure to contested debates. As such, they act as an acceptable convention for the collective, against the subjective perceptions of the individual (Parker, 1999, p. 86), allowing journalists and their editors to quantify uncertainty and scrutinise the consequences of that uncertainty in society. For a profession that normatively aims at providing answers, the use of statistics is assumed as a panacea for truth.

This power of statistics to legitimise news resides in their external appreciation as an objective and quasi-scientific source of information, which is able to provide consensus among the audiences while setting the parameters for conventions among those publicly debating policy and social issues. The ability of those using statistics to underpin socially constructed reality is such, at least among journalists working in the mainstream news media, that one is perhaps inclined to set statistics apart from any other news source.

Indeed, journalists constantly use statistics to generate, substantiate and/or legitimise their news stories. They see them as a scientific tool to scrutinize government and society. Great weight is accorded to statistical findings seeing as they are usually disseminated by reputable scholars and so "look and sound" scientific (Zuberi, 2001, p. x). Therefore an official document or access to a dataset is considered by many journalists as a news source in itself (Kapuscinski, 2002, p. 44). It is in this last category in which we can place statistics as a news source, which in terms of articulating news is—in the mind of many practitioners—both "a source" of information and a legitimate set of "facts".

This double role, we argue, makes statistics an atypical source of information in journalism practice. For example, and contrary to what occurs with other news sources, they are seldom crossed-referenced to be verified and they are more often than not taken at face value. Moreover, due to what some authors describe as increasing pressures and limited resources in the newsroom (Davies, 2008, p. 394), these editors and journalists also tend to accept uncritically the interpretations and explanatory frameworks provided by those who produce these statistics and their spin-doctors: something that is detrimental for public policy scrutiny—a fundamental role of the press—as isolated data has no meaning or worse, "can be made to mean anything" (Robert & Zauberman, 2009, p. 8).

In addition to this, we are confronted with the issue of credibility of the news sources, which is pivotal in allowing us to understand the role of statistics in the legitimisation of news. Credibility is considered to be the extent to which the source is perceived as possessing an expertise relevant to the communication topic; therefore being able to be assumed as trustful and objective when communicating a message or supporting an opinion (Goldsmith, Lafferty, & Newell, 2000, p. 43). To be that, the news source has to have perceived characteristics such as trustworthiness, expertise, respect for privacy, honesty and neutrality. Statistics seem to comply with all of these attributes and consequently news people see them as a legitimate and credible source of information.

The appreciation of statistics as credible sources has led the news media to a constant search for data to legitimise their stories. This in turn has created a demand for government officials and a variety of institutions to produce statistical information (Higgs, 2013) regardless of the area or the pertinence of carrying out quantitative measurement. All in all, in the journalistic imagination, statistics are the ultimate "fact" in assessing public policy as they are the "science of the nation" (Desrosieres, 1993). Accordingly, statistical data guides the analysis of all other possibilities of expression, as well as its variations, in an attempt to assimilate the effort put into this search for the imposition of meanings (Fisher, 1996).

Moreover, as statistics is often studied as an exact science, one that can be quantified and re-traced, they secure for themselves and those providing them a unique sense of credibility and legitimacy in what they say or express as news. Consequently, statistics are perceived as "expert" evidence from which news people are allowed to legitimately infer as they, presumably, reflect general trends in society. Finally, as they are normally accompanied by a technical explanation of how they were gathered and processed, they are also conceived as a "neutral" element from which journalists can draw "honest" conclusions and "anyone who understands [mathematical] terms will agree to [their] truth" (Davis & Hersh, 1986, p. 57).

As a consequence, statistics in the news play a pivotal role in the construction of social reality as those who use them exercise "a very specific power over society and the interpretation of society" (Ernest, 1997). Let us not forget that "all sources of statistical information about crime reflect social construction of the phenomenon under study" (Van Dijk, 2009) in a way that is far from deprived of ideology. In this sense, Pierre Bourdieu (1998) said that placing the public at large at the recipient end of this phenomenon creates a cycle of fear and collective insecurity, "which promotes policy measures that end up violating constitutional covenants and creating an increasingly more and more punitive state" (1998, p. 12). This suggest that the use of crime statistics is in fact a covenant for political conservativism, as it intrinsically leads to news that makes the public increasingly at ease and in favour of a "crime and punishment" approach.

As our own analysis suggests, most official figures published by journalists in their stories reinforce the views on crime as those depicted by law enforcement agencies, politicians, spin-doctors and prosecuting attorneys rather than those held by social workers, parole officers, academics and offenders. Crime surveys, for example, tend to reflect the situation as viewed by the public at large (Van Dijk, 2009) which tends to widely reinforce victimisation, fear of "others" and moral panics. Because of this innate "conservativism" the understanding of the dynamics and processes that take place around the news reporting of official statistics needs to be examined more critically. Particularly considering that crimes statistics are recorded by the police and are therefore well-known to be affected by inbuilt limitations (Van Dijk, 2009, p. 13) and biases of authority: something that has been highlighted by the UK Statistics Authority which has refused to certify the data generated by most police authorities in the UK for its lack of compliance with the set standards.[1] Thus a more critical and sound analysis of the way in which these statistics are reported is needed in order to improve the process of policy formulation and decision; one that provides a better understanding of the role of the media in fostering public anxieties that create unnecessary pressures and distortions on the process of policy making. We know, for example, that many officials and segments of the media have used statistics in past political campaigns to mobilise voters (Gest, 2001; Lee, 2013).

This is a matter of increasing concern given the fact that successive governments have used crime statistics to promote and legitimise their ideologies on crime while calling it a "research-lead policy" (Hope, 2008, p. 46). One of the best known examples of this practice is that of former New York Mayor, Rudy Giuliani, who used statistics in order to advance his own political career, something that has been well documented in both scholarly work and the news media (Greene, 1999; Harcourt, 1998; Newburn & Jones, 2007). In relation to this, Battersby (2010) argues that critical knowledge and awareness is necessary not only to understand the data given but also, and perhaps most importantly, to distinguish useful from deceptive information.

General Findings

Our initial expectation was that knife crime statistics would be mainly reported in terms of a "hard news" style as this is the prevalent genre in news reporting (Rudin & Ibbotson, 2002, p. 52). This was in fact confirmed by the findings as over 82% of the news containing crime statistics was published as hard news stories, because most of the news stories were produced the same day that the crime statistics were released by officials, and published or broadcast the next day. This is despite the fact that these statistics reflect past events rather than current ones, suggesting that the "newness" that prompted publication did not come from the data itself, but from the performance of releasing the data to the public.

This suggest to us that crime stories are considered in the newsroom as a particular type of news. What makes them a "hot" topic, despite reflecting past events, is that crime statistics are perceived to be a measurement of the degree of success of a government in terms of justice and crime policy. The release of statistics to the general public is used by officials and by those in opposition to assert narratives of failure or success of the incumbent government and therefore is carefully staged by the PR machinery of the Home Office.

The prevalent use of "hard news stories" as a journalistic genre to disseminate crime statistics also reflects the fact that they are presented to the public in a certain manner.[2] Indeed, the release of crime statistics is orchestrated by the authorities as "media events", which by nature are exercises of "hegemonic manipulations" (Dayan & Katz, 1994, p. vii). In so doing, the agenda on crime statistics is set by those who provide the statistics in the first place rather than by the journalists or news media outlets. What should be a reflective process of public social analysis derived from the analysis and processing of numerical data becomes instead a descriptive reproduction of assumptions made by others. Only on a few occasions did we find in our sample in-depth critical analysis produced by journalists (less than 12%) that was published at times when the data had not been released the same day by official sources. These pieces were mostly produce in weekend editions and published as feature articles.

Our study also shows that the Home Office in London was the main source, providing the statistics in most news stories. It not only provided the statistical dataset but also complementary information packages with analysis, press releases and other elements to support and facilitate the work of journalists. One exception is *The Scotsman* in Edinburgh, which follows instead the agenda set by the Scottish Government rather than the Home Office. However, even in this case the gathering and production of news followed similar patterns; that is publishing the day after the Scottish Government had released the data.

Overall, access to news sources in terms of who provides the statistics indicates that in 73% of cases, the statistics were from government sources, while in 24.5% of cases the source of the statistics was not mentioned (although in many of them one could infer that it was also from an official source). As mentioned above, the news source mostly quoted is the Home Office which is also the main provider of these statistics (Table 5.1).

Table 5.1 Who presented the statistics?

Valid	Percentage	Valid percentage	Cumulative percentage
Home Office	43.9	43.9	43.9
National Office for Statistics	2.4	2.4	46.3
University	4.9	4.9	51.2
Other	7.3	7.3	58.5
Unknown	41.5	41.5	100.0
Total	100.0	100.0	

Source: Lugo-Ocando and Faria Brandão (2017)

This data confirms something that has been observed in other news beats; journalists' over-reliance on official sources to articulate news stories (Brown, Bybee, Wearden, & Straughan, 1987; Goldacre, 2009; Lewis, Williams, & Franklin, 2008; Manning, 2001). Likewise, close reading suggests that most sources consulted by the journalists were either the officials providing the statistics or other voices offering a human dimension to the story. In neither case did these "alternative" sources refer directly to the numerical data or question its validity and reliability. In only a few cases did we find stories that incorporated other sources contradicting or questioning the data itself (less than 5% of the entire sample). On this, our interviewees have a consistent explanation:

> In truth, the only access we have to the most current crime statistics is by the Home Office. I mean…they give us this data and to be honest is such volume of data that at times is difficult to handle. I simply don't have the time as I have also to produce a couple of stories for that same day too. Before, we were three people in this beat, now it is only me and sometimes an intern. To me to include two or more sources more would require a couple of hours that I simply don't have. I am being totally honest here.[3]

Other interviewees also pointed out time pressures and limited resources as the main causes for the lack of variety:

> When I do other stories, I tend to double check by phone. I call two or maybe three people by phone. Nowadays, you know…one has little time to go there in person, particularly in a city like London where you can easily waste a couple of hours going from one part [of the city] to the other. But with crime statistics [it] is different, I would have to sit down face to face with an expert because we would have to look at it together. It simply wouldn't work by phone, I have tried it.[4]

Our content analysis confirms this practice as in 56.1% of the cases there was only one or no primary sources, which we define here as "one that is personally researched by the journalist" (Rudin & Ibbotson, 2002, p. 32) (Table 5.2).

Table 5.2 Number of primary sources quoted

Valid	Percentage	Cumulative percentage
One	29.2	29.2
Two	17.1	46.3
Three	9.8	56.1
Four or more	17.1	73.2
None	26.8	100.0
Total	100.0	

Source: Lugo-Ocando and Faria Brandão (2017)

Indeed, most journalists interviewed said that they tended to use a fewer number of sources than in other news beats mostly because of "time pressures":

> Normally we get the statistics and have to work with them all day. In some bigger newspapers you tend to get support and time to deal with that news story on the day. However, that is not our case. We are a medium size newspaper struggling. We don't have enough staff so I have to single-handedly produce the whole story with what I have while often having also to write something else that day. I am lucky if I manage to include one additional source.[5]

This lack of diversity of news sources is further problematised by the over-dependency on official sources, which as we have discussed is a characteristic of journalism in general, but that in this case seems even more challenging. In fact, we carried out a comparative close reading of published news against press releases made available by the Home Office on the same day. In many cases, we saw that news stories referreing to crime statistics basically reproduced these press releases to a large degree or were very similar, in terms of news angle and data used, to the press release of the day. This is not a surprising finding given the over-dependency of journalists in current times on PR, which has come to fill the information deficit produced by diminishing resources (Davies, 2008; Lewis et al., 2008).

Our close reading of the sample also showed that there is a lack of investigative reporting around knife crime statistics and there is hardly any indication that journalists engage in more advanced ways of using statistics to develop a more in-depth analysis of crime and society. Indeed, very few of the articles (only eight) showed explicitly or suggested implicitly any type of test related to regressions, correlations or factor analysis. This indicates that in most cases the journalists did not explore fully the potential of the data to inform about policy and outcomes.

When asked about this lack of "tests" in the sample, three of the journalists interviewed claimed time pressure and other prerogatives in the newsroom as the main reason. However, one of the interviewees pointed out a lack of knowledge:

> To process that type of data in that way, I would probably need additional training in both using the software and developing the analytical skills necessary to process them. Otherwise, I would have to seek expert advice and there is simply not time to do that under the current pressures we are under. I have covered this beat now for a couple of years and frankly I don't know any of my colleagues who could do that…no one that I know working on this beat would know how to do these tests.[6]

All of the interviewees agreed that more training is necessary although they all recognised the need to make better use of the data made available in the newsroom:

> We do need to make a greater effort in the newsroom to assess better this data, even if that means breaking the cycle of having to publish everything on the day. As a [Home Affairs] correspondent I believe that we could do a better service if we did that. Now…I am not sure how that would be possible under the current situation, perhaps, reflecting on ourselves we are too fixed to the idea that these statistics have to be published tomorrow. Perhaps…I think, we could agree among the media to [impose an] embargo [on] the news as to give us all more time to digest them…I don't know if that is possible, but perhaps it is an idea.[7]

When asked why their own newsrooms did not spend as much time and resources in examining crime statistics as they do with election polls, they all said the same thing: one is considered more important than the other and therefore the coverage of elections is allocated far more resources than the crime beat. As one of the interviewees put it:

> You cannot compare the two things! An election is a huge event you know...all the newsroom stops in order to cover that. Resources are poured into making sure that we don't miss anything, particularly what the polls says about who is going to win. In my own place [of work], they cleared an office for two experts they brought [in]...and it wasn't even part of the rest of the open space. The office was our meeting room, we have to meet in one of the corridors. That tells you how important it is. That would never happen in a million years in relation to crime statistics.[8]

Additional close reading of the sample points out that knife crime statistics are mostly accessed by journalists and news editors by means of "media events" (Couldry et al., 2009; Dayan & Katz, 1994), which are staged and managed by officials with a vested interest in "spinning" the news. Instead, only a small number of news stories on knife crime are contextualised historically as most of them tend to focus on snapshot data provided in media events by officials (Table 5.3).

In other words, journalists tend to concentrate on statistics that refer to what is happening "now", making it difficult for the public to see trends or understand their relationship with specific circumstances and policies. Journalists interviewed contested these findings:

> But we do offer historical perspective! We use crime statistics from longitudinal datasets. I myself always try to compare today's statistics with yesterday's, particularly in relation to previous governments. Well...I wouldn't go as far as ten years, because that doesn't make sense. Our readers want to

Table 5.3 Time scale of the statistics used

Valid	Percentage	Valid percentage	Cumulative percentage
Longitudinal data	26.8	26.8	26.8
Cross sectional/snapshot	68.3	68.3	95.1
Not specific	4.9	4.9	100.0
Total	100.0	100.0	

Source: Lugo-Ocando and Faria Brandão (2017)

know what is going on today and certainly they are interested in what this data says in relation to last year. I might include a decade [of data], but as part of a larger piece, not on that day.[9]

In other words, they believe that they do provide context by interpreting short longitudinal data as "historical" while dismissing longer historical sets as irrelevant for their audiences.

Another important finding from our close reading is the lack of follow-up as few stories tend to link with previous explanations or are contrasted with past policy. In our sample, it was *The Guardian* and *The Observer* which published more follow-ups to the initial stories and these titles were also at the forefront in developing stories based on knife crime statistics that were independent of the agenda set by the release of statistics by the Home Office. However, even in these cases, it was only a few stories (only 12 in the whole period) that were re-assessed by other sources, contrasted against a distinctive set of evidence or compared to what officials had said in previous years.

Overall, news on crime statistics rarely has a follow-up the next day. That is not to say that news on knife crime did not appear for several days as a news theme in the same newspaper but it did so either as a campaign or as independent (although somehow related) stories. Only a tiny proportion of stories based on crime statistics received the type of follow-up, scrutiny or historical contextualisation that stories from other beats get (less than 4%). Moreover, looking at these findings, they suggest that historical context—in terms of longitudinal data analysis, news follow-up and policy assessment—is the great absentee in the reporting of crime statistics.

These findings are particularly significant in light of the prevalent news culture among journalists which assumes that these types of shortcomings can be corrected the next day (Bugeja, 2007, p. 50). In other words, there is an understanding in the newsroom that if a story is somehow incomplete, slightly inaccurate or something else needs to be said, journalists and editors can always correct this the following day. But, as we have seen here, this does not happen. This, to us, is indicative of one of the great paradoxes we found: that when it comes to scrutinising statistics and cross-referencing the sources that produce them, the traditional procedures paraded as part of pragmatic objectivity and which demand cross-referencing and contextualisation are rarely applied, despite the aura of scientific truth that journalism claims for itself.

Conclusions

Overall, the news media tends to presents itself as the "mirror of reality" (Broersma, 2010; Mindich, 1998), as it claims to offer a factual representation of the world out there that is as comprehensive and as unbiased as possible. However, by looking at this sample, what we find is a very different picture: one that is largely dominated by the sources producing the statistics and by the editorial dynamics, prerogatives and agendas of the news media itself rather than by a system of checks and balances of public policy. What we see here is that the statutory duty to produce these statistics and present them to the public in a democratic society so as to foster self-criticism is instead a practice done in ways that reinforce prevalent discourses and particular agendas.

What we were also able to see here is how, contrary to the assumptions of objectivity and factuality that journalists bear on crime statistics, these numbers are instead subject to the same type of agency and power games which are pretty much present in other news beats. More importantly, we were able to highlight how the lack of criticality towards statistics opens the possibility that official sources use news people to advance their own agendas in a manner that serves their own interests rather than those of society as a whole. In addition, there seems to be, based on our findings, a faster pace of information. This creates repetition in a sort of mimicry within the general news media of what those in power want them to say. Information provided by the sources, in the form of press releases and information packages, is then replicated—almost unchanged in some cases—by media outlets. It is in this context that the reporting of crime data rather than being an exercise of accountability for public policy in order to assess current circumstances in society seems to have become instead a repetitive ritualistic performance in which journalists covering crime statistics pretend to be reporting objectively and authorities pretend to be fulfilling their obligation of informing the public. Thus both journalists and officials are ill-serving a society that so desperately needs to dissipate the fog of moral panic that crime reporting has created over the decades.

Notes

1. As explained by Andrew Dilnot CBE, Chair of the UK Statistics Authority, during the Knoop Lecture, Numbers and Policy, at the University of Sheffield on 11 November 2014. http://www.sheffield.ac.uk/economics/events/knoop/14 [accessed on May 12, 2015]
2. All the interviewees agreed with this statement.
3. Sources anonymised by request of the interviewee on 14 November 2013 in London.
4. Sources anonymised by request of the interviewee on 15 November 2013 in London.
5. Interview on 21 March 2013. Identity of the interviewees withheld at their request.
6. Interview on 21 March 2013. Identity of the interviewees withheld at their request.
7. Interview on 21 March 2013. Identity of the interviewees withheld at their request.
8. Interview on 3 September 2012. Identity of the interviewees withheld at their request.
9. Interview with Jamie Beatson, editor of Kingdom News Agency on 22 January 2013.

References

Banks, M. (2005). Spaces of (in) security: Media and fear of crime in a local context. *Crime, Media, Culture, 1*(2), 169–187.

Bardin, L. (1977). *Análise de Conteúdo*. Lisbon: Edicoes 70.

Battersby, M. (2010). *Is that a Fact?* Peterborough, ON: Broadview Press.

Blastland, M., & Dilnot, A. (2008). *The Tiger that isn't—Seeing through a world of numbers*. London: Profile Books.

Bourdieu, P. (1998). *On television and journalism*. London: Pluto.

Boyle, D. (2000). *The Tyranny of numbers*. London: HarperCollins Publishers.

Broersma, M. (2010). The unbearable limitations of journalism on press critique and journalism's claim to truth. *International Communication Gazette, 72*(1), 21–33.

Brown, J. D., Bybee, C. R., Wearden, S. T., & Straughan, D. M. (1987). Invisible power: Newspaper news sources and the limits of diversity. *Journalism Quarterly, 64*(1), 45–54.

Brummett, B. (2010). *Techniques of close reading.* London: Sage.

Bugeja, M. (2007). Making whole: The ethics of correction. *Journal of Mass Media Ethics, 22*(1), 49–65.

Carvalho, A. (2008). Media(ted) discourse and society. *Journalism Studies, 9*(2), 161–177.

Chibnall, S. (1977). *Law-and-order news. An analysis of crime reporting in the British press.* London: Tavistock Publications.

Conboy, M. (2001). *The press and popular culture.* London: Sage.

Couldry, N., Hepp, A., & Krotz, F. (2009). *Media events in a global age.* London: Routledge.

Davies, N. (2008). *Flat earth news: An award-winning reporter exposes falsehood, distortion and propaganda in the global media.* London: Random House.

Davis, P. J., & Hersh, R. (1986). *Descartes' dream: The world according to mathematics.* London: Penguin Books.

Davis, N. (2008). *Flat earth news.* Londres: Chatto & Windus.

Dayan, D., & Katz, E. (1994). *Media events.* Cambridge, MA: Harvard University Press.

Desrosieres, A. (1993). *The politics of large numbers: A history of statistical reasoning.* London: Harvard University Press.

Devlin, K. (1998). *The language of mathematics: Making invisible visible.* New York: W. H. Freeman and Company.

Ditton, J., & Duffy, J. (1983). Bias in the newspaper reporting of crime news. *The British Journal of Criminology: An International Review of Crime and Society, 23*(2), 159–165.

Dorling, D., & Simpson, S. (1999). *Statistics in society: The arithmetic of politics.* London: Arnold.

Dowler, K. (2003). Media consumption and public attitudes toward crime and justice: The relationship between fear of crime, punitive attitudes, and perceived police effectiveness. *Journal of Criminal Justice and Popular Culture, 10*(2), 109–126.

Durham, M. G. (1998). On the relevance of standpoint epistemology to the practice of journalism: The case for "strong objectivity". *Communication Theory, 8*(2), 117–140.

Eberstadt, N. (1995). *The Tyranny of numbers: Mismeasurement and misrule.* Washington, DC: AEI Press.

Ericson, R., Baranek, O., & Chan, J. (1987). *Visualising deviance.* Buckingham: Open University Press.

Ernest, P. (1997). *Social constructivism as a philosophy of mathematics.* New York: State University of New York Press.

Feilzer, M. (2007). Criminologists making news? Providing factual information on crime and criminal justice through a weekly newspaper column. *Crime, Media, Culture, 3*(3), 285–304.

Fioramonti, L. (2014). *How numbers role the world. The use and abuse of statistics in global politics.* London: Zed Books.

Fisher, N. (1996). *Statistical analysis of circular data.* Cambridge: Cambridge University Press.

Frankin, B. (2011). Sources, credibility and the continuing crisis of UK journalism. In B. Franklin & M. Carlson (Eds.), *Journalists, sources, and credibility* (pp. 90–106). London: Routledge.

Gest, T. (2001). *Crime & politics: Big government's erratic campaign for law and order.* New York: Oxford University Press.

Goldacre, B. (2009). *Bad science.* London: Fourth State.

Goldsmith, R. E., Lafferty, B. A., & Newell, S. J. (2000). The impact of corporate credibility and celebrity credibility on consumer reaction to advertisements and brands. *Journal of Advertising, 29*(3), 43–54.

Gomes de Melo, C. (2010). Mídia e Crime: liberdade de informacao jornalística e presuncao de inocencia. *Revista do Direito Público, 5*(2), 106–122.

Greene, J. (1999). Zero tolerance: A case study of police policies and practices in New York City. *Crime & Delinquency, 45*(2), 171–187.

Hall, S. (1975). *Newsmaking and crime.* Birmigham: Centre for Contemporary Cultural Studies.

Harcourt, B. (1998). Reflecting on the subject: A critique of the social influence conception of deterrence, the broken windows theory, and order-maintenance policing New York style. *Michigan Law Review, 97*(2), 291–389.

Higgs, M. D. (2013). Do we really need the S-word? *American Scientist, 101*, 6–9.

Hohl, K., Stanko, B., & Newburn, T. (2012). The effect of the 2011 London disorder on public opinion of police and attitudes towards crime, disorder, and sentencing. *Policing, 7*(1), 12–20.

Hope, T. (2004). Pretend it works evidence and governance in the evaluation of the reducing burglary initiative. *Criminal Justice, 4*(3), 287–308.

Hope, T. (2008). Dodgy evidence—Fallacies and facts of crime reduction, Part 2. *Safer Communities, 7*(4), 46–51.

Hough, M., & Roberts, J. (2005). *Understanding public attitudes to criminal justice*. New York: McGraw-Hill Education.

Jaffe, A., & Spirer, H. (1987). *Misused statistics: Straight talk for twisted numbers*. New York: Marcel Dekker, Inc.

Jewkes, Y., & Yar, M. (2010). Introduction: The Internet, cybercrime and the challenges of the twenty-first century. In Y. Jewkes & M. Yar (Eds.), *Handbook of internet crime* (pp. 1–8). Devon: Willan Publishing.

Josselson, R. (2013). *Interviewing for qualitative inquiry. A relational approach*. New York: The Guildford Press.

Kaplan, R. (2009). The origins of objectivity in american journalism. In S. Allan (Ed.), *The Routledge companion to news and journalism studies*. New York: Routledge.

Kapuscinski, R. (2002). *Los cinicos no sirven para este oficio*. Barcelona: Editorial Anagrama.

Karabell, Z. (2014). *The leading Indicators. A short hitory of the numbers that rule our world*. New York: Simon & Schuster.

Kidd-Hewitt, D., & Osborne, R. (1995). *Crime and the media: The post-modern spectacle*. London: Pluto Press.

Koch, T. (1990). *The news as a myth: Fact and context in journalism*. Westport, CT: Greenwood Press.

Krippendorff, K. (2013). *Content analysis. An introduction to its methods*. London: Sage.

Lee, M. (2013). *Inventing fear of crime*. London: Routledge.

Levi, M., & Jones, S. (1985). Public and police perceptions of crime seriousness in England and Wales. *British Journal of Criminology, 25*(3), 234–250.

Lewis, J., Williams, A., & Franklin, B. (2008). A compromised fourth estate? UK news journalism, public relations and news sources. *Journalism Studies, 9*(1), 1–20.

Lindgren, S. (2008). Crime, media, coding: Developing a methodological framework for computer-aided analysis. *Crime, Media, Culture, 4*(1), 95–100.

Lippmann, W. (1922). Public opinion. New York: Hartcourt Brace.

Lugo-Ocando, J., & Brandão, R. F. (2016). Stabbing news: Articulating crime statistics in the newsroom. *Journalism Practice, 10*(6), 715–729.

Manning, P. (2001). *News and news sources: A critical introduction*. London: Sage.

Manning, P. (2006). There's no glamour in glue: News and the symbolic framing of substance misuse. *Crime, Media, Culture, 2*(1), 49–66.

Maras, S. (2013). *Objectivity in journalism*. Hoboken, NJ: John Wiley & Sons.

Martin, J. D. (Producer). (2010). Journalists need to do the math—CJR. Retrieved from http://www.cjr.org/behind_the_news/journalists_need_to_do_the_math.php

Mindich, D. T. Z. (1998). *Just facts: How objectivity came to define American journalism*. New York: University Press.

Newburn, T., & Jones, T. (2007). Symbolizing crime control: Reflections on zero tolerance. *Theoretical Criminology, 11*(2), 221–243.

O'Keefe, G., & Reid-Nash, K. (1987). Crime news and real-world blues the effects of the media on social reality. *Communication Research, 14*(2), 147–163.

Parker, I. (1999). Qualitative data and the subjectivity of 'objective' facts. Research fails unless it engages with subjectivity. In D. Dorling & L. Simpson (Eds.), *Statistics in society. The arithmetic of politics* (pp. 83–88). London: Arnold.

Paulos, J. A. (1996). *A mathematician reads the newspaper*. London: Penguin Books.

Porter, T. (1996). *Trust in numbers: The pursuit of objectivity in science and public life*. Princeton, NJ: Princeton University Press.

Porter, T. (1997). The triumph of numbers: Civic implications of quantitative literacy. In L. Steen (Ed.), *Why numbers count: Quantitative literacy for tomorrow's America*. New York: College Board.

Randall, D. (2000). *The universal journalism*. London: Pluto Press.

Robert, P., & Zauberman, R. (2009). Introduction. In P. Robert (Ed.), *Comparing crime data in Europe: Official crime statistics and survey based data*. Brussels: Brussels University Press.

Rowbotham, J., Stevenson, K., & Pegg, S. (2013). *Crime news in modern Britain: Press reporting and responsibility, 1820–2010*. New York: Springer.

Rubin, D. M. (1987). How the news media reported on Three Mile Island and Chernobyl. *Journal of communication, 37*(3), 42–57.

Rudin, R., & Ibbotson, T. (2002). *An introduction to journalism: Essential techniques and background knowlegde*. Oxford: Focal Press.

Schlesinger, P., & Tumber, H. (1994). *Reporting crime. The media politics of criminal justice*. Oxford: Oxford University Press.

Schudson, M. (2001). The objectivity norm in American journalism. *Journalism, 2*(2), 149–170.

Sparks, R. (1992). *Television and the Drama of Crime*. Buckingham: Open University Press.

Thomas, G., & Durant, J. (1987). Why should we promote the public understanding of science. *Scientific Literacy Papers, 1*, 1–14.

Tuchman, G. (1972). Objectivity as strategic ritual: An examination of newsmen's notions of objectivity. *American Journal of sociology, 77*(4), 660–679.

Tuchman, G. (1980). *Making news*. New York: Free Press.

Utts, J. (2003). What educated citizens should know about statistics and probability. *The American Statistician, 57*(2), 74–79.

Utts, J. (Producer). (2010). Unintentional lies in the media: Don't blame journalists for what we don't teach. Retrieved from http://citeseerx.ist.psu.edu/viewdoc/summary?doi=10.1.1.205.227

Van Dijk, J. (2009). Approximating the truth about crime: Comparing crime data based on general population surveys with police figures of recorded crime. In P. Robert (Ed.), *Comparing crime data in Europe: Official crime statistics and survey based data*. Brussels: Brussels University Press.

Wilby, P. (Producer). (2007). Damn journalists and statistics. *The Guardian*. Retrieved from http://www.theguardian.com/media/2007/nov/05/monday-mediasection.pressandpublishing

Williams, P., & Dickinson, J. (1993). Fear of crime: Read all about it? The relationship between newspaper crime reporting and fear of crime. *British Journal of Criminology, 33*(1), 33–56.

Zuberi, T. (2001). *Thicker than blood: How racial statistics lie*. Minneapolis: Minnesota Press.

6

News, Public Policy and Crime Statistics

Popular myth echoed in the mainstream media often refers to the famous law enforcement agent Eliot Ness (1903–1957) who is credited with putting behind bars the no-less famous gangster Al Capone (1899–1947), ending his reign of terror and corruption in Chicago. As a prohibition agent, Ness led the team of law enforcement officers nicknamed "The Untouchables", who inspired many films and television series (Gagne, 2015; Tucker, 2000). What is less known and perhaps more important is the fact that Ness was above all a policy maker who revolutionised policing in the USA. For example, in 1935 he introduced the patrol car, equipped with radio, which rapidly took over the traditional role of cops walking the beat. He also introduced innovations in forensics and ballistics into criminal investigation by using cameras as to reconstruct crimes and by examining more closely bullet damage and angles. As Douglas Perry (2014) points out, his investigators pioneered the use of lie detectors and his work on automobile traffic, introducing speed limits and checks on drunk drivers, with severe penalties, was directly responsible for one of the most dramatic reductions in road deaths in that city, to the point that many claim that this action in itself saved more lives that all the rest of his policing work combined.

© The Author(s) 2017
J. Lugo-Ocando, *Crime Statistics in the News*,
DOI 10.1057/978-1-137-39841-3_6

However, for many, his greater contribution to fighting crime was the introduction of statistics to design and implement crime policy, something that the Federal Bureau of Investigation (FBI) and other police departments would only manage to do many years later. Indeed:

> A firm believer in crime data, his precinct captains were ordered to accrue and then analyse statistics on a monthly basis—including the volume, nature, location and time of wrongdoing in their areas. Utilizing that data, Cleveland's most dangerous neighbourhoods soon were more precisely identified and thus saw a steadier stream of those flashy squad cars during peak bad-guy hours. And at the most dangerous intersections, curbs were rounded, safety islands built and traffic signals installed. (Kane, 2014)

This is a crucial fact that is often overlooked in popular culture and in particular by the media, which prefers to focus on the myth of an anti-prohibition crusader confronting crime with macho force and machine guns rather than the much subtler and effective man who took scientific measures to reduce crime. For the purpose of this book, however, his real story, that of a sophisticated policy maker, illustrates perfectly what has happened to the news reporting of crime statistics, which overall tends to emphasise the "hard core" and "scandalous" aspects of these numbers instead of using them to map a picture of what has to be done and which types of policies and approaches are required to address the key issues around crime and social deviation.

In relation to this, journalism ought to play a pivotal role as it helps set the agenda of the discussion while mediating the key debates taking place in society around key issues, including crime (Ettema & Glasser, 1998; Hall, 1975). Consequently, journalism should perform the function of bringing to the public's attention what the matters that urgently need to be address are, gathering together the views and voices that can address these issues, and mediating between them to allocate the necessary resources and promote the most adequate strategies and policies. This might not, of course, be the case in practice but this is definitely the role that journalism is expected to undertake in a democratic society.

On the ground, however, most of us would have to accept that the news coverage of crime statistics seems to have a very different impact on the articulation and implementation of crime policy, making it far from sound and comprehensive. This is not because of what these numbers can do to inform policy makers, but because of the way they are reported to the public and the subsequent pressure that public reactions put upon policy makers. This chapter discusses how the way crime statistics are reported by the news media can affect the design and implementation of public policy in general and how it can influence public policy thinking in particular.

In so doing, the chapter deliberates about the way crime statistics are used in the political debate and examines how they translate into public policy. It tries to explain why crime statistics become so important under certain circumstances and why they are almost ignored in others.

One typical example of this is the use of immigration statistics to both criminalise and link immigrants to crime. Take for example the following lead from a story in the London-based *Daily Mail* from 18 February 2012 under the headline "Immigrant crimewave warning: Foreign nationals were accused of a QUARTER of all crimes in London", in which it is claimed that:

> Foreigners are accused of more than one in four crimes committed in London, an investigation reveals. Astonishingly, they make up nine out of ten drug suspects and are responsible for more than one in three sex offences. Nationals of Poland, Romania and Lithuania are most likely of all foreigners to be prosecuted by the police. The figures will give force to warnings of a growing 'immigrant crime wave'. Four years ago, foreign nationals were found to commit one in five crimes.[1]

The ways in which these numbers are reported allow journalists to present immigration and crime as a single thematic area. This area tends to receive far more attention and resources from legislators, policy makers and law enforcement agencies than other much more urgent areas such as domestic abuse or rape. Indeed, the reporting of these numbers has had, in the past, a detrimental impact on public attitudes and public policy which become skewed against immigration, as we saw in the case of the Brexit vote in Britain and the US presidential elections in 2016. On the other hand, we also know that the reporting of crime statistics feeds the process of policy making (Tim Hope, 2004, p. 288) and therefore, improving its coverage could have positive effects on the process of policy formulation and decision making by fostering a better informed public, which consequently will reduce public anxiety and undue political pressure.

Therefore, this chapters aims to explain the importance of reporting crime statistics in the current political context whereby the process of public policy design and implementation seems to be influenced by public opinion and media representations more so than in the past. This is significant, given that the use of statistical evidence in policy design has proven to be problematic in relation to the so-called "evidence-led crime policy" implemented by various governments (Mears, 2007; Tilley, 2001). In so doing, it explores important cases in which the reporting of crime statistics was at the centre of a news story that had significant impact on the process of policy making. It looks at how certain areas of legislation tend to receive more attention than others when crime reporting of these issues mobilises public opinion, and examines specific topics such as prison policy, rape and drugs, among others, as examples of a strong link between policy making and crime reporting. By doing so, the chapter puts a particular emphasis on the way statistical data on crime is used in the political debates to articulate specific discourses and how these discourses translate into policy.

The Policy Numbers

Let us start by recognising that the numbers that land on policy makers' desks can sometimes be problematic. We know, to cite a well-known example, that some police forces in the UK wrote off almost a third of the crime in the past based on technicalities or simple sloppiness (Taylor, 2011). We also have to acknowledge that the labelling of certain crimes or the rules used to record them changed over the years, making historical comparisons nothing less than a guessing game. We can also argue that crime statistics do not always communicate what they say they do—there is at times a lack of validity—while the process of collection and testing used to examine the data does not have the necessary rigour—that is it lacks or has weak reliability.

Therefore, journalists reporting crime in many countries have to start with data that is not as dependable as it should be and that at times does not communicate the facts it is supposed to. This does not exculpate, however, the fact that sometimes news coverage itself can add to the distorted picture that crime statistics can create. In many cases news has contributed to blurring rather than elucidating the debates around crime. Take for example the following story under the headline of "FBI stats back up Trump's warning on crime", which appeared in *The New York Post* on 26 September 2016:

> The FBI confirmed Monday that Donald Trump's right: America's murder rate is spiking. New data show homicides rose 11 per cent in 2015, with overall violent crime up 4 per cent. Trump rightly warned that this is a particular crisis for poor minorities, since the rise is mainly an urban one: "Homicides last year increased by 17 per cent in America's 50 largest cities," he said. "That's the largest increase in 25 years." Critics huffed—but the fact-checkers had to concede he's right. The Washington Post confirmed Trump's figure in July. The New York Times this month said murders soared 14 per cent in the 100 biggest cities, with half the jump coming from just seven: Baltimore, Chicago, Cleveland, Houston, Milwaukee, Nashville and Washington.[2]

These numbers were, of course, distorted. Instead, the crime rates in 2016 were nearly the same as in the previous year, with crime remaining at an all-time historical low, according to the Brennan Center for Justice at NYU School of Law. In its report, *Crime in 2016: A Preliminary Analysis* (Friedman, Grawert, & Cullen, 2016), released in the Center's "Election 2016 Controversies" series the specialists presented data from the 30 largest US cities which was analysed by a team of economics and policy researchers. The Center's report found no substance for Donald Trump's claims. This, however, did not stop these distorted claims about raising crime numbers from playing a role in many people's intention to vote for Trump by creating totally unsubstantiated moral panics.

Indeed, the way some politicians and the news media reports crime statistics can have a truly detrimental effect upon the design and implementation of public policy. Take for example the way the "zero tolerance" approach has been underpinned by a particular interpretation of crime statistics that assumes cause-effect when there has not been any indication of a link between one and the other, and where studies have indicated that community-centred approaches are in fact far more effective (Bowling, 1999; Greene, 1999). The end result is that countries such as the USA and UK, where the "tough-macho" approach to crime has been paraded as political propaganda using crime statistics, now have some of the highest levels of incarceration and re-offending in the whole of the Western world.

Another case is that of how, for years, child abuse statistics were often misreported or not reported at all. Because of this, abuses against children have been constructed in the news media as "horror stories" (Johnson, 2003, p. 267) rather than examined as a structural issue that needs an institutional approach. What statistics show in this case is that child abuse is perpetrated predominantly by adults with close proximity, power and access to the children rather than by strangers. In fact, it is estimated that the great majority of child sexual abuse victims know the perpetrator in some way and that a large proportion of these children are abused by a family member (CFCA, 2014). However, over the years, the media has focused instead on the "other" or the stranger and tended to use a tone that brought about moral panic. In so doing, the media has portrayed child abuse and molestation as a random act that, although it can happen to anyone and any family, is mostly the product of random encounters.

Consequently, the public's reaction has been one of demanding longer terms of incarceration and isolation of the "random" individuals who have committed such horrible crimes. The consequence in terms of public policy has been precisely that—longer terms of incarceration—and the societal effect has been that children are increasingly kept at home glued to electronic gadgets and watching television rather than playing outside. Overall, the news coverage of child abuse has promoted a culture of fear and distrust.

But perhaps the worst effect of this lack of use of statistics when reporting child abuse is that for the past five decades the mainstream news media was unable or unwilling to spot the biggest stories in relation to child abuse. It was only after years of neglecting evidence of systematic abuse in the Catholic Dioceses in Boston and Ireland that some journalists finally started to understand that there was a pattern of institutional abuse and cover-up. And, it was only after his death that many reporters openly acknowledged that Jimmy Savile (1926–2011), the former BBC presenter and celebrity, was part of a vast network of child abuse. Moreover, it was only recently, after current and former footballers came out one by one to denounce that as youths they were sexually abused, that the news media in general came to accept its own blindness to the fact that child abuse in our society is a structural and widespread problem.

Without that particular understanding—that child abuse needs to be understood as an institutionalised issue in the same way that institutionalised racism is—the media was unprepared to exercise properly its role as a watchdog. It was incapable, therefore, of providing sound scrutiny and proper examination of the root causes of child abuse. Consequently, public policy and power remained unchecked and thousands of people suffered permanent physical and psychological damage that scars them for life. It did not need to be like that, as the statistics were always available to show that institutional power (family, organisation, etc.) is key in explaining patterns in child abuse. So why did so many journalists decide to ignore these statistics and focus instead on the narrative of the "other"? To be sure, the process of "othering" is pivotal in explaining why stories of abuse and rape tend to centre upon narratives of individual victimisation, hence ignoring or downplaying structure and context. It is also central in understanding why journalists—intentionally or inadvertently—cherry-pick certain crime statistics.

Take the case of the multiple rapes in the English town of Rotherham, where over 1400 young women—most of them under-age—were systematically abused and sexually exploited between 1997 and 2013. Because many of the men involved belonged to the Pakistani community, the data presented by many journalists over and over again tried to suggest that Asian Muslims of Pakistani origin were more likely to rape than other communities. As some authors have expressed, the development of the British Muslim as a racialised threat is a current and on-going legacy of colonialism in which this group experiences discriminatory "othering" processes resulting in their marginalisation (Tufail, 2015, p. 30). What made this case even more problematic, however, was that indirect reference to data highlighted in a Home Office (2013) report seemed to suggest that British Muslims were more likely to commit these crimes than other groups. The report itself described these cases as "[showing] a particular model…of organised, serious exploitation and abuse that involves predominantly Pakistani-heritage men grooming and abusing predominantly white British girls", although the report did stress that the government does not believe "localised grooming" is intrinsic of any culture, religion, and/or race. Many journalists ignored the last warning and jumped into the early suggestion of a "cultural" pattern.

This conclusion, however, goes against wider statistical evidence that suggest that child abuse is very present in all groups in society. Indeed, as freelance journalist and political activist Julie Bindel pointed out:

> The media coverage of that case, and of previous prosecutions in which the defendants were all or primarily of Pakistani origin, was so focused on race that it might lead the public to imagine that all we need to do to eradicate child sexual abuse is to lock up all Pakistani men. The committee is hearing evidence, however, that online grooming, abuse within the home, within gangs, and elsewhere takes place and is perpetrated by predominantly men (and some women) from every demographic. (Bindel, 2012)

Moreover, the actual data suggests that most societies face high levels of child abuse. In Britain, for example, one study carried out by the Child and Woman Abuse Studies Unit at London Metropolitan University found that 59% of young women and 27% of young men disclosed, in a survey of 1244 attending further education colleges, that they had experienced at least one sexually intrusive incident before the age of 18. The study also found that 21% of young women and 7% of young men experienced sexual abuse involving physical contact. Some 14% of the perpetrators were close relatives, 68% more distant relatives and other previously known people, and only 18% were strangers. Conclusion: child abuse is a domestic problem not one that would statistically happen because of the "other".

Nevertheless, it is precisely the stories of "strangers" abducting children that are the ones that get more news coverage and consequently more public attention. That was evident in the case of the disappearance in 2007 of the then four-year-old British girl Madeleine McCann, who vanish from her parents' hotel room when they were dining in a restaurant just outside the hotel. Hundreds of newspaper pages and thousands of minutes of broadcast airtime were devoted to highlighting this particular case. Other similar cases in the past that also received high levels of media attention include that of the 1994 murder of seven-year-old Megan Kanka in New Jersey, USA by Jesse Timmendequas, a sex offender with two previous convictions of sex crimes against small children living across the street. The public outcry led to the implementation of a subsection of the Jacob Wetterling Crimes Against Children and Sexually Violent Offender Registration Act of 1994, which required sex offenders to register with local law enforcement agencies. Research around this law is far from conclusive, but broadly suggest that it has had very limited impact. First, because is very difficult to implement and secondly because most abuses against children are perpetrated by people who know the child and have no sex convictions (Levenson & Cotter, 2005; Prescott & Rockoff, 2008; Vásquez, Maddan, & Walker, 2008).

Moreover, cases such as the disappearance of Madeleine McCann highlight a series of very problematic issues in relation to the way the media reports crime. For example, on 30 May 2007 the McCanns and a group of journalists flew to Rome in a Lear jet belonging to British businessman Philip Green to meet Pope Benedict XVI (Formicola, 2011; Robertson, 2010). (The Pope would later be accused of providing a systematic cover-up of dozens of paedophiles priests in Ireland and the USA.) The journalists and their editors happily jumped onto the bandwagon of placing Madeleine on the front pages of British newspapers, enabling them to sell up to 30,000 extra copies a day. Consequently, her story was on the front page of several British tabloids every day for almost six months and became one of Sky News's menu options (Greer & McLaughlin, 2013; Stillman, 2007). At the time, these journalists seemed to have no ethical qualms regarding the way this particular story was facilitated by those in power (who should themselves have been under scrutiny), as long as it sold newspapers and increased ratings.

The main problem with this type of coverage is not only that it sends the wrong message to the public but that it also mobilises public opinion and policy makers in the wrong direction. Hence, while we have seen a stark decrease in resources being allocated towards supporting individuals at risk—i.e. general cuts to welfare provisions, cuts to legal aid to families, reduction in housing provisions for vulnerable women and children at risk—we have seen instead an increasing tendency to develop legislation and the allocation of resources to areas such as immigration control and the war on drugs, which are supposedly aimed at controlling "the other"—the stranger. However, these approaches have little or no impact on reducing violence against the child or on child exploitation. In other words, news coverage of these types of events, in the way it happens, makes for very ineffectual public policy.

The relationship between news reporting of crime statistics and public policy is not only characterised by misuse and misrepresentation, but also by the absence of data in cases in which it should be displayed. In many cases, the use of statistics in crime reporting and public policy is one of "constant missed opportunities": those situations in which the news media could have highlighted statistics to encourage and foster public discussion about certain crime-related topics but that it did not do so. Instead, in these cases, the media tends to individualise the story, depriving it of almost all structural analysis and socio-political context.

Take, for example, the case of Nigella Lawson, the daughter of the former UK Chancellor of the Exchequer Nigel Lawson, who made a name as a celebrity television chef. The news media got hold of pictures which apparently showed her then husband and advertising tycoon, Charles Saatchi, trying to strangle her, although he would later claim that this event was out of context and was only a "playful tiff". The Crown Prosecution Service (CPS) did not press charges against Saatchi nor did large segments of the news media, at the time, contextualise the issue in terms of violence against women as being a widespread problem.

Instead, the news coverage limited itself to presenting this as an isolated case. Moreover, when Nigella Lawson was invited onto one of BBC Radio 4's flagship programmes *Woman's Hour* a few months after the incident, not a single question was asked about or reference was made to the abuse, nor was the programme followed by any special announcement of support lines available for women who have suffered from domestic violence. Few statistics were brought into the overall coverage of her abuse, nor was it pointed out—again with a few exceptions—that violence against women is endemic and structural in society.

Newspapers such as *The Mirror* and *The Sunday People*, would use terms such as "Assault victim Nigella Lawson" only a year later to describe how she was backing a domestic violence charity (Hind, 2014), but no data was incorporated in order to illustrate how this problem is much more widespread that many are led to believe. In fact, the overall news coverage of this particular incident of violence against women lacked statistical data. Moreover, the overall tone of news reports was that this incident was somehow unusual given the "status" of those involved, as if domestic violence is somehow confined to the working classes. *The Daily Mail*, in its coverage of a completely separate trial of two acquaintance who stole from the celebrity couple, refer to the context of the abuse in these terms:

> The couple may have lived in a huge £27 million home in Chelsea, with white flagstone floors and immense art installations, but it was a gilded cage in which, by Nigella's own account, she existed in a state of emotional distress. Saatchi was characterised by Nigella in court as "brilliant but brutal". She sought therapy and used anxiety medication. Her dope-smoking was caused, she said, by their failing marriage. She also claimed that a sole experiment with cocaine in 2010 had been driven by "intimate terrorism" on his part which had left her feeling "isolated and in fear". (Boshoff, 2013)

Overall, the coverage of this incident was particularly flawed given the missed opportunities to raise awareness of how this is an issue that can happen to women of any background rather than being presented as an unusual case of a "bad marriage". Given her personal links to the political elites and her celebrity status, the news coverage could have been directed towards mobilising resources and efforts towards providing safety, protection and options for vulnerable women who face increasing limitations given the cuts in welfare and legal aid. Statistics could have helped to create a link between Nigella Lawson and other women as well as exposing the double standards of successive governments that claim to care about people at risk of violence but do very little to support them.

Paradoxically, when it comes to violence against women committed by "other" communities or individuals, statistics seem to magically multiply. Female genital mutilation (FGM) and the so-called "honour killings", for example, tend nowadays to receive much more news coverage. As important and dreadful as these crimes are, they are far from being the most predominant forms of violence against women in the West, but are nevertheless utilised to frame public discourse on Muslim immigrant integration in Europe in terms of the presumed incompatibility of Islamic and Western values (Korteweg & Yurdakul, 2009, p. 218). Things are made worst by the fact that journalists tend to detach these stories from wider patterns of violence against women across society, leaving the public thinking that these are isolated trends that have "nothing to do with us" and everything to do with a specific "culture" or "religion". However, both honour killings and FGM are at the bottom of the statistical data while manslaughter committed by "white" men against their spouses or partners is at the top. According to data from 39 out of 52 police forces, there were 11,744 incidences of so-called honour killing and FGM crimes in the five-year period between 2010 and 2014 (inclusive) in the whole of the UK (Talwar & Ahmad, 2015). Compare this with 117,568 violent crimes against women, in England and Wales, just in 2015–2016 (Laville, 2016). At no point are we suggesting that these very deplorable crimes committed by a tiny minority of the population should be somehow let off the hook. On the contrary, they deserve important attention and resources in order to be eradicated from all societies. However, it might be worth reminding journalists and politicians of a biblical question: "Why do you see the speck that is in your brother's eye, but do not notice the log that is in your own eye?" (Mathew 7:3) The answer, as in the biblical tale, is because recognising a problem inherent to us is for more difficult than displacing it to the "other". Moreover, by not using statistics to contextualize these crimes, the news media is actually helping criminalise these segments of society. If people think that these types of horrible crimes, artificially labelled as "honour killings"—as in all fairness a white atheist man killing his spouse because of jealousy should also then be labelled as an "honour killing"—are limited to certain religious communities or groups, then not only will they reject those communities but also assume that those crimes do not happen elsewhere in society.

Consequently, the larger segments of society will be less willing to support and put pressure on law makers to produce policy and allocate resources towards the areas where they are actually needed. In the specific case of the news coverage of honour killings and FGM we have seen, in fact, how resources for law enforcement and draconian surveillance have increase while resources to support women in general to get out of the trap of domestic violence—closely linked to the lack of property ownership, access to housing, legal assistance and support for children—are diverted or cut altogether. That makes for the worst kind of policy possible.

Conclusion

Overall, the reporting of crime statistics is important to inform the public about public policy and decision making, because it facilitates democratic accountability and allows the public to assess the risk of crime in their neighbourhoods. Fully validated and quality assured national statistics that comply with the Code of Practice for Official Statistics are essential for these purposes at a national level (Matheson, 2011, p. 3). However, as we have discussed in this chapter, statistics can also be reported by the news media in ways that can distort the public's understanding of crime and subsequently skew the process of policy making.

This, as we have seen, can have a detrimental effect on both the delivery of justice and, more importantly, on people's lives. Moreover, the process of public policy design and implementation is nowadays extremely mediatised (Esser & Strömbäck, 2014; Mazzoleni & Schulz, 1999). This means that media logics have an enormous influence upon how politicians engage with each other and with the public. It is because of this, as we have seen in the examples used here, that the reporting of statistics or the lack of reporting has become so important. This increasing dominance of media logic in the process of policy design and implementation, referred to as mediatisation, is problematic as nowadays crime statistics are presented to the public in ways in which they support narratives and discourses of power. In more simple terms, crime statistics are constantly "spun" by those in charge so they are perceived and reported in ways that

do not challenge power. For spin-doctors the dissemination of these statistics confers a scientific aura and a sense of neutrality to policies and
approaches that are nevertheless mostly based on ideology. In times of
managerial politics and pseudo-technocratic governments, all politicians
want to appear to be delivering evidence-based policy, and the way crime
statistics are spun enables precisely that.

Notes

1. Doyle, Jack and Wright, Stephen (2012). Immigrant crimewave' warning:
   Foreign nationals were accused of a QUARTER of all crimes in London.
   The Daily Mail. http://www.dailymail.co.uk/news/article-2102895/
   Immigrant-crimewave-warning-Foreign-nationals-accused-QUARTER-
   crimes-London.html#ixzz4SR5oEggQ [Accessed on 2 March 2017].
2. Post Editorial Board (2016). FBI stats back up Trump's warning on crime.
   The New York Post. http://nypost.com/2016/09/26/fbi-stats-back-up-
   trumps-warning-on-crime/ [Accessed on January 12, 2017].

References

Bindel, J. (2012). Sexual abuse of children is widespread—Let's confront the
difficult truth. *The Guardian.* Retrieved from https://www.theguardian.com/
commentisfree/2012/jun/13/sexual-abuse-children-difficult-truth

Bosshoff, A. (2013). Inside Nigella's toxic marriage: She was haunted by depression. He was a terrible bully driven mad by jealousy of her children. The bitter
truth behind Nigella and Saatchi's marital breakdown. *The Daily Mail.*
Retrieved from http://www.dailymail.co.uk/news/article-2527397/Inside-
Nigellas-toxic-marriage-She-haunted-depression-He-terrible-bully-driven-
mad-jealousy-children-The-bitter-truth-Nigella-Saatchis-marital-breakdown.
html#ixzz4TeaLb6EI

Bowling, B. (1999). The rise and fall of New York murder: Zero tolerance or
crack's decline? *British Journal of Criminology, 39*(4), 531–554.

CFCA. (2014). Who abuses children? Retrieved February 2, 2017, from https://
aifs.gov.au/cfca/publications/who-abuses-children

Esser, F., & Strömbäck, J. (2014). *Mediatization of politics.* Basingstoke: Palgrave
Macmillan.

Ettema, J., & Glasser, T. (1998). *Custodians of conscience: Investigative journalism and public virtue*. New York: Columbia University Press.

Formicola, J. R. (2011). Catholic clerical sexual abuse: Effects on Vatican sovereignty and papal power. *Journal of Church and State, 53*(4), 523–544.

Friedman, M., Grawert, A., & Cullen, J. (2016). *Crime in 2016: A preliminary analysis*. New York: NYU School of Law.

Gagne, T. S. (2015). *Eliot Ness*. Newark, DE: Mitchell Lane Publishers, Inc.

Greene, J. (1999). Zero tolerance: A case study of police policies and practices in New York City. *Crime & Delinquency, 45*(2), 171–187.

Greer, C., & McLaughlin, E. (2013). La giustizia mediatica nel Regno Unito: il caso Madeleine McCann. *Sicurezza e scienze sociali, 2*(1), 151–164. doi:10.3280/SISS2013-002012.

Hall, S. (1975). *Newsmaking and crime*. Birmigham: Centre for Contemporary Cultural Studies.

Hind, K. (2014). Nigella Lawson uses high public profile to back domestic violence charity after split from Charles Saatchi. *The Mirror*. Retrieved from http://www.mirror.co.uk/tv/tv-news/nigella-lawson-domestic-abuse-campaign-3222401

Home Office. (2013). The government responses to the second report from the Home Affairs Committee Sesssion 2013–14 HC68. Childe sexual explotation and the responses to localised grooming. Home Office, London.

Hope, T. (2004). Pretend it works evidence and governance in the evaluation of the reducing burglary initiative. *Criminal Justice, 4*(3), 287–308.

Johnson, J. (2003). Horror stories and the construction of child abuse. In D. Loseke & J. Best (Eds.), *Social problems: Constructionist readings* (pp. 267–279). New York: Aldine de Gruyter.

Kane, M. (2014). Eliot Ness' revolutionary police work goes far beyond Al Capone. Retrieved February 2, 2016, from http://nypost.com/2014/02/22/eliot-ness-didnt-take-down-al-capone-but-what-he-did-is-better/

Korteweg, A., & Yurdakul, G. (2009). Islam, gender, and immigrant integration: Boundary drawing in discourses on honour killing in the Netherlands and Germany. *Ethnic and Racial Studies, 32*(2), 218–238.

Laville, S. (2016). Violent crimes against women in England and Wales reach record high. Retrieved November 9, 2016, from https://www.theguardian.com/society/2016/sep/05/violent-crimes-against-women-in-england-and-wales-reach-record-high

Levenson, J. S., & Cotter, L. P. (2005). The effect of Megan's Law on sex offender reintegration. *Journal of Contemporary Criminal Justice, 21*(1), 49–66.

Matheson, J. (2011). *National statistician's review of crime statistics: England and Wales*. London: Government Statistical Service.

Mazzoleni, G., & Schulz, W. (1999). "Mediatization" of politics: A challenge for democracy? *Political Communication, 16*(3), 247–261.

Mears, D. P. (2007). Towards rational and evidence-based crime policy. *Journal of Criminal Justice, 35*(6), 667–682.

Perry, D. (2014). *Eliot Ness: The rise and fall of an American hero.* London: Penguin.

Prescott, J. J., & Rockoff, J. E. (2008). *Do sex offender registration and notification laws affect criminal behavior?* NBER Working Paper No. 13803. Retrieved December 13, 2016, from http://www.nber.org/papers/w13803

Robertson, G. (2010). *The case of the Pope: Vatican accountability for human rights abuse.* London: Penguin.

Stillman, S. (2007). 'The missing white girl syndrome': Disappeared women and media activism. *Gender & Development, 15*(3), 491–502.

Talwar, D., & Ahmad, A. (2015). 'Honour crime': 11,000 UK cases recorded in five years. Retrieved December 2, 2016, from http://www.bbc.com/news/uk-33424644

Taylor, J. (2011, June 1). Force writes off a third of crimes. *Metro,* p. 12.

Tilley, N. (2001). Evaluation and evidence-led crime reduction policy and practice. In *Crime, disorder and community safety* (pp. 81–97). London: Routledge.

Tucker, K. (2000). *Eliot Ness and the untouchables: The Historical reality and the film and television depictions.* London: McFarland.

Tufail, W. (2015). Rotherham, Rochdale, and the racialised threat of the' Muslim Grooming Gang'. *International Journal for Crime, Justice and Social Democracy, 4*(3), 30–43.

Vásquez, B. E., Maddan, S., & Walker, J. T. (2008). The influence of sex offender registration and notification laws in the United States: A time-series analysis. *Crime & Delinquency.* doi:10.1177/0011128707311641.

7

Spinning Crime Statistics

Over the past decades, we have witnessed the increasing influence of public relations (PR) in setting the news agenda (Davies, 2008; Lewis, Williams, & Franklin, 2008; Miller & Dinan, 2007). This has been particularly the case in relation to the interaction between government officials, the news media and the public. Something has happened in the context of the increasing "mediatization" of politics; a process in which the power of prevailing influential institutions such as governments and political parties becomes subordinated to the logic and dynamics set by the news media (Hjarvard, 2008; Livingstone & Lunt, 2014). Hence, political communication is performed, framed and defined by the media rather than traditional actors such as political parties.

This is partly because the media, as a social institution, has become the main provider of information for the individuals not only mediating but also shaping the construction of social reality (Fuchs, 2013; Gamson, Croteau, Hoynes, & Sasson, 1992). Hence, people not only see the political world through the lenses of the media, but also rely on it to make sense of reality. Indeed:

In earlier societies, social institutions like family, school and church were the most important providers of information, tradition and moral

© The Author(s) 2017
J. Lugo-Ocando, *Crime Statistics in the News*,
DOI 10.1057/978-1-137-39841-3_7

orientation for the individual member of society. Today, these institutions have lost some of their former authority, and the media have to some extent taken over their role as providers of information and moral orientation, at the same time as the media have become society's most important story-teller about society itself. (Hjarvard, 2008, p. 13)

It is in this context that PR has emerged as a key player in defining the way stories are told to us (Austin & Jin, 2015; Lloyd & Toogood, 2014).

Overall, PR work involves persuasive communication and advocacy, lobbying, source–media relations, reputation and relationship management, and issues and crisis management (L'Etang, 2008). In this sense, the history of PR is closely linked to that of modern propaganda, although it is not constrained to the political sphere (L'Etang, 2004, p. 15). In the case of policing, PR practice, conceived as an orchestrated effort to develop professional organisational communications, is relatively recent. In the UK, the professional management of public affairs and communications—or professional communications—had already become "an integrated part of policing" by 2007 (Mawby, 2012) although professional communication efforts to improve the image of the police can be traced back to the early twentieth century in the light of the role of the police in confronting the striking miners (Miller & Dinan, 2007).

Overall, the police uses the media to reaffirm its own status as law enforcers and sole legitimate administrators of violence. Consequently, law enforcement organisations invest resources to influence the way crime is reported and presented to the public while improving their own reputation in order to gain influence and power. Some studies have found that police categorisation of crime, for example, is self-promoting and supportive of traditional responses, while reporters are not critical of police (Chermak, 1995, p. 21). Indeed, "the media portrayal of policing is juxtaposed with both positive and negative representations. As a result, a complex relationship exists between media consumption and public attitudes towards the police" (Dowler & Zawilski, 2007, p. 193). This relationship, as complex as it is, is managed by professionals within the police enforcement agencies and political spheres whose normative function is to provide accessibility and transparency to the police organisations but whose real job, in many cases, is to spin facts and news to reaffirm the status quo and power of the police.[1] It is within this context in which the communication of crime statistics happens in most societies.

This chapter, therefore, examines the dynamics and process that take place among those who present these statistics to the news media. In so doing, the chapter looks at the role of PR and in particular that of spin in presenting crime statistics in the news and how professional communication helps to shape public perception with regards to crime in general. It assesses the methods and approaches undertaken by those managing communications within the police organisations in dealing with crime statistics in order to extract political advantage from its presentation. The chapter looks at particular problems and ethical dilemmas and tensions which derive from the PR efforts to articulate press releases and support materials regarding statistical data relating to crime against the tension generated by the resistance of the news media to accept these accounts uncritically. In so doing, it examines particular examples in which there have been tensions and conflicts derived from the different approaches undertaken by both parties. The chapter does so in order to understand the different difficulties and issues around providing journalists with the data and support materials relating to crime.

Crisis Time

On 6 April 2006, a group of journalists sent a letter to Julia Simpson the then Director of Communications of the UK Home Office, in charge of policing, to share their collective disquiet over the Home Office's practice of issuing all its statistics on a single day each month. This was due to the difficulty of processing the volume of statistics provided. The issue was highlighted by the UK Statistics Commission in 2006 after a group of news media associations and companies in Britain published an open letter to the Home Office in which it accused the government of "dishonourable tactics" in releasing a large number of statistics and research reports in such a way that made it impossible for journalists to digest them in such a short time. The members of the group, which included the Press Association, the BBC and some of the most prominent national newspapers in Britain, said that by providing all the statistics at once in bulk, the government made it very difficult for journalists and news editors to process them appropriately. Those who signed the letter suggested that this was a government tactic so that it could "bury bad news" by overwhelming reporters with statistical information on the last Thursday of every month; a day that became known as "research Thursday".

This was perhaps one of the few times in decades that journalists were complaining about having too much information. However, this episode highlights the fact that for many journalists, quantitative data can be overwhelming, both due to its nature and proliferation. However, what was more revealing from this, not isolated, incident is the degree to which many government officials and corporations go to avoid a close and critical examination by the news media of their numbers. It also highlights common practices that, regrettably, are still prevalent in many areas. These practices derive from an understanding of media dynamics which is then utilised to "manage" the dissemination of statistics in order to "spin" issues. This is an approach that still prevails in many countries around the world.

In the UK, one must acknowledge that the manner in which officials manage statistics has come a long way since 2006 and important progress has been made. In this sense, the way officials now make this data available to the public is much better regulated and transparent. Indeed, the creation of the UK Statistics Authority under the Statistics and Registration Service Act 2007 was an important step in avoiding, as much as possible, manipulation and opacity in the way official statistics were treated and then presented to the public. As an independent statutory body, the UK Statistics Authority reports directly to the UK Parliament, the Scottish Parliament, the National Assembly for Wales and the Northern Ireland Assembly, and therefore is totally independent of the Executive. Indeed, according to the 2007 Act of Parliament, the Authority has a statutory objective to promote and safeguard the production and publication of official statistics that "serve the public good" as well as regulating quality and publicly challenging the misuse of statistics. Moreover, one of Andrew Dilnot's first actions as newly appointed head of the Authority in 2011 was to impose restrictions on government officials so they could not disseminate statistics without a proper balance and checking, to guarantee more transparency and accuracy in the way data was being reported to the public. Thanks to the Authority's actions and set of new policies, today Britain can present data that is far more transparent and accessible to its citizens in almost all areas; that is, with the exception of crime statistics.

Regrettably, crime statistics produced by the Home Office in Britain continues to present numerous problems and it is still not completely regulated by the Authority despite repeated calls to surrender power and oversight to the independent body. Instead, government after government has been reluctant to cede its ability to control and comply with the Authority's request to produce and manage the statistical data in an appropriate manner. This has meant that until 2016, at the time of writing this book, the UK Statistics Authority had still not certified crime statistics in the UK. Consequently, further erosion of credibility and trust around crime numbers on the part of the public and legislators has endured. Furthermore, the Public Administration Select Committee of the British Parliament published a report following an inquiry into the quality of crime statistics under the title "Caught Redhanded: Why we can't rely on Police Recorded Crime" in which it raised "serious concerns about the crime-recording process" (RSS, 2014).

So the question is: why are some police enforcement agencies so reluctant to have external oversight of their statistics? One possible answer is that it gives them power to set the agenda and establish the core narrative. In an ideal world, crime numbers should be there to inform the public and for policy makers to undertake sound policies and approaches. In the real world, however, these numbers are used to "manufacture consent" (Cottle, 2006; Herman & Chomsky, 2010 [1984]) and mobilise public opinion and politicians in favour of the police.

For the police forces from around the world, this is not a small matter and the fact that they themselves have oversight and control over the gathering, management and dissemination of crime statistics is very important. It is a way of reaffirming their status as the central bureaucracy of power in relation to the administration of violence and legal authority in civil life. Indeed, as Michael Foucault (1979 [1977]) pointed out, the compilation of detailed information about many aspects of social life was a crucial factor in the development of modernity, and closely tied up with the consolidation of governments' control over their populations. It was unsurprising, therefore, that the collection and analysis of crime data soon became predominantly the province of government employees, rather than academic scientists. Despite this practice originating in France in the Napoleonic era, it soon expanded across Europe and the rest of the world as "the idea was also highly compatible with the aims and practices of the centralized bureaucracies that were expanding across Europe in support of the emerging nation states" (Maguire, 2012, p. 207).

Professional Communication

Today, police forces in many countries possess large communication teams that professionally manage public affairs and spin facts and events to "facilitate" the work of their officers, which in practice means "manufacturing" the necessary consent to guarantee power for the organisation, as that is the function of many PR practitioners (L'Etang, 2008; Pieczka & L'Etang, 2006). Indeed, on the one hand, there is the normative claim that the professionalisation of police force communications is carried out in order to make these forces more transparent and accountable. On the other hand, we face the fact that these efforts are often aimed at obscuring malpractices, such as the Phone Hacking Scandal and payment of police bribes by the press in the UK, highlighted in recent years.

In recent times, the way professional communication, in the form of PR, is carried out has become increasingly relevant to how crime is reported by the mainstream media (Davies, 2008; Lewis et al., 2008). In particular, in the way crime statistics are presented to the public. It is possible to argue that among officials and policy makers the process of dissemination of this type of data has become, over the years, mediatised. In other words, the logics and dynamics of the news media shape the way law officials and enforcement agencies present data to the public. This seems to be irrespective of whether such officials are elected politicians or designated civil servant officials, in all cases mediatisation has set the logic according to which the media now defines the way crime statistics are communicated to the public.

Indeed, over the past few years a wide range of organisations have adopted PR as part of their organisational structure as a means of achieving particular goals through media coverage and the professional management of current affairs. At the same time media institutions, operating under tighter editorial budgets, have become more dependent on information supplied by external sources in what is call an "information deficit" (Anderson, 2015; Sumner et al., 2014). This deficit of what the news media is now able to produce, has translated into the growth of the professional PR sector and changes to existing patterns of source access (Davis, 2000, p. 39) where PR professionals have come to fill the information gap left by the newsrooms increasingly deprived of resources. Consequently, these trends are affecting the way various sources gain and manage media access while facilitating this access to those who have the economic resources and skills to muscle their way in (Davis, 2000, p. 54). In other words, although non-official sources, such as non-governmental organisations (NGOs) and pressure groups, can practise PR to gain access to the media, the increasing news media dependency upon PR is ultimately benefiting governments and corporations.

In the case of the dissemination of crime statistics the situation is made even more problematic because the production of these numbers is carried out by the official sources themselves, a process that is often left unaccountable and lacks, in many cases, sufficient transparency. Consequently, journalists covering crime, who are presented with press releases and news packages in order to disseminate this data, are often unable to cross-reference the statistics or bring into question key approaches and methodologies used to produce such numbers. In most cases, the numbers are simply "reproduced" without proper critical analysis, as they are presented, and central issues such as validity and reliability of these statistics are left unchecked.

The control and oversight of how crime numbers are gathered, managed and disseminated is therefore pivotal as an interface of power between the police authorities, the government and the general public. It allows officials to articulate narratives that seem legitimate enough to set the boundaries around the explanatory frameworks that define the discursive regimes within which journalists produce their stories. This is referred in PR scholarship as being a function of communication professionals in setting the "regimes of truth" which place emphasis on producing highly coherent regimes of "truth" (Edwards & Hodges, 2011, p. 13).

These discursive regimes define the boundaries of what is acceptable and what is not, particularly in relation to defining reality in terms of objective and factual truth. To give an example, the police PR official often provides crime statistics that show that more arrests are being made and that targets to confiscate drugs are being met. But where are these raids taking place? Traditionally, the police tend to carry out raids in poor areas where it is easier to proceed without a written warrant or avoid a backlash from the public. Consequently, when one correlates the number of drug-related arrests made against the geographical area where these are being carried out, it is immediately noticeable that poor people, and in the case of the USA particularly black neighbourhoods, are being disproportionally targeted. This is despite the fact that studies show that the levels of drug use among blacks and whites are very similar. In so doing, the police authorities and the government give the impression that they are tackling the drug problem across the board, which is not the case. However, once that matrix is created in the public sphere, journalists covering the War on Drugs will find it very difficult to step outside those parameters of "truth" and therefore are incapable of challenging authority about its core narratives. The news coverage then focuses on assessing the War on Drugs in terms of measurable variables such as arrest and consumption, and thus turns these regimes of truth—based on statistical data—into straightjackets for public debate.

One of the reasons for this is that PR practitioners see statistics as "facts" in the same way as journalists do. Indeed the Chartered Institute of Public Relations in the UK points out that "statistics is the word used for the facts or data that are collected, measured and/or calculated of things of interest" (CIPR, 2016, p. 2). This definition therefore lacks the critical approach needed to understand that these numbers are a representation and summary of many events and should not necessarily be taken as facts. This is not to suggest that PR practitioners will use numbers deliberately to manipulate public opinion or restrict critical debate about the operations of the organisations they represent. On the contrary, organisations such as the CIPR itself have produced very clear guidelines about the ethical use of numbers when dealing with the press. Nevertheless, the tension between providing public transparency and protecting the interests of the organisations PR practitioners represent often tips the balance towards the latter and that is when the misuse of statistics tends to happen the most.

Not Only About Communication

Having said that, the way these numbers are communicated to the public by means of the intervention of PR practitioners within the mainstream media realm is only one aspect of this relationship. Indeed, another very important area where PR uses statistics is in lobbing. It is important, therefore to define what exactly we understand by this practice.

Lobbying is the act of attempting to influence decisions made by officials in the government, most often legislators or members of regulatory agencies. Lobbying is carried out by many different types of people and organised groups, including individuals in the private sector, corporations, fellow legislators or government officials, or advocacy/interest groups (Baumgartner, Berry, Hojnacki, Leech, & Kimball, 2009; Potters & Winden, 1992). The police enforcement agencies having to compete with other government bodies for resources and public support are no different.

It is imperative to start acknowledging the often "unseen power" of PR, which in many cases had a detrimental effect on public policy in countries such as the USA and UK (Cutlip, 2013; Miller & Dinan, 2007). The hidden or opaque source of PR power derives from its organisational ability to lobby governments and individuals in order to favour corporate interests. Some studies have confirmed that corporate lobbying is often instigated by company chief executive officers (CEOs) but the PR manager often plays a crucial role (Haug & Koppang, 1997, p. 233). This "direction" does not have to be explicit as many PR practitioners assume that their job is to "spin" the facts in order to advance their company's cause.

These studies have also shown that lobbying has a marked effect on policies and a disproportionate effect on policy making (Godwin, Godwin, Ainsworth, & Godwin, 2012; Helpman & Persson, 2001). In the case of the use of statistics by police forces they are often used to gain greater public support and mobilise political support to access resources.

Numbers, therefore, are a key element in convincing key constituencies to adopt a specific approach or to challenge opposing views to that of the organisation that the PR practitioners represent.

Lobbying is closely connected to PR (Black, 2013; Davidson, 2015). Those who practise it attempt to influence legislators, policy makers and key actors in developing legislation and policy that supports the organisation in question, thus encouraging the institutions to produce policies and legislation that are beneficial to their employers. In a nutshell, lobbying is all about communicating with policy makers and networking to proactively or reactively deal with legislative controls that are perceived to be detrimental to those who lobbyists represent. Most lobbyists work for private organisations, advocacy organisations or even government departments where they can promote their own agendas by meeting with members of congress, legislative aides and leaders of other government agencies.

In the case of crime statistics, there are several lobby and pressure groups that use them to promote their own agendas. In the UK, for example, there is the Police Federation, which effectively represents police officers as a non-official union, and the British Security Industry Association which represents government outsourced private companies that operate in areas such as crime, prisons and the justice system. Other smaller players are pressure groups and think-tanks that are either charities, NGOs or a political front for other players. Among these are some very well-known bodies, such as the National Rifle Association in the USA, which represents the gun industry in that country, the Police Foundation, a think-tank based in Oxford, UK, the Centre for Policy Studies, a conservative think-tank, and many others entirely focused or partially focused on crime prevention policy.

In most cases, these organisations lobby and make use of statistics to do so. In almost all cases, the statistics they use are those produced by the authorities themselves but in other cases they produce their own statistics. However, contrary to journalists, these organisations have the time and resources to disect the numbers and re-package data within narratives that are far more effective in advancing their own agendas. To do so, they use statistics to underpin or challenge particular views and approaches. Contrary to common assumption, however, lobbying is not always carried out behind closed doors. In some cases, such as the NRA, lobby groups operate in an opaque manner, in others they act very openly and lobbyists are required to register their interests, such as in the case of MEPs in the European Union Parliament. The problem is that, even when carried out openly, lobbing as a political activity entails far more than canvassing for a cause. In many cases, it means bribes and even unlawful pressure and blackmail, giving lobbying overall a terrible reputation.

In countries such as the USA, lobbying is widespread throughout the political system. Lobbying expenditure at the federal level is estimated to be approximately five times that of political action committee (PAC) campaign contributions. For instance, in 2012, organised interest groups spent over US$3.5 billion annually lobbying the federal government, compared to approximately US$1.55 billion in campaign contributions from PACs and other organisations over the two-year (2011–2012) election cycle. Moreover, corporations and trade associations comprise the vast majority of lobbying expenditure by interest group—more than 84% at the federal level—compared with issue-ideology membership groups, which make up only 2% of these expenditures (De Figueiredo & Richter, 2014).

In many cases, these lobby interventions allow pro-gun organisations and companies to validate and legitimise their ideological positions and views by developing supportive statistical evidence. In this way, the views advanced by these organisations are presented as scientific conclusions and become harder to challenge. However, it should be noted that the most common use of statistical evidence among lobbyists is to create doubt. This is to postpone as much as possible regulatory legislation that could affect their profits. In other words, the data is used to delay political intervention (Oreskes & Conway, 2011).

Take the example of gun control in the USA. In this area, lobbyists deploy vast armies of analysts to scrutinise the available data and help them create their own data to "factualise" their narratives. Both anti- and pro-gun groups use statistics to legitimise their positions and convince the public and legislators to restrain (or not) from issuing additional controls upon the sale of guns in the USA. In some cases, they use the same set of statistics to argue something completely different. For example, the NRA often claims that violent crime in the USA has decreased as gun control restrictions have been eliminated or rolled back at the federal, state and local levels, and that people who use guns to defend themselves against robbery and aggravated assault are less likely to be injured than people who use other means, or no means, of self-defence. In the first case, the NRA lobbyists use these numbers to "demonstrate" that less restrictions on the sales of guns—and presumably higher sales—do not translate into more violent crimes. In the second case, there is the assumption that cor-relations translates into causation. Both cases, of course, are more com-plex than what the NRA would make us believe.

It might be the case that weapon sales are not correlated at all with increases in crime. But that was rarely the point made by anti-gun groups, which were far more concern with random shootings over the years; such as the Columbine High School massacre of 1999, the 2012 Aurora shoot-ing and the San Bernardino attack of 2015. That is to say that these anti-gun groups were far more concerned with the "probability" that people not mentally fit to own a gun were nevertheless able to buy one. They were also concerned about the calibre of the guns being sold and with the increasing use of semi-automatics assault weapons. None of these con-cerns were addressed in the statistics used by the NRA.

This use of statistics by lobbyists not only has an effect on policy making but also, and fundamentally, on the public as it creates and reinforces particu-lar views and opinions of the issue. This has meant that, over the years, people in the USA have changed the reasons as to why they want to own guns. A Pew Research Center survey conducted in February 2013 pointed out that about half (48%) of gun owners said the main reason they owned a gun was for protection while about one in three (32%) said they owned a gun for hunting. This is a fundamental change from 1999, when 49% said they owned a gun for hunting and only 26% said they had a gun for protection.

A Force for Good?

It is worth clarifying that PR is not only about spin, manipulation and undue lobbying, and that in many cases it has proven to be a force for good. In the European Union, for example, the biggest registered lobby group is Greenpeace and the way it has used statistics and data to inform debate in the European Parliament has positively contributed in many cases to more robust and better European environmental legislation. Indeed, PR can also contribute to grassroots democracy through activism and radical politics; these practitioners use tools and approaches taken from PR to advance their organisations' and groups' agendas (Holtzhausen, 2000, p. 93). These tools can helps activists establish important spaces for dialogue and provide some symmetry—although rarely equality—in the terms of engagement between powerful institutions and the ordinary citizen.

In the realm of crime statistics, PR practitioners from both the police and Third Sector Organisations (TSOs) could potentially use these numbers to ensure that the terms of the debate are far more transparent and are established with more accuracy and rigour. However, as we seen in this chapter, there are important obstacles that hinder this noble objective. On the one hand, the quality and interpretation given to the numbers is under question and so is the way they are accessed both by the news media and the public. On the other hand, the majority of power and resources deployed in PR is held by organisations and corporations that have an agenda that is not really in the public interest. No anti-gun group in the USA comes close to matching what the NRA deploys in lobbying in the USA nor can any civic group in Western Europe compete with what security companies allocate for PR and lobby efforts. Therefore the issue of "asymmetry" in PR practice (L'Etang, 1994; Murphy, 1991) is crucial in understanding why, on the whole, professional communication is not good for the public understanding of crime statistics.

However, one should also note that the key problem is not to do with private corporations, pressure groups or think-tanks but with the police and government itself. The exponential growth of PR resources in police forces around the world in times of decreasing investment in newsrooms is a danger not only to the reporting of crime but to the delivery of justice and to democracy itself. The fact that those who are filling the information gap and complementing the democratic deficit are precisely those who have a vested interest in establishing particular news accounts, means that power narratives coming from the police are left unaccounted for and adopted as "truth". In these cases the weak end up being effectively silenced in favour of the powerful and, sadly, statistics then become a fundamental part of the setting in which injustices steam from inequality.

Notes

1. The notable case of this was of course the Hillsborough disaster at Hillsborough football stadium in Sheffield, England on 15 April 1989, during the 1988–1989 FA Cup semi-final game between Liverpool and Nottingham Forest where 96 people died and 766 others were injured. For years the police spun these events to avoid any responsibility, blaming the victims instead.

References

Anderson, A. (2015). Reflections on environmental communication and the challenges. *Science, 1*(2), 199–230.

Austin, L., & Jin, Y. (2015). Approaching ethical crisis communication with accuracy and sensitivity: Exploring common ground and gaps between journalism and public relations. *Public Relations Journal, 9*(1), 2.

Baumgartner, F. R., Berry, J. M., Hojnacki, M., Leech, B. L., & Kimball, D. C. (2009). *Lobbying and policy change: Who wins, who loses, and why*. Chicago: University of Chicago Press.

Black, S. (2013). *Practice of public relations*. Abingdon, OX: Routledge.

Chermak, S. (1995). Image control: How police affect the presentation of crime news. *American journal of police, 14*(2), 21–43.

CIPR. (2016). Using statistics in public relations. Retrieved February 12, 2017, from https://www.cipr.co.uk/content/cpd/summer-cpd/using-statistics-public-relations

Cottle, S. (2006). Mediatized rituals: Beyond manufacturing consent. *Media, Culture & Society, 28*(3), 411–432.

Cutlip, S. M. (2013). *The unseen power: Public relations—A history*. London: Routledge.

Davidson, S. (2015). Everywhere and nowhere: Theorising and researching public affairs and lobbying within public relations scholarship. *Public Relations Review, 41*(5), 615–627.

Davies, N. (2008). *Flat earth news: An award-winning reporter exposes falsehood, distortion and propaganda in the global media.* London: Random House.

Davis, A. (2000). Public relations, news production and changing patterns of source access in the British national media. *Media, Culture & Society, 22*(1), 39–59.

De Figueiredo, J. M., & Richter, B. K. (2014). Advancing the empirical research on lobbying. *Annual Review of Political Science, 17*, 163–185.

Dowler, K., & Zawilski, V. (2007). Public perceptions of police misconduct and discrimination: Examining the impact of media consumption. *Journal of Criminal Justice, 35*(2), 193–203.

Edwards, L., & Hodges, C. E. (2011). Introduction: Implications of (a radical) socio-cultural 'turn' in public relations scholarship. In L. Edwards & C. E. Hodges (Eds.), *Public relations, society & culture: Theoretical and empirical explorations* (pp. 1–15). Abingdon, OX: Taylor & Francis.

Foucault, M. (1979 [1977]). *Discipline and punish.* New York: Vintage.

Fuchs, C. (2013). *Social media: A critical introduction.* Thousand Oaks, CA: Sage.

Gamson, W. A., Croteau, D., Hoynes, W., & Sasson, T. (1992). Media images and the social construction of reality. *Annual Review of Sociology, 18*(1), 373–393.

Godwin, R. K., Godwin, K., Ainsworth, S., & Godwin, E. K. (2012). *Lobbying and policymaking.* London: Sage.

Haug, M., & Koppang, H. (1997). Lobbying and public relations in a European context. *Public Relations Review, 23*(3), 233–247.

Helpman, E., & Persson, T. (2001). Lobbying and legislative bargaining. *Advances in Economic Analysis & Policy, 1*(1). doi:10.2202/1538-0637.1008

Herman, E. S., & Chomsky, N. (2010 [1984]). *Manufacturing consent: The political economy of the mass media.* London: Random House.

Hjarvard, S. (2008). The mediatization of society. *Nordicom Review, 29*(2), 105–134.

Holtzhausen, D. R. (2000). Postmodern values in public relations. *Journal of Public Relations Research, 12*(1), 93–114.

L'Etang, J. (1994). Public relations and corporate social responsibility: Some issues arising. *Journal of Business Ethics, 13*(2), 111–123.

L'Etang, J. (2004). *Public relations in Britain: A history of professional practice in the twentieth century.* Abingdon-on-Thames, OX: Routledge.

L'Etang, J. (2008). *Public relations.* Hoboken, NJ: Wiley Online Library.

Lewis, J., Williams, A., & Franklin, B. (2008). A compromised fourth estate? UK news journalism, public relations and news sources. *Journalism Studies, 9*(1), 1–20.

Livingstone, S., & Lunt, P. (2014). Mediatization: An emerging paradigm for media and communication studies. In K. Lundby (Ed.), *Mediatization of communication. Handbooks of communication science* (Vol. 21, pp. 703–724). Berlin: De Gruyter Mouton.

Lloyd, J., & Toogood, L. (2014). *Journalism and PR: News media and public relations in the digital age.* London: IB Tauris.

Maguire, M. (2012). Criminal statistics and the construction of crime. In M. Maguire & R. Morgan (Eds.), *The Oxford handbook of criminology* (Vol. 5, pp. 206–244). Oxford: Oxford University Press.

Mawby, R. C. (2012). Crisis? What crisis? Some research-based reflections on police–press relations. *Policing, 6*(3), 272–280.

Miller, D., & Dinan, W. (2007). *A century of spin: How public relations became the cutting edge of corporate power.* London: Pluto Press.

Murphy, P. (1991). The limits of symmetry: A game theory approach to symmetric and asymmetric public relations. *Journal of Public Relations Research, 3*(1-4), 115–131.

Oreskes, N., & Conway, E. M. (2011). *Merchants of doubt: How a handful of scientists obscured the truth on issues from tobacco smoke to global warming.* London: Bloomsbury Publishing.

Pieczka, M., & L'Etang, J. (2006). Public relations and the question of professionalism. In J. L'Etang (Ed.), *Public relations: Critical debates and contemporary practice* (pp. 265–278). Mahwah, NJ: Lawrence Erlbaum Associates, Inc.

Potters, J., & Winden, F. (1992). Lobbying and asymmetric information. *Public Choice, 74*(3), 269–292.

RSS. (2014). PASC sets out criticism of police-recorded crime statistics. Retrieved March 28, 2017, from https://www.statslife.org.uk/news/1352-pasc-sets-out-criticism-of-police-recorded-crime-stats

Sumner, P., Vivian-Griffiths, S., Boivin, J., Williams, A., Venetis, C. A., Davies, A., … Dalton, B. (2014). The association between exaggeration in health related science news and academic press releases: Retrospective observational study. *BMJ, 349*(g7015), 1–8.

8

Visualising Crime Statistics

Let us start by reminding ourselves that data graphics or data visualisation is the display of measured quantities by means of combining points, lines, a coordinate system, numbers, symbols, words, shading and colour. Overall, producing excellent statistical graphics consists of being able to communicate complex ideas with clarity, precision and efficiency (Tufte, 2001). Indeed, one of the key advantages of presenting visual data to the general public instead of the statistics themselves in a basic manner is that graphics tend to be intuitive and do not require the understanding of complex mathematical or statistical algorithms or parameters (Keim, 2002, p. 1). Hence, visualising the data makes it easier for officials and journalists to communicate the meaning of crime statistics to the public. In so doing, data visualisation permits the detection of subgroups: for example, criminal networks can often be partitioned into subgroups consisting of individuals who closely interact with each other (Xu & Chen, 2005). These graphics can also provide an understanding of the hierarchy of crime clusters while elucidating the most common methods used by criminals as well as assisting in the discovery of patterns of interaction both nationally and locally. They can also help in revealing patterns of behaviour between groups, interactions and associations, and can help to

© The Author(s) 2017
J. Lugo-Ocando, *Crime Statistics in the News*,
DOI 10.1057/978-1-137-39841-3_8

expose the overall structure of criminal networks under investigation. Indeed, as Nathan Yau points out:

> One of the best ways to explore and try to understand a large dataset is with visualisation. Place the numbers into a visual space and let your brain or your readers' brain find the patters. We are good at that. You can often find stories you might never have found with just formal statistics methods. (Yau, 2011, p. xvi)

All in all, the visualisation of crime data permits a better communication of meaning and makes numbers more accessible to the public understanding of crime. Therefore, this chapter examines the way crime statistics are visually presented in the news media. It starts by looking at the most basic and traditional ways of representing crime statistics graphically, while defining which are the most common and predominant forms of graphic display. It discusses how and why visualisation of statistical data has become such an important feature in the process of communicating crime statistics to the wider public and how it has affected the way people understand and react to this type of information. In so doing, it also assesses how the rise of data journalism has affected the way crime statistics are presented in graphic terms, while examining the use of key communication elements and resources such as infographs. In thus offers an explanatory framework as to how crime statistics are presented to the audiences of the mainstream media and how this helps shape the public imagination. The aim is to contextualise this analysis in the wider context of theory and practice associated with visual communication of news, while assessing how these graphic representations make crime statistics more accessible (or not) to the public.

Graphic Understanding

Traditionally, journalists reporting crime statistics have used graphs to communicate these numbers to the public. They assume that by presenting the statistics in a graphical manner people will be able to understand them better and this data will somehow become more accessible. This assumption is based upon the fact that the visualisation of data is the most effective method to convey its meaning in an accessible and transparent manner. Numbers organised in bars or in a pie chart can, it is often claimed, make up for the shortfall in the public's understanding of numbers.

The idea of data visualisation however is not new and statisticians have used graphs since the early stages of statistics as a science. Neither is the use of this visual representation to influence politicians or the public new. As Edward Tufte reminds us:

> The use of abstract, non-representational pictures to show numbers is a surprisingly recent invention, perhaps because of the diverse skills required—the visual-artistic, empirical-statistical, and mathematical. It was not until 1750–1800 that statistical graphics—length and area to show quantity, time-series, scatterplots, and multivariate displays—were invented, long after such triumphs of mathematical ingenuity as logarithms, Cartesian coordinates, the calculus, and the basics of probabilistic theory. The remarkable William Playfair (1759–1823) develop or improved upon nearly all the fundamental graphical designs, seeking to replace conventional tables of numbers with the systematic visual representation of his "linear arithmetic". (Tufte, 2001, p. 9)

Moreover, Florence Nightingale (1820–1910), years later, would develop a diagram of the causes of mortality in the British army in the East to convince both the Army and the Medical establishment of the need for more strict sanitation procedures. She was a pioneer in the visual presentation of information and statistical graphics and used methods such as the pie chart to illustrate her points and influence politicians. Her polar area diagram allowed her to illustrate seasonal sources of patient mortality in the military field hospital she managed during the Crimean War to Members of Parliament and civil servants who would have been unlikely to read or understand traditional statistical reports. Having said that, many of the capabilities to support computerised mapping and spatial statistical analyses emerged only during the 1990s (Anselin, Cohen, Cook, Gorr, & Tita, 2000, p. 43). It was in the twentieth century, in fact, that the full potential of data visualisation started to emerge.

Today, the visual representation of numbers is no longer only done to communicate their meaning. It is also increasingly utilised to analyse the data itself. For example, using spatial data to explore the relationship between crime and place is nowadays a key feature of investigative reporting in that beat. In a piece under the headline "Murder Rates Rose in a Quarter of the Nation's 100 Largest Cities"[1] in *The New York Times*, reporters Haeyoun Park and Josh Katz wrote that:

> Murder rates rose significantly in 25 of the nation's 100 largest cities last year, according to an analysis by The New York Times of new data compiled from individual police departments. The findings confirm a trend that was tracked recently in a study published by the National Institute of Justice. "The homicide increase in the nation's large cities was real and nearly unprecedented," wrote the study's author, Richard Rosenfeld, a criminology professor at the University of Missouri-St. Louis who explored homicide data in 56 large American cities.

The piece is accompanied by a set of graphs that allows readers to view exactly where these increases are taking place and easily make a comparison between states, cities and local communities.

In this sense, journalists are using data visualisation not only to report news but also to incentivise analysis and discussion among their audiences (Gray, Chambers, & Bounegru, 2012; Yau, 2013). Consequently, news media outlets are developing provisions such as interactive infographs that allow their users to examine and explore data in terms that are meaningful to them (Daniel & Flew, 2010, p. 186). Looking at, for example, crime across a particular city, people can make decisions about housing or write to their representatives or councillors to ask for something to be done in a particular area. Visualising data is in fact changing the relationship between the news media and its audiences, who are expected to engage more fully with the facilities now provided (Krum, 2013; Nguyen & Lugo-Ocando, 2015).

Interactive visualisation of crime statistics is in fact a trend that seems to have come to stay and software developers are constantly producing new tools to allow people to access and use numbers in ways that give them more information. These tools include a series of packages that allows us to cross-reference, for example, data with geography as in the

The New York Times case above. However it also allows us to highlights hierarchies and key aspects of the data that otherwise would be imperceptible to most readers. Having said that, there is very little evidence that the greater public is making full use of these tools or the data itself (Borges-Rey, 2016, 2017); or at least not to the degree and at the level that many had expected. Therefore, for a while, it seems that journalists reporting crime are still bound to use traditional methods of visualising data.

Key Graphics

Journalists reporting crime statistics often use charts (or graphs) to represent this data. In so doing, they use different types of graphics such as histograms, bar charts, pie charts or line charts. Each one of them conveys a particular meaning to the story. Is important to highlight that the primary function of graphic design in journalism is to communicate the core idea of the news (Evans, 1973) and this is the main criterion that prevails in the news media—or at least that should prevail—in relation to why news people choose a particular chart. Consequently, the selection of a particular graphic to communicate a story is undertaken not so much to facilitate the analysis but to convey a particular message. Hence, a pie chart would be better to use when reporting about budget cuts among different government bodies while a line chart would be better placed to highlight an increase or decrease of crime in general. Therefore, it is important to understand the communication function of each of these charts.

To start with, the bar chart is perhaps the most used in the reporting of crime statistics. This chart, with rectangular bars, can be presented vertically or horizontally, and is normally used to communicate a sense of distribution. So, journalists will use bar charts to explain, for example, how violent crime compares to non-violent crime. Bars charts are distinguished from histograms, in that they do not display continuous developments over an interval; they are only a snapshot of what is happening then and there. A bar chart tells the reader how many crimes of a particular nature occurred at a given time. The bar chart used by *The Chicago Tribune* in its editorial "What's behind Chicago's surge in violence?"

(2017) published on 17 January 2017 gives a perfect example of this as it shows the way these type of charts are normally used by journalists and news editors.

The other bar-type graph used by journalists, albeit not that often, is the histogram. This chart is used to represent distribution of the data. It consists of tabular frequencies, shown as adjacent rectangles, erected over discrete intervals with an area equal to the frequency of the observations in the interval. It is used to present continuous data, where the "bins" represent ranges of data, while a bar chart is a plot of categorical variables. It conveys the representation of the distribution of numerical data allowing us to estimate the probability distribution of a continuous variable. While a bar chart is a plot of categorical variables,[2] the histogram is used instead for continuous data, where the bins represent ranges of data. Therefore it allows us to explore the distributions of frequency (i.e. how many under-age persons were stabbed last year). A histogram in the news media would look like this (Fig. 8.1).

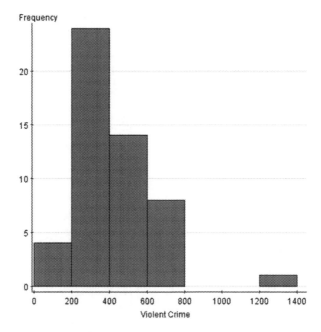

Fig. 8.1 A histogram in the news media. Source: Federal Bureau of Investigation

With no spaces between the bars the axis values convey information about the way the frequencies of an occurred event are distributed in relation to a particular crime. Journalists do not often make use of histograms to visualise data given that they are a poor way to display distributions because of the arbitrary definition of class intervals, which is invariably biased. It is also visually difficult to read and does not convey the clarity of meaning that a bar chart does. However, in the newsrooms histograms might be useful for journalists themselves to analyse the data that is being presented.

The other type of graph that tends to be very popular in the media is the line chart, which is a two-dimensional scatterplot of ordered observations where the observations are connected following their order. In the news media outputs, these lines provides temporality to the data and communicate how things are evolving. Journalists reporting crime use them to tell the story of peaks and troughs in crime. For example, in a report under the headline "Why are European kids are committing fewer crimes? They're too busy on their phones" by Rick Noack (2017) from *The Washington Post* a line chart is used to show the decrease in crime among young people. Indeed, in crime reporting, line charts are perhaps the most used as many stories involving crime statistics are about trends. Journalists use line charts because they also offer a political message; that is, if trends are up this means trouble for the incumbent authorities. If over the years, the overall trend in crime in most Organization for Economic Cooperation and Development (OECD) countries is down, then recent increases in countries such as the USA and some Western European countries have fuelled particular debates and generated anti-immigration rhetoric.

Finally, we have the pie chart, which is a graph that communicates proportions. In crime reporting, this means showing—for example—the percentage of crimes that were violent against those which were non-violent. The pie chart is circular and is divided into slices to illustrate numerical proportion. In a pie chart, the arc length of each slice is proportional to the quantity it represents. One example of this is the pie charts produced regularly by the press department of the US Federal Bureau of Investigation (FBI) and later reproduced and used across many media outlets in the USA (Fig. 8.2).

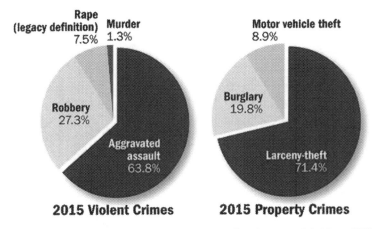

From *Crime in the United States, 2015*

Fig. 8.2   FBI pie chart. Source: Federal Bureau of Investigation

One problem with pie charts is that they cannot show more than a few values and this might be a limitation when reporting particular areas of crime that require a more nuanced understanding of the complexity of social deviation. Many specialists regard pie charts as a poor method of displaying information and do not tend to use them. As Walter Hickey (2013) points out:

> The pie chart is easily the worst way to convey information ever developed in the history of data visualization. Sure, there are other more cumbersome ways to articulate data. But none have the credibility nor the widespread use that the pie chart has (…). The one single thing pie charts are good at is when you're comparing 2–3 different data points with very different amounts of information.

Having said that, and despite a barrage of criticism, journalists and the news media in general continue to use pie charts widely when reporting crime because they appear easy to understand and are effective in putting things in perspective. They are also good at simplifying narratives about conflicting and competing issues.

Other Forms of Representation

Give the process of digitalisation, news media outlets are now more likely to experiment with a variety of forms when it comes to the presentation of crime statistics. In so doing, they make use of particular graphics that communicate ideas in a clear and understandable manner. Take the newspaper *The Guardian* in the UK which, by using proportion and colour, was able to provide a better and clearer idea of who the victims of rape are (Burn-Murdoch, 2013). This use of proportion to highlight quantities is becoming increasingly fashionable and useful among the news media.

The news media is also making increasing use of interactivity in the visualisation of crime statistics. This allows their audiences to tailor the data around what they need to know and explore it in relation to their own interests. People using these interactive features can look at crime data relating to their own local communities and analyse both trends and categories. It can also help organisations such as local governments, charities and non-governmental organisations (NGOs) to plan better the type of interventions that are needed. However, so far there is very little evidence that these features are being widely used by the communities or the audiences at large, except for a very few data enthusiasts (Borges-Rey, 2017; Chung & Yoo, 2008; Larsson, 2011; Williams, Wardle, & Wahl-Jorgensen, 2011). In fact, in some cases the news media outlets have made data available to audiences to use in ways that fulfil their particular needs and interests. In a series of interviews with news people, Borges-Rey has pointed out:

> In a very limited number of cases, informants provided audiences with easy access to raw data and filtering tools to make sense of this data, in an attempt to democratise both the databases that serve as inputs for stories and the news workflow that produces such stories. When asked about the subject, informants mentioned they have attempted crowdsourcing at least once, by identifying local communities of online users that actively aided them in disseminating, analysing or generating information. However, in most of the cases they seemed to fail to attract numbers significant enough to deem the practice successful. (Borges-Rey, 2017)

Indeed, the use of interactive facilities around data and statistics remain under-used by the audiences across all news beats. Crime statistics are no different and the question, therefore, remains as to why crime statistics need these types of provisions. One of the answers is that news audiences do not exist, they are created. Indeed, news audiences only exist in relation to particular uses and gratifications that they can extract from the stories and news provisions that the media can offer them. The uses and gratifications approach continues to be an important explanatory framework in understanding the theoretical link between audience motivations and news consumption (Lee, 2013, p. 313). At the moment, the uses and gratifications of interactive features are still limited, particularly in relation to crime.

However, this is not a static story and there are important developments in this field. One example is the "Murder Mysteries" project led by Tom Hargrove of the Scripps Howard News Service. Building from government data and public record requests his team produced a demographically-detailed database of more than 185,000 unsolved murders across the USA, and then designed an algorithm to search it for patterns suggesting the possible presence of serial killers.

Tom Hargrove, Lee Bowman, Isaac Wolf, Elizabeth Lucas and Jason Bartz used the statistical technique of cluster analysis and social science to develop a unique algorithm to expose patterns in suspected serial killings. They grouped homicides by metro area, method of killing, age group and gender. The software then analysed the 540,000 murders listed on the most recent supplementary homicide report (SHR) and narrowed them down to 160 clusters in which women of a similar demographic were killed by similar means. The team identified 10 cities in their algorithm and contacted those police forces, sometimes using Freedom of Information laws to gather details. Police in eight of those 10 cities acknowledged that the clusters found by Hargrove's team were either confirmed serial cases, or are likely to be such. The database was then placed online so that law enforcement personnel and ordinary people from communities across the USA could use it to make connections. Already, one armchair detective in upstate New York has used the data to find a cluster that police acknowledge is the work of a previously unacknowledged serial killer.[3] If this interactive feature is not yet used widely by the general public, it is nevertheless contributing greatly to the public's overall safety.

Moreover, in the UK a website which lets users in England and Wales see reported crimes in their streets and which covers public places received over 450 million hits in its first year alone (between 2011 and 2012). Using the information from those crime maps, "people can attend their local neighbourhood beat meeting and hold their local police to account for their performance" pointed out the then Home Secretary Theresa May. For her, the expectation was this map "will help drive up local policing standards and help drive down local crime". Indeed, the crime mapping site, which allows users to see the offences reported in their local streets by entering a street name or postcode, receives more hits than most other government sites. The website also maps crimes to other locations including airports, airfields, bus and coach stations, ferry terminals, motorway service stations, petrol stations and sports and recreation areas. Other sites include race tracks, adventure parks, parking areas, higher education buildings, shopping areas, supermarkets, theatres, conference centres, hospitals and prisons.[4]

Now, it would be naïve to take these interactive features at face value given that the data that underpins them is mostly derived from official sources and therefore suffers from many of the same problems that most crime statistics present. Just because data is displayed as an interactive feature or visually presented in a more accessible way does not make it better data. The fact of the matter remains, that visual and interactive presentation of data is only as good as the quality of the data in the first place. Many misplaced assumptions that are made by people looking at charts or toying with interactive features are a direct consequence of incomplete or flawed statistical data in the first place. In other words, despite all the technological facilities that visualisation offers nowadays, the ability of journalists to critically assess the data continues to be paramount.

Conclusion

There is no doubt that data visualisation can provide meaning to the numbers by establishing different interfaces with the general public. In so doing, it allows the reader to become aware of how information that has been abstracted in some schematic form can be displayed in a graphical manner so as to facilitate or direct interpretation. All in all, the visualisation of statistics is perhaps one of the most interesting and promising developments for journalism. Not only because it makes this data appealing and interesting for the general public but because also it facilitates the analysis and interpretation performed by journalists themselves.

Though, as we have seen in this chapter, there is a caveat to this. The visualisation of data is only as good as the basic data. Too often journalists working with data visualisation get absorbed by the aesthetics and neglect the substance. Visualisation of data will not in itself address the issues, but it is contributing to change and in some cases is improving the relationship between journalists, statistical data and the public. As Eddy Borges-Rey points out:

> Despite generalised claims in favour of journalistic authority over computing skills, data journalism has potentially disrupted an otherwise quite normative practice by gradually infusing the performativity and reflexivity of traditional journalists with traces of computational thinking. The clearest indication of this is the progressive replacement of linear storytelling by more interactive and engaging forms of informational user experience that offer multi-layered, multiplatform, gamified, database-linked dynamic content. This informational experience appears to be heavily mediated by the ontologies of user-interface design, user-experience design and human–computer interaction, which signals the pervasiveness of computational thinking in data journalists' reflexivity. (Borges-Rey, 2016, p. 841)

In the case of crime statistics, their power and influence derives from their reliability, validity and above all their relevance to the public. That relevance is not intrinsically given by the abstraction itself, one that summarises a given phenomenon in a simple number, but by the contextualisation and interpretation that journalists provide. Displaying this data either in charts or as an interactive feature does no good to public service unless there is a story behind the data that is both appealing and comprehensive. Journalism can benefit greatly from data visualisation but only if it develops a better and more critical understanding of how the numbers behind the graphics are gathered and what they really mean in the context of society.

Notes

1. Park, Haeyoun and Katz, Josh (09/09/2016). Murder Rates Rose in a Quarter of the Nation's 100 Largest Cities. *The New York Times.* https://www.nytimes.com/interactive/2016/09/08/us/us-murder-rates.html?hp&action=click&pgtype=Homepage&clickSource=story-heading&module=photo-spot-region&region=top-news&WT.nav=top-news&_r=1 [Accessed on 20 February 2017].
2. A categorical variable (sometimes called a nominal variable) is one that has two or more categories, but there is no intrinsic ordering to the categories. For example, gender is a categorical variable having two categories (male and female) and there is no intrinsic ordering to the categories.
3. Crawley, Michelle (2015). Thomas Hargrove's award-winning methods. *Scripps News Online.* http://escrippsnews.scrippsnet.com/node/2468 [Accessed on 3 March 2017].
4. BBC (2012). Crime map website to reveal hotspots. *BBC Online.* http://www.bbc.co.uk/news/uk-16804001 [Accessed on 4 February 2017].

References

Anselin, L., Cohen, J., Cook, D., Gorr, W., & Tita, G. (2000). Spatial analyses of crime. *Criminal Justice, 4*(2), 213–262.

Board, E. (2017). Editorial: What's behind Chicago's surge in violence? *The Chicago Tribune.* Retrieved March 26, 20017, from http://www.chicagotribune.com/news/opinion/editorials/ct-chicago-crime-increase-causes-edit-0118-md-20170117-story.html

Borges-Rey, E. (2016). Unravelling Data Journalism: A study of data journalism practice in British newsrooms. *Journalism Practice, 10*(7), 833–843.

Borges-Rey, E. (2017). Towards an epistemology of data journalism in the devolved nations of the United Kingdom: Changes and continuities in materiality, performativity and reflexivity. *Journalism.* doi:10.1177/1464884917693864.

Burn-Murdoch, J. (2013). 69,000 female, 9,000 male rape victims per year: Get the full data. Retrieved March 21, 2017, from https://www.theguardian.com/news/datablog/2013/jan/11/male-female-rape-statistics-graphic

Chung, D. S., & Yoo, C. Y. (2008). Audience motivations for using interactive features: Distinguishing use of different types of interactivity on an online newspaper. *Mass Communication and Society, 11*(4), 375–397.

Daniel, A., & Flew, T. (2010). *The Guardian reportage of the UK MP expenses scandal: A case study of computational journalism.* Paper presented at the Record of the Communications Policy and Research Forum 2010.

Evans, H. (1973). *Newspaper design.* London: Holt, Rinehart & Winston.

Gray, J., Chambers, L., & Bounegru, L. (2012). *The data journalism handbook: How journalists can use data to improve the news.* Newton, MA: O'Reilly Media, Inc.

Hickey, W. (2013). The worst chart in the world. Retrieved March 23, 2017, from http://www.businessinsider.com/pie-charts-are-the-worst-2013-6?IR=T

Keim, D. A. (2002). Information visualization and visual data mining. *IEEE Transactions on Visualization and Computer Graphics, 8*(1), 1–8.

Krum, R. (2013). *Cool infographics: Effective communication with data visualization and design.* Indianapolis, IN: John Wiley & Sons.

Larsson, A. O. (2011). Interactive to me—Interactive to you? A study of use and appreciation of interactivity on Swedish newspaper websites. *New Media & Society, 13*(7), 1180–1197.

Lee, A. M. (2013). News audiences revisited: Theorizing the link between audience motivations and news consumption. *Journal of Broadcasting & Electronic Media, 57*(3), 300–317.

Nguyen, A., & Lugo-Ocando, J. (2015). Introduction: The state of statistics in journalism and journalism education—Issues and debates. *Journalism, 17*(1), 3–17.

Noack, R. (2017). Why are European kids are committing fewer crimes? They're too busy on their phones. Retrieved February 23, 2017, from https://www.washingtonpost.com/news/worldviews/wp/2017/02/22/why-are-european-kids-are-committing-fewer-crimes-theyre-too-busy-on-their-phones/?utm_term=.f4ee7c070405

Tufte, E. (2001). *The visual display of quantitative information.* Chesire, CT: The Graphic Press.

Williams, A., Wardle, C., & Wahl-Jorgensen, K. (2011). "Have they got news for us?" Audience revolution or business as usual at the BBC? *Journalism Practice, 5*(1), 85–99.

Xu, J., & Chen, H. (2005). Criminal network analysis and visualization. *Communications of the ACM, 48*(6), 100–107.

Yau, N. (2011). *Visualize this. The flowing data guide to design, visualisation and statistics*. Indianapolis, IN: Wiley Piblishing, Inc.

Yau, N. (2013). *Data points: Visualization that means something*. Hoboken, NJ: John Wiley & Sons.

9

Crime Statistics and the Public

One of the key reasons as to why we need a better public understanding of crime statistics is because "the pervasiveness of statistics poses a problem, as statistics is a difficult discipline associated with misunderstandings, which ruin trust and lead to misgivings" (Von Roten, 2006, p. 243). Therefore, misunderstanding and misuse of crime statistics can lead to all sorts of political interpretations and public pressures that rather than contributing towards a constructive debate around crime prevention could instead hinder the formulation and implementation of sound crime and justice policy. In this sense, existing scholarly research regarding the public's knowledge and awareness regarding crime statistics suggests overall that the way these numbers are presented to the general public in the news media not only affects and shapes the ability of the average citizen to grasp what these numbers mean but also distorts altogether the environment in which public policy is discussed.

This chapter deals with how people read, understand and react to crime statistics in the news. It looks at issues such as "moral panics" in relation to the way crime statistics are reported by the news media. In this sense, vital work has been done by scholars and polling organisations that indicates an important gap between what the statistics say and what the

© The Author(s) 2017
J. Lugo-Ocando, *Crime Statistics in the News*,
DOI 10.1057/978-1-137-39841-3_9

media and the general public make of them (Best, 2004; Miller, 2004; Slovic, 1986; Von Roten, 2006). In bringing these contributions into the discussion, the chapter aims to provide a comprehensive picture of these issues. Overall, it also seeks to offer insight into the reasons for the gap and the issues of perceptions and pre-conceptions that also define the interpretation of statistics by the public. These issues are explored in the light of wider theories of public opinion such as the role of crime statistics in reinforcing the "spiral of silence"; theories that could help explain, in part, how and why people react to these statistics in the way they do.

The chapter then goes on to provide a political account of how statistics are interpreted by the public and how they help change and/or reinforce perceptions about issues and policies relating to law and order. It offers examples of news stories containing crime statistics that have been important in the shaping of the public's views regarding crime while looking at how they influence, over the time, crime policy. In looking at the way the public engages with crime statistics through news media reports, this chapter also explores how this reporting affects economic behaviour, such as tourism flows, particular industries, such as leisure, and security-related areas of the economy. The intention is to offer a comparative analysis of the gap between what people perceive to be the main issues according to their views derived from what statistics say within news reports and what they actually mean in terms of "hard evidence". All in all, the chapter will try to examine how the way crime statistics are reported by the news media influences how the general public sees crime.

The Importance of Numbers

Let us start by acknowledging that the reporting of crime statistics in the news media has two main purposes. First, it brings about accountability for government policy and hopefully triggers both the judicial system and police authorities to address crime in specific areas and around specific issues. Secondly, the reporting of these numbers informs the public about the societal risks posed by crime. In fact, one of the most important goals of any crime statistics system is to convey a sense of the risk that crime poses to residents and others, and do this in a way that can inform public, and perhaps private, efforts to control the risk of criminal victimisation (Lynch & Addington, 2006, p. 62). The news reporting of crime statistics, therefore, helps contextualise crime news in the wider framework of society's problems while offering a sense of collective needs and responses.

By providing statistics in the news, reporters allow their stories to transcend the anecdotal space and to be placed instead at the core of the political debate. It also permits the news media to go beyond the narrow use of statistics on crime and develop a news agenda that incorporates other, perhaps more important, issues such as white-collar crime. This because crime statistics, in these cases, have the power to make an issue relevant to the audiences that otherwise would be missed owing to the pressures placed upon journalists by the commercial needs of narration and storytelling.

This was certainly the case of the journalist Paige St. John of the *Sarasota Herald-Tribune* in the USA who in 2011 won the Pulitzer Prize thanks to her examination of weaknesses in the murky property-insurance system affecting Florida homeowners. Her data brought the issue to the attention of the authorities, regulators and, more importantly, to thousands of residents who would otherwise not have engaged with this type of crime story. Without the use of statistics, her work would have seemed irrelevant to most citizens who might have perceived it as a minor crime compared to, for example, the murder rates in their communities. However, as her work showed, this was a generalised type of fraud that not only had become endemic in those communities but that were in fact putting in danger the livelihood of the entire community. This particular example shows the real power and potential of crime statistics in the news; that is to subvert and reshape the news agenda.

Crime statistics are also used to underpin attitudes and political agendas that favour certain sectors. In this sense, crime statistics have been used to promote scaremongering and moral panics among the public. For example, in a 2012 story about how increasing numbers of immigrants in London are pushing a "wave" of crime, the London-based newspaper, *The Daily Mail* issued an "Immigrant crimewave" warning on its front pages which claimed that foreign nationals "were accused of a quarter of all crimes in London". According to statistics cited by this newspaper:

> Foreigners are accused of more than one in four crimes committed in London, an investigation reveals. Astonishingly, they make up nine out of ten drug suspects and are responsible for more than one in three sex offences. Nationals of Poland, Romania and Lithuania are most likely of all foreigners to be prosecuted by the police. The figures will give force to warnings of a growing 'immigrant crime wave'. Four years ago, foreign nationals were found to commit one in five crimes. (Doyle & Wright, 2012)

These numbers were of course presented without context regarding the way in which they are recorded or their meaning in the wider framework of national statistics on crime. The numbers reported also had serious issues around validity, as they did not really underpin what the newspaper claimed they were suggesting. Sufficient to say that most crimes in the UK are committed by British nationals and that foreigners who offend are in fact a tiny minority of the crime and deviation spectrum. (In the past five years the percentage of crimes committed by foreign national is less than the 5% of the overall numbers of crimes in England and Wales.) However, after years of several media outlets using statistics to frame crime with this particular angle, it is not surprising to see a strong correlation between this type of news coverage and adverse public perceptions of foreign nationals (Jewkes, 2015; McCombs, 2013).

Most evidence from surveys indicate that there are very high levels of opposition to immigration in many Western countries (Hainmueller & Hopkins, 2014; Schlueter, Meuleman, & Davidov, 2013; Valentino, Brader, & Jardina, 2013). They suggest that a great majority of respondents think that there are "too many migrants", that "fewer migrants should be let into the country", and that legal restrictions on immigration should be tighter. For example, the 2013 British Social Attitudes survey, one of the most important independent surveys carried out in the UK, highlights how nowadays the majority of Britons endorse reducing immigration. Indeed, over 56% chose "reduced a lot", while 77% chose either "reduced a lot" or "reduced a little". The same question yielded similar results in the British Social Attitudes survey in 2008, adding confidence that these are reliable estimates. One of the key elements in explaining these views, according to the researchers, is "fear of crime" (Chandler & Tsai, 2001; Hagan, Levi, & Dinovitzer, 2008; Sklansky, 2012).

Fear of crime is in fact crucial in shaping both attitudes and discourses around immigration. For example, panel survey data from Germany about immigration has shown that, over time, consternation about crime is a significant predictor of anxiety about immigration and that it has a greater substantive impact than any other explanatory factor, such as concerns about the economy. This research also highlighted an interactive effect: the connection between these two issues is especially strong among those interested in politics (Fitzgerald, Curtis, & Corliss, 2012, p. 477). In this context, notions such as that of "social cohesion" (Joseph Chan, To, & Chan, 2006; Cheong, Edwards, Goulbourne, & Solomos, 2007) have become paramount in the narratives of those in power or aspiring to it as "the lack of it" allows politicians and the media at large to single out crime as a consequence of immigration rather than as the result of a series of structural causes such a poverty and inequality.

This is because the relationship between attitudes towards immigration and crime are deeply shaped by the process of "othering". In this sense, othering refers to the process in which people or groups of people are made to seem mildly or radically different. The representation of "otherness" is based on a duality described by Karl Marx as *Vertretung* and *Darstellung*. From a political-economic point of view, *Vertretung* refers to someone representing others, embodying them and speaking for them. *Darstellung*, on the other hand, refers to the act of representing the others by shaping the image of who they are or how they are (Spivak, 1988, p. 275). The news media plays a central role in making and reinforcing those distinctions between "them" and "us", while negatively framing immigration as a whole in the context of debates around crime (Bailey & Harindranath, 2005; Breen, Devereux, & Haynes, 2006). This is explained by the political role that the othering of immigration and its subsequent link with crime has had in mobilising public opinion and creating fear in recent history (Fetzer, 2000; Simon & Sikich, 2007).

The impact of this gap between media representation and hard facts in relation to crime statistics has become crucial in politics in many countries. Events such as the massive losses in the local elections by the ruling CDU party in Germany (Kirschbaum & Shalal, 2016), the vote to leave the European Union by the British public, known as Brexit (Bennett, 2016) and the rise of Donald Trump as a presidential candidate in the USA elections in 2016 were unequivocally linked to the theme of immigration (Clement & Tankersley, 2016), where crime statistics played a crucial role in shaping and legitimising populist discourses around immigration (Agerholm, 2016; Asthana, 2016). So the question remains: why have statistics as a scientific tool become misappropriated by these political sectors in the way they have, and how and why have these populist groups been able to subvert their meaning? To start with, let us examine the ability of the general public to understand and manage these numbers and how they help to construct public imagination.

One of the possible factors to consider is the level of understanding that both the public and the media have of crime statistics. Particularly, the gap between what the statistics state and the public's perceptions. For example, while German statistics of police-recorded crime show a decline in total offences over the 10 years up to 2003, survey-based evidence shows that the German public assumes, on balance, that crime has increased. Moreover, according to studies, the proportion of people in that country who are in favour of tougher sentencing has increased and they would prefer stiffer penalties. This data shows that the pattern of television viewing is associated with the belief that crime is rising (Pfeiffer, Windzio, & Kleimann, 2005, p. 259). There is further evidence to suggest that these perceptions in relation to crime "waves" have further deepened in the case of Germany since it has taken over one million refugees from Syria.

Understanding Numbers

Germany is not alone in this and it is no secret that in most countries there is a general lack of understanding of crime statistics among the general public. Indeed, one of the few longitudinal research studies on public perceptions around the reporting of crime numbers suggested that public fear—because of these numbers—was more a product of the way the media presented these numbers than a reflection of the real world of crime that these numbers conveyed. According to the authors of this study, news variables alone accounted for almost four times more variance in the public perception of crime as the "most important problem" of society than the actual crime rates did. The way these numbers were presented, rather than the numbers themselves, could easily explain the sharp jump from 5% to an unprecedented 52% in crime fear among the general public in a very short time span (Lowry, Nio, & Leitner, 2003, p. 61).

One of the key characteristics of the relationship between media, crime statistics and public opinion is that "style" is more important than substance. In other words, it is all about how statistics are presented to the public. This explains why, for example, readers of popular newspapers (tabloids) have the highest levels of fear of crime. Indeed, a report from the UK's Home Office pointed out that attitudes to crime are hugely influenced by newspaper reports, with tabloid readers almost twice as likely to be worried about crime as those who favour broadsheets, according to government figures. This survey of 40,000 adults in the UK showed that:

> The tabloids' penchant for human interest stories involving violence and law-breaking have had a marked effect as 43% of tabloid readers believe crime has increased "a lot" compared with just 26% of broadsheet readers. Tabloid readers were more than twice as likely to fear being mugged, with 16% admitting they were "very worried" about a possible assault compared with just 7% of broadsheet readers. When it came to the threat of physical attacks, the difference was even more marked with 17% of tabloid readers claiming to be "very worried" compared with just 6% of broadsheet readers. (Cozens, 2003)

These problems with presentation and style are worsened by the general lack of understanding and poor numeracy skills of the general public. Indeed, other studies have looked at how the media disseminates crime statistics and have suggested that interest in, take-up, and retention of factual information on crime and criminal justice is not as high as previous empirical research had suggested (Feilzer, 2007, p. 302). Therefore, the ability to process and understand these numbers is limited and in most cases insufficient to allow the public to fully engage with the discussions and policies surrounding crime. According to Mark Liberman, when referring to the ability of the public to deal with statistics:

> Even today, only a minuscule proportion of the U.S. population understands even the simplest form of these concepts and terms. Out of the roughly 300 million Americans, I doubt that as many as 500 thousand grasp these ideas to any practical extent, and 50,000 might be a better estimate. The rest of the population is surprisingly uninterested in learning, and even actively resists the intermittent attempts to teach them, despite the fact that in their frequent dealings with social and biomedical scientists they have a practical need to evaluate and compare the numerical properties of representative samples. (Liberman, 2007)

In most countries, the great number of people would be unable to comprehend crime statistics without the context and explanation offered by journalists when using or referring to them in their news reports. Consequently, the issues of how these statistics are framed and to what degree they are trusted are crucial in the circulation of knowledge that comes about from the dissemination of these numbers.

Indeed, trust is a pivotal aspect in the dissemination and understanding of crime statistics, although it is a complicated one. Recent studies show that most people tend to trust the source of the statistics more than the actual statistics. In a survey carried out by Ipsos-MORI (2013) in the UK, members of the public were asked "[Do] politicians use official statistics accurately when talking about their policies?" Over 69% answered no to this question. However, when the same statistics were presented by more reputable sources, such as scientists, the levels of trust dramatically increased. Hence, in the perception of crime statistics the issue is not so much about what the statistics say, but who presents them.

Having said that, let us not forget that crime statistics are, one way or another, reported by the public and that the police only record them

(Bottomley & Coleman, 1981, p. 8). Therefore, crime statistics represent what people report as being committed crimes (in the case of the statistics recorded by the police) or feel about crime (in the case of the crime surveys). In both cases, they tell the story of what is happening in terms of crime; a story that is in many ways reported directly by people themselves. The fact that there are issues of trust around crime statistics has little to do with the source itself and everything to do with how numbers are recorded, processed and presented to the public.

The first two of these key problems, recording and processing, have been widely debated across different countries at various times. For example, some scholars have raised questions about the reliability of current data for estimation and forecasting purposes (particularly in relation to estimating economic models of crime). They have highlighted the disparity between crime rates suggested by victimisation surveys and the rates suggested by Official Statistics (in the case of the UK), and concluded that this is primarily a consequence of under-reporting by victims and under-recording by the police (MacDonald, 2002, p. 85). In addition to this, over the years there has been a series of reports and recommendations made in order to improve the recording and processing of crime statistics in different countries (Biderman & Lynch, 2012; Lynch & Addington, 2006; Matheson, 2011). More recently, for example, Bernard Jenkin MP, Chair of the Public Administration Select Committee said that:

> Poor data integrity reflects the poor quality of leadership within the police. Their compliance with the core values of policing, including accountability, honesty and integrity, will determine whether the proper quality of Police Recorded Crime data can be restored. (2014)

Indeed, the Public Administration Select Committee (PASC) in its 2014 report following the inquiry into the quality of crime statistics pointed out unequivocally that "there is strong evidence that the police under-record crime, particularly sexual crimes such as rape in many police areas" and that this was due to "lax compliance with the agreed national standard of victim-focused crime recording". As a result of

PASC's inquiry, the report adds, the UK Statistics Authority has already stripped police recorded crime data of the quality kite mark, "National Statistics".

Where there has been far less work carried out is in relation to the dissemination and presentation of crime statistics by the news media to the general public, and in particular in relation to how news audiences react and interact with this data. In this sense, the UK Government Statistical Service, a network of professional statisticians and their staff, operating both within the Office for National Statistics and across more than 30 other government departments and agencies to ensure transparency and quality of official statistics, recommended in a 2011 report that:

> The body responsible for the publication of crime statistics should seek to improve the presentation of the statistics to give users and the public a clearer understanding of the overall picture of crime, by providing the major and other sources of crime statistics together with additional contextual information. (Matheson, 2011, p. 4)

Also in the UK, the Royal Statistical Society has worked intensively with a variety of institutions and professional bodies, including universities and the Home Office, to improve the ability of journalists and public relations (PR) practitioners to ensure that the statistics not only have the necessary quality but are also sufficiently contextualised and accessible for the average citizen. At the time of writing this book, this was in fact an ongoing process and further research is needed to understand better what ought to be done and the impact of these efforts in improving the public's understanding of crime statistics.

However, one thing is clear: the worst thing that can happen in any society is that no one does anything about public awareness and understanding of and engagement with crime statistics. This is because, as we have discussed here, statistics have the power to shape public views while legitimising particular discourses. In this sense, it is worth noting that crime statistics are closely linked to "fear of crime" and play a very important role in the creation of "moral panics" a phenomenon often linked to crime reporting (Cohen, 2002; Hier, 2011; Thompson, 2013). In this sense:

> Moral panic is such a well-established term, both in academic and everyday vocabulary that it is surprising to recall that it has only become widely used since the work of Stan Cohen in the early 1970s on youth subcultures. Since then the term has been regularly used in the media to refer to all sorts of anti-social and/or criminal behaviours. Essentially, a moral panic refers to an exaggerated reaction, from the media, the police or wider public, to the activities of particular social groups. These activities may well be relatively trivial but have been reported in a somewhat sensationalised form in the media; and such reporting and publicity has then led to an increase in general anxiety and concern about those activities. So a moral panic is an exaggerated response to a type of behaviour that is seen as a social problem—the term indicates an over-reaction on the part of the media and/or other social institutions. Furthermore, this over-reaction magnifies the original area of concern. (Marsh & Melville, 2011, p. 1)

Generally speaking, the term is traditionally understood as process of arousing social concern over an issue, especially in the light of news media framing of the issue. It is nevertheless a wider phenomenon historically connected to "fear" of particular groups of people or ideas (Bourke, 2005; Robin, 2004) and which is closely linked to the emergence of both modernity (Plamper & Lazier, 2010, p. 58) and the society of risk (Beck, 2010 [1998]; Bernstein, 1996; Luhmann, 1993). As Murray Lee, a Professor of Criminology at the University of Sydney, explained:

> There is little doubt that the genealogy of fear of crime as a concept is intimately entwined with the development and deployment of crime statistics more generally—statistics we might say are a broad but vital continuity of its emergence. The enumeration of offence rates, of crime itself, has a complex genealogy upon which I can only touch, but without this development it would be unthinkable that fear of crime would be enumerated as it was to be in the 1960s, and without enumeration fear of crime, the concept, would be rendered unthinkable. (Lee, 2013)

This very close historical and sociological link between crime statistics and public fear of crime is quintessential in understanding why crime statistics are such a powerful discursive tool; one that is capable of activating and directing political mobilisation. Having said that, it is important to reiterate that not enough research has been carried out in this area of news audiences and statistics, let alone in relation to audiences and crime statistics, and more work is needed in order to advance our understanding of this phenomenon (Chiricos, Eschholz, & Gertz, 1997; Jensen, 1987). This is not only for the sake of bridging the knowledge gap but also for very practical reasons.

Certainly, there is an increasing number of opportunities to hold governments and public bodies to account using evidentiary data, by allowing the public to engage more actively in data-driven and data-informed policy design, formulation, implementation and assessment. With so much data out there nowadays, and the technological possibilities to make it accessible to all, there is the possibility of narrowing the gap as never before. This means offering ways of combining and interrogating policy, and executing policy at many different levels, while being able to ask from a global and local perspective new and more pertinent questions about crime, policing and justice. The data revolution and, in particular, the accessibility that technology now offers is creating opportunities for informed citizens to make real contributions in the same way that amateur astronomers had done for years in science. However, to fulfil this potential, we need to understand that what we also need from the public is "critical engagement" rather than simply "awareness and understanding". Member of the public needs to be able to operationalise crime statistics in ways that allow them to discern and evaluate the authorities, interact with their representatives and engage in meaningful and constructive discussion. Thus leaving behind the irrational—although sometimes grounded—fears that crime statistics have historically created. This also means accepting the fact that statistics largely consists of methodologies for exploring questions that are not themselves really part of statistics, and so it is even more important to persuade people that engaging with statistics in a critical manner is becoming a pre-requisite for democratic engagement and debate. Only then can we can start moving towards a sounder and subtler discussion around deviance and public policy. However, this is a task that cannot be left to journalists alone.

References

Agerholm, H. (2016). Brexit: Wave of hate crime and racial abuse reported following EU referendum. Retrieved September 10, 2016, from http://www.independent.co.uk/news/uk/home-news/brexit-eu-referendum-racial-racism-abuse-hate-crime-reported-latest-leave-immigration-a7104191.html

Asthana, A. (2016). Vote Leave releases list of serious crimes by EU citizens in Britain. Retrieved September 2, 2016, from https://www.theguardian.com/politics/2016/mar/28/vote-leave-releases-list-of-serious-crimes-by-eu-citizens-in-britain

Bailey, O. G., & Harindranath, R. (2005). Racialized 'othering'. In S. Allan (Ed.), *Journalism: Critical issues* (pp. 274–286). Meidenhead: Open University Press and McGraw-Hill Education.

Beck, U. (2010 [1998]). *La Sociedad del Riesgo. Hacia una nueva modernidad.* Madrid: Paidos Surcos.

Bennett, A. (2016). Did Britain really vote Brexit to cut immigration? Retrieved October 10, 2016, from http://www.telegraph.co.uk/news/2016/06/29/did-britain-really-vote-brexit-to-cut-immigration/

Bernstein, P. L. (1996). *Against the Gods. The remarkable history of risk.* New York: John Wiley and Sons, Inc.

Best, J. (2004). *More damned lies and statistics: How numbers confuse public issues.* Berkeley: University of California Press.

Biderman, A. D., & Lynch, J. P. (2012). *Understanding crime incidence statistics: Why the UCR diverges from the NCS.* Berlin: Springer Science & Business Media.

Bottomley, A. K., & Coleman, C. (1981). *Understanding crime rates: Police and public roles in the production of official statistics.* Farnborough, Hampshire: Gower.

Bourke, J. (2005). *Fear: A cultural history.* Berkeley, CA: Counterpoint Press.

Breen, M. J., Devereux, E., & Haynes, A. (2006). Fear, framing and foreigners: The othering of immigrants in the Irish print media. *International Journal of Critical Psychology, 16,* 100–121.

Chan, J., To, H.-P., & Chan, E. (2006). Reconsidering social cohesion: Developing a definition and analytical framework for empirical research. *Social Indicators Research, 75*(2), 273–302.

Chandler, C. R., & Tsai, Y.-M. (2001). Social factors influencing immigration attitudes: An analysis of data from the General Social Survey. *The Social Science Journal, 38*(2), 177–188.

Cheong, P. H., Edwards, R., Goulbourne, H., & Solomos, J. (2007). Immigration, social cohesion and social capital: A critical review. *Critical social policy, 27*(1), 24–49.

Chiricos, T., Eschholz, S., & Gertz, M. (1997). Crime, news and fear of crime: Toward an identification of audience effects. *Social Problems, 44*(3), 342–357.

Clement, S., & Tankersley, J. (2016). Even if Trump loses, this poll shows why hard-line immigration positions are here to stay. Retrieved October 10, 2016, from https://www.washingtonpost.com/news/wonk/wp/2016/10/06/even-if-trump-loses-this-poll-shows-why-hard-line-immigration-positions-are-here-to-stay/

Cohen, S. (1972 [2002]). *Folk devils and moral panics: The creation of the mods and rockers.* New York: Psychology Press.

Cozens, C. (2003). Tabloids 'stoke fear of crime'. Retrieved March 11, 2016, from https://www.theguardian.com/media/2003/jul/17/pressandpublishing.politics

Doyle, J., & Wright, S. (2012). 'Immigrant crimewave' warning: Foreign nationals were accused of a QUARTER of all crimes in London. Retrieved August 1, 2016, from http://www.dailymail.co.uk/news/article-2102895/Immigrant-crimewave-warning-Foreign-nationals-accused-QUARTER-crimes-London.html

Feilzer, M. (2007). Criminologists making news? Providing factual information on crime and criminal justice through a weekly newspaper column. *Crime, Media, Culture, 3*(3), 285–304.

Fetzer, J. S. (2000). *Public attitudes toward immigration in the United States, France, and Germany.* Cambridge: Cambridge University Press.

Fitzgerald, J., Curtis, K. A., & Corliss, C. L. (2012). Anxious publics worries about crime and immigration. *Comparative Political Studies, 45*(4), 477–506.

Hagan, J., Levi, R., & Dinovitzer, R. (2008). The symbolic violence of the crime-immigration nexus: Migrant mythologies in the americas. *Criminology & Public Policy, 7*(1), 95–112.

Hainmueller, J., & Hopkins, D. J. (2014). Public attitudes toward immigration. *Annual Review of Political Science, 17*, 225–249. doi:10.1146/annurev-polisci-102512-194818.

Hier, S. P. (2011). *Moral panic and the politics of anxiety.* Abingdon, OX: Routledge.

Ipsos MORI. (2013). Ipsos MORI public understanding of statistics. Retrieved February 2, 2016, from https://www.ipsos-mori.com/Assets/Docs/Polls/rss-kings-ipsos-mori-trust-in-statistics-topline.pdf

Jenkin, B. (2014). Why we can't rely on police recorded crime statistics. Retrieved March 2, 2017, from http://www.parliament.uk/business/committees/com-

mittees-a-z/commons-select/public-administration-select-committee/news/
crime-stats-substantive/

Jensen, K. B. (1987). News as ideology: Economic statistics and political ritual in television network news. *Journal of Communication, 37*(1), 8–27.

Jewkes, Y. (2015). *Media and crime.* London: Sage.

Kirschbaum, E., & Shalal, A. (2016). German anti-immigrant party beats Merkel in her home district. Retrieved September 4, 2016, from http://www. reuters.com/article/us-germany-election-idUSKCN1190XG

Lee, M. (2013). *Inventing fear of crime.* London: Routledge.

Liberman, M. (2007). The pirahã and us. Retrieved April 21, 2016, from http:// itre.cis.upenn.edu/~myl/languagelog/archives/004992.html

Lowry, D. T., Nio, T. C. J., & Leitner, D. W. (2003). Setting the public fear agenda: A longitudinal analysis of network TV crime reporting, public perceptions of crime, and FBI crime statistics. *Journal of Communication, 53*(1), 61–73.

Luhmann, N. (1993). *Communication and social order: Risk: A sociological theory.* Piscataway, NJ: Transaction Publishers.

Lynch, J. P., & Addington, L. A. (2006). *Understanding crime statistics: Revisiting the divergence of the NCVS and the UCR.* Cambridge: Cambridge University Press.

MacDonald, Z. (2002). Official crime statistics: Their use and interpretation. *The Economic Journal, 112*(477), 85–106.

Marsh, I., & Melville, G. (2011). Moral panics and the British media—A look at some contemporary 'folk devils'. *Internet Journal of Criminology, 1*(1), 1–21.

Matheson, J. (2011). *National statistician's review of crime statistics: England and Wales.* London: Government Statistical Service.

McCombs, M. (2013). *Setting the agenda: The mass media and public opinion.* Oxford: John Wiley & Sons.

Miller, J. D. (2004). Public understanding of, and attitudes toward, scientific research: What we know and what we need to know. *Public Understanding of Science, 13*(3), 273–294.

Pfeiffer, C., Windzio, M., & Kleimann, M. (2005). Media use and its impacts on crime perception, sentencing attitudes and crime policy. *European Journal of Criminology, 2*(3), 259–285.

Plamper, J., & Lazier, B. (2010). Introduction: The phobic regimes of modernity. *Representations, 110*(1), 58–65. doi:10.1525/rep.2010.110.1.58.

Robin, C. (2004). *Fear: The history of a political idea.* Oxford: Oxford University Press.

Schlueter, E., Meuleman, B., & Davidov, E. (2013). Immigrant integration policies and perceived group threat: A multilevel study of 27 Western and Eastern European countries. *Social Science Research, 42*(3), 670–682.

Simon, R. J., & Sikich, K. W. (2007). Public attitudes toward immigrants and immigration policies across seven nations. *International Migration Review, 41*(4), 956–962.

Sklansky, D. A. (2012). Crime, immigration, and ad hoc instrumentalism. *New Criminal Law Review: In International and Interdisciplinary Journal, 15*(2), 157–223.

Slovic, P. (1986). Informing and educating the public about risk. *Risk analysis, 6*(4), 403–415.

Spivak, G. (1988). Can the subaltern speak? In C. Nelson & L. Grossberg (Eds.), *Marxism and the Interpretation of Culture* (pp. 271–313). Urbana; Chicago: University of Illinois Press.

Thompson, K. (2013). *Moral panics.* London: Routledge.

Valentino, N. A., Brader, T., & Jardina, A. E. (2013). Immigration opposition among US Whites: General ethnocentrism or media priming of attitudes about Latinos? *Political Psychology, 34*(2), 149–166.

Von Roten, F. C. (2006). Do we need a public understanding of statistics? *Public Understanding of Science, 15*(2), 243–249.

10

Conclusion

On 7 February 2017, US President, Donald Trump, claimed during a meeting with sheriffs at the White House that the US murder rate in that country "is the highest it's been in 47 years":

> I'd say that in a speech and everybody was surprised because the press doesn't like to tell it like it is. It wasn't to their advantage to say that. The murder rate is the highest it's been in I guess 45–47 years. (Diamond, 2017)

However, as pointed out by a CNN report later that day, the reality is that the US murder rate in 2015, the latest full year available, was lower than it was 45 years before. CNN reporters then went on to clarify that if the US had experienced its highest one-year increase in the murder rate in half a century, between 2014 and 2015, then the murder rate in 2015 was just 4.9 per 100,000 people. Moreover, that figure is dwarfed by crime figures in the 1990s when the murder rate hovered between eight and 10 murders per 100,000 people. In this particular case, the news media acted appropriately by calling out what by all means was a misuse of crime statistics and unmasking an attempt by the US President himself to disseminate "fake news". The tragedy, however, for the US public,

© The Author(s) 2017
J. Lugo-Ocando, *Crime Statistics in the News*,
DOI 10.1057/978-1-137-39841-3_10

regardless of one's political preferences, is that it did not do so as vehemently during the presidential elections when Trump, then as a candidate, repeated this same pack of lies over and over again.

In a news age that seems dominated by "fake news" and the strange appeal of conspiracy theories, serious, well-informed and sound journalism is needed more than ever (Allcott & Gentzkow, 2017; Kucharski, 2016). In this context, statistics is a central aid for journalists to fulfil their watchdog role, bringing about accountability and rigour to the political debates and public agenda around crime and law and order. However, this—as we have seen in this book—has not always been the case and too often crime statistics are used uncritically to underpin the prevalent discourses of those in power or, even worst, they are misused to manipulate and "manufacture consent" (Herman & Chomsky, 2010 [1994]) around agendas that could not be further away from the public's interests.

It is also clear that contrary to common assumptions, the misuse of crime statistics cannot be only attributed simply to "journalistic innumeracy" (Maier, 2003). Instead, there are in fact structural issues that shape the news cultures within which crime statistics are gathered and then incorporated into the news. On top of this, there are important political interests that are all too often prone to use crime statistics to obscure rather than to elucidate reality and political debate. Police constables and law enforcement agencies from around the world, for example, are incentivised to manipulate these numbers to retain power and access to resources. The police know that, as do the politicians, but they are nevertheless submerged into a web of deception that allows many of them to retain certain power privileges in a society that is increasingly hooked on moral panics to explain itself.

However, above all these problems, it is perhaps the way journalists conceive crime statistics that is paramount and needs most urgently to be addressed. Overall, the news media likes to incorporate statistics in news stories because numbers seem to be hard facts. Little nuggets of indisputable truth (Maier, 2003) that somehow are seen both as "hard facts" and "sources" of information (Nguyen & Lugo-Ocando, 2015). As we have seen here, this conceptualisation of what crime statistics are has become extremely pernicious to the way journalists deal with these numbers.

Mainly because it fosters a framework in the newsroom that is uncritical while promoting a narrow understanding of these numbers. Crime statistics, in this context, then become an element to underpin and reinforce pre-existing views rather than a tool to explore and deconstruct the world outside. In this sense, journalists are no different from the rest of people who tend to use statistics to support their own point of view and to bring others around to their way of thinking through a "rhetorical" use of the data.

We must note, however, that this uncritical approach towards statistics seems to occur far more with crime than with other news beats. Indeed, one of the most interesting aspects to observe in the overall discussion centres around comparing the way journalists treat statistics and use it in other news beats—such as science—against the way they cover crime statistics. In the science news beat, for example, journalists are more prone to challenge statistics even when they show that a particular issue, such as climate change, is overwhelmingly single sided within the science community. This is because, as Dunwoody (2014, p. 33) points out, journalistic norms of objectivity and balance arise as surrogates of "validity" to compensate for the inability of journalists to confirm what the source presents as truth. So this scepticism and criticality does happen more or less in many other areas, although not always as much as it should. However, this is not the case with crime statistics, where journalists tend to assume these numbers are hard facts and use them to underpin pre-conceived explanatory narratives. In other words, if the reporting of statistics in general is overall uncritical, it is even more so in the case of crime statistics.

Hence the need to explore the ethics involved in the communication of crime statistics by policy makers, criminologist, statisticians and journalists. Foremost, it is important to understand the deontological ethics—or deontology—that relates to the use of crime statistics by news reporters. As we can assume, this is characterised by a normative ethical position that judges the morality of an action based on rules. For journalists, the deontology is one based on the duty to present the "facts" as they are regardless or in spite of the consequences. They see these statistics as facts that need to be presented as they are regardless of anything else.

Consequently, and this is one of the key problems, journalists adopt a Kantian view that crime statistics are a factual object that is intrinsically good, without qualification. These numbers, in their deontological practice, are tools to elucidate reality and it is assumed that as neutral/objective things they could never make a situation ethically worse. Hence, journalists covering statistics see these numbers as an expression of reality and they feel compelled to take them and present them at face value. Particularly given the sensationalist past of crime reporting that made the personalisation of crime a detestable practice as the suffering of the victims and the gruesomeness of violence was openly exploited to boost sales and ratings.

As we discussed in our own historical interpretation of the evolution of crime statistics reporting, these numbers came to de-sensationalise crime reporting, allowing journalists to re-configure crime news in more policy-based terms. This was in fact a great improvement that saw crime reporting undergo an important ethical shift from the bloody back pages littered with corpses to a more nuanced approach that prefers context when reporting crime. In ethical terms, the incorporation of statistics into news reporting brought about important changes, drawing a line between crime reporting being sensational and being sound policy. Crime reporting, thanks to statistics, became far more committed to seeing the whole picture.

Yet, these numbers were never entirely free from the dichotomy between informing and entertainment that we pointed out in an earlier chapter. Hence, they also became a tool to advance moral panics by helping articulate narratives of fear. They help to create distorted social realities that somehow appear to be far more legitimate while feeding prejudices, xenophobia and racism to say the least.

One emblematic example of this was an article on the front page of the London-based tabloid, *The Sun*, in which it was claimed that one in five British Muslims supported people who have gone to Syria to fight for jihadi groups such as Islamic State. This, as it was later acknowledged, was significantly misleading. In fact, the Independent Press Standards Organisation (Ipso)—the main self-regulatory body of the printed news media in the UK—determined that a front page article from 23 November 2015—as well as more coverage inside the paper—misrepresented the results of the poll on which the article was based because the relevant question in the poll did not support the claim. Ipso pointed out in its ruling that:

> While the newspaper was entitled to interpret the poll's findings, taken in its entirety, the coverage presented as a fact that the poll showed that one in five British Muslims had sympathy for those who left to join Isis and for Isis itself," Ipso said. In fact, neither the question, nor the answers which referred to 'sympathy', made reference to [Isis]. The newspaper had failed to take appropriate care in its presentation of the poll results and, as a result, the coverage was significantly misleading.[1]

The key issue here is that by making these types of number misrepresentations the newspaper criminalises de facto whole sections of society, presenting Muslims as keen on terrorists and therefore reinforcing negative stereotypes. This is a case in which the normative deontology does not work because of the fact that by the action itself things are made ethically worse.

All in all, crime statistics are now an intrinsic feature of modern journalism and therefore we need to understand how the politics of statistics shapes news reporting. In so doing, we need to critically examine the relationship between those who produce these numbers, those who disseminate them and how audiences make sense of them. It is not only that those involved can ethically make things worse but that they are, in fact, reshaping the way we understand crime and the manner in which crime is created. Needless to point out the profound distortions that the political communication of crime statistics is creating among law enforcement agencies and police officers in the USA and the UK, for example, who deliberately target poor areas with random stop and search trawls for drugs so they can meet their statistical targets. These areas offer less resistance to police questionable interventions as they have less access to legal advice and are more prone to accept guilt in court, therefore helping the police to boost their targets (O'Neil, 2016). The bottom line is that crime statistics are abused by many parties including government officials, special interest groups and journalists in order to advance their own agendas. Over time, data has proven to be as susceptible to sensationalism and manipulation as any other element of the crime beat. The problem now is that data is everywhere.

"Datafication" of Life

In today's society, we face the challenge of public life being "datafied"; our lives are being increasingly quantified by data (Ruckenstein & Pantzar, 2015; Yang, 2016). It is a phenomenon that has seen the emergence of so-called "big data" thanks to the increasing use of technology to monitor and provide a degree of predictability about people's behaviour. This is fundamentally—although not exclusively—based upon gathering data on people's use of Information and Communication Technologies (ICTs) when shopping, speaking to others or accessing the Internet. This data is then processed and analysed using specific algorithms, which permits both analysis and prediction of behaviour patterns as well as data mining from different databases. Data mining means, in this case, the technological capacity of these algorithms to search and detect data that can then be brought together and correlated with other sets of data.

Indeed, many aspects of our lives are nowadays being turned into computerised data that is then exchanged and used as a commodity in the market place. In the case of crime data, as Cathy O'Neil (2016) has already warned us, one of the key problems is how big data follows very flawed models to wrongly assign criminal records to innocent people and negatively affects the credit scores of thousands of people in the USA because of flawed predictability and even more problematic assumptions made by computers with no human intervention. Meanwhile, José van Dijck (2014) has suggested that this process of "datafication" is deeply rooted in problematic ontological and epistemological claims. For him, "datafication" has now become an accepted new paradigm to understand sociality and social behaviour as part of a larger "social media logic", one that, we must add, is characterised and defined by the market. In so doing, "datafication" has now become effectively a widespread secular belief that claims to explain the world and provide order to what it sees as chaotic reality. In this context, adds Dijck, the notion of "trust" becomes more problematic because people's faith in data is then extended to other public institutions such as law enforcement officials who handle their data. Consequently, we have witnessed an extended level of permissibility in allowing law enforcement agencies to encroach upon our private data—and our private lives—in the name of the fight against crime and in the form, for example, of the wars against terror and drugs. However, as Dijck reiterates, the interlocking of government, business and academia in the adaptation of this ideology should make us look more critically at the entire ecosystem of connective media.

In addition to this, I might suggest, datafication in crime has also affected the way we conceive and see crime statistics in the news. In the current mode, crime statistics are no longer only those compiled by the law enforcement agencies, as used to be in the past. As problematic as they were and as unregulated as they remain, they were somehow far more representative of reality as they summarised the reporting of social deviation both by police forces—in the case of national crime statistics— as well by the public's perception of crime based on the national crime survey in each country. These were and continue to be imperfect models, but nevertheless were based on actual events and/or on perceptions around these events. However, we are now entering a new phase in which people arriving at an airport terminal are required to open their Facebook or Twitter account to an immigration official even when a visa has been granted to an individual (Gibbs, 2016). This data is then used to criminalise individuals and whole segments of society. Thus ascribing to them, by means of predictability and probability, assumed patterns that infer the likelihood of some individuals committing a crime. This is nothing new, of course, as stop and search of young Afro-Americans in the USA and heavier sentences upon blacks and Latinos are a testament to deeply flawed and very biased policing models of the past (Chin, 2002; Dowden, Ethridge, & Brooks, 2016; Miller, 1996). The aggravation today, however, is that with the use of "big data" law enforcement agencies can now claim legitimacy by presumably removing human agency while continuing with the same practices (Chan & Moses, 2016; Crawford & Schultz, 2014). We live, in fact, in a time in which one can have "big data and small ideas" in relation to crime and crime prevention (Crawford & Schultz, 2014; Sampson, 2013).

These are indeed, times in which crime "big data" is being created instead of reported. This data, which is processed by algorithms that are rarely updated or tested for their effects on people's lives, serves no purpose in crime other than distorting the fundamental principle of law enforcement: that everyone is innocent until proven the contrary. In fact, as Cathy O'Neil (2016) has eloquently summarised, the more efficient the algorithm processing the data, the less fair it becomes. Indeed, the management and processing of big data is based upon the mathematical notions of predictability and probability, neither of which should be ethically or morally applied to law enforcement, as effective as this might seem. As in Tom Cruise's blockbuster *The Minority Report*, the final dystopian message is absolutely clear (spoiler alert!): under no circumstances can the ends justify the means when it comes to the delivery of justice and crime prevention. Moreover, given the fact that with even less regulation and oversight than traditional statistics, big data has very limited claims to validity or reliability. Under these circumstances, any presumption of producing "scientific" knowledge about crime and therefore informing the police about their strategies and approaches, must be taken with extreme caution.

It is in this context that we need to revisit the professional ethics that drive journalism and discuss approaches and strategies in the newsroom to deal with these pressing issues and challenges. As we have discussed in this book, the impact of technology on the reporting of crime statistics— and in particular the process of digitalization, interactivity and convergence—are affecting the way reporters gather, produce and disseminate crime statistics in ways that were unthinkable only 10 years ago. Journalists, for example, now have access to data visualisation technology that facilitates access and understanding of these numbers in ways that were undreamt of in the past. Nevertheless, let us not forget that as appealing and aesthetically useful that it might seem, data visualisation of crime statistics still remains rooted in data that remains inappropriately regulated and in many cases flawed. Because of this, the reporting of crime statistics has become increasingly complex as technological changes have also facilitated the reporter's access and ability to manage crime statistics while not really improving the quality of the statistical data at all. Indeed, the process of "datafication" has brought about increasing complexity to the reporting of crime statistics.

However, from the ethical point of view, it is important to remind ourselves that datafication did not somehow come out of the blue thanks only to technology. On the contrary, it is the logical consequence of a very long-standing project referred to as the "mathematisation" (Debreu, 1991; Keitel, Kotzmann, & Skovsmose, 1993) of society that ran hand in hand with the enlightenment as a political project. In this sense, mathematisation refers to the formatting of production, decision making, economic management, means of communication, war power, medical techniques and others by means of mathematical insights and techniques (Skovsmose, 2014). By assuming that everything can be mathematically defined and measured, the process of mathematisation is then able to provide particular meaning to objects and dynamics in our society.

Mathematisation is now widespread in most disciplines of social sciences, especially in economics and criminology, where supporters have tried to legitimise this process by arguing the inherent and axiological neutrality of mathematics (Brandao, 2017, p. 506). This process is broadly grounded in positivism claims that knowledge derives from sensory experience and that this should be interpreted through reason and logic. It only sees verified data (positive facts) received from the senses as "empirical evidence" as a legitimate source of knowledge. In this sense, positivism extends this principle to society, which is interpreted and understood as part of the physical world and therefore operating according to general natural laws. For one of its main proponents, Auguste Comte (1798–1857), much as the physical world operates according to gravity and other absolute laws, so does society (Macionis, 2017). In this context, mathematical language became the language of science and without quantification there are no legitimate claims to truth, at least not within the boundaries established by current discursive regimes in social science. Hence, this explains why statistics became such a paramount element in discourses around crime; moreover, as crime reporting embraces more and more the idea of subtle and scientific analysis of social deviation.

Is equally important to underline the fact that the "datafication" of public life is not a neutral or just technologically-driven phenomenon, nor that it is—as it pretends to be—deprived of human agency and intervention. On the contrary, it is a process closely linked to the increasing marketisation of society as well as with the colonisation of people's private spheres by consumerism. This because the "datafication" trend, in a way, is a derivative of the "great transformation" enunciated by Karl Polanyi (1957 [1945]) and which saw the logic of the market overtaking the rest of society. This raises important questions about the central assumption of statistical neutrality. Statistics and the rest of data are neither politically neutral nor devoid of distinctive interpretations from the moment that a particular set of data is conceived to the moment it is disseminated. All in all, statistics are not a hard fact but just another representation in the human imagination used to construct social reality.

We also need to acknowledge that the mathematisation of public life can contribute only in a very limited way to the comprehension of historical and current processes associated with crime. In this sense, mathematical models are unable to describe the origin, development or decline of social relations. A model might be useful as a description of quantitative patterns of events when social relations stay stable (Brandao, 2017) but it tells us very little about context and root causes. Yes, crime statistics provides a picture of social deviation. However, contrary to common assumptions, it is not a model upon which we should rely solely as a society to undertake predictive approaches towards crime. This is because social changes, even the smallest ones, are often outside the explanatory scope of numbers regardless of what data scientists, seeking to describe and ultimately control human behaviour, claim. Journalists, therefore, face the challenge of not succumbing to the temptation that by using numbers alone they can understand patterns of crime. As most criminologists would probably agree, social deviation is too much of a political and complex issue to be reduced to mere numbers.

Daily Crime

Ultimately, the main challenge for journalists continues to be how to engage with crime statistics constructively and critically while making them appealing, relevant and accessible at the same time. Journalists need this data to help them and their audiences make sense of a world that at times seem increasingly complex and chaotic. But in building that picture, journalists should never forget that crime statistics are just another piece in a jigsaw that is constantly changing. It is precisely because of this challenge that journalists dealing with crime statistics need to think about them not as facts. Instead, they need to embrace them as an open invitation to constantly and critically reflect upon issues of conceptualisation, definitions and operationalisation of crime and social deviation itself. In this sense, the name of the game continues to be substance rather than style; a game in which journalism can only win if it is able to perform critical thinking around the data and make no assumption except for the fact that truth is never eternal and needs to be constantly challenged (Popper, 1972, 2002).

Having said that, I would not want to leave readers with a postmodernist impression that crime statistics are "too relative" as to be useful in helping us understand the world. On the contrary and broadly speaking, the issue remains that, although the quality of crime statistics continues to be flawed and therefore the statistics are open to misinterpretation and manipulation, they are nevertheless the best we have to create links between individual crime stories and the wider society. Therefore, the priority for journalists is to be able to assess these numbers critically and interpret them in a sound manner. Indeed, to be able to read them, interpret them and deconstruct the numbers in order to analyse crime. Everything else follows from that and as promising as data visualisation might be, nothing would substitute for the need to see through these numbers and call it as it is. They represent a particular view of what crime is, a view that might be helpful in understanding crime and crime policy but one that will also be at times partial, distorted and incomplete. For journalism as a social practice and journalists as a professional body, the challenges in relation to the use and news coverage of crime statistics are diverse. But it is not a task that can be left to them alone. For example, academics also have to play their part by focusing some of their research agenda on these pressing issues. The news media organisations, government officials and other actors also need to understand that despite the rise of social media and other technologies, journalists continue to be the key mediators between crime policy and the public. Therefore, they need to participate proactively in facilitating access, dissemination and use of crime statistics so as to support better informed citizens. However, above all, as we have discussed in this book, the urgent priority for those studying these themes and for those practising journalism is to firmly commit ourselves that we shall never, ever again, allow our ignorance of crime statistics to condemn the innocent.

Notes

1. Rawlinson, Kevin (2016). Sun ordered to admit British Muslims story was 'significantly misleading'. *The Guardian*. https://www.theguardian.com/media/2016/mar/26/ipso-sun-print-statement-british-muslims-headline [Accessed on 11 February 2017].

References

Allcott, H., & Gentzkow, M. (2017). *Social media and fake news in the 2016 election*. Cambridge, MA: National Bureau of Economic Research.

Brandao, R. F. (2017). The uses of science statistics in the news media and on daily life. In M.-S. Ramírez-Montoya (Ed.), *Handbook of research on driving STEM learning with educational technologies* (pp. 506–523). Hershey, PA: IGI Global.

Chan, J., & Bennett Moses, L. (2016). Is big data challenging criminology? *Theoretical Criminology, 20*(1), 21–39.

Chin, G. (2002). Race, the war on drugs, and the collateral consequences of criminal conviction. *Journal of Gender, Race & Justice, 6*(1), 255–278.

Crawford, K., & Schultz, J. (2014). Big data and due process: Toward a framework to redress predictive privacy harms. *BCL Review, 55*, 93–128.

Debreu, G. (1991). The mathematization of economic theory. *The American Economic Review, 81*(1), 1–7.

Diamond, J. (2017). Trump falsely claims US murder rate is 'highest' in 47 years. *CNN Online*. Retrieved March 12, 2017, from http://edition.cnn.com/2017/02/07/politics/donald-trump-murder-rate-fact-check/index.html.

Dowden, A. R., Ethridge, G., & Brooks, M. (2016). The impact criminal history has on the employability of African American and Latino populations with disabilities receiving state vocational rehabilitation services: Implications for adding a criminal history variable to the RSA-911 data. *Journal of Vocational Rehabilitation, 45*(2), 213–224.

Dunwoody, S. (2014). Science journalism: Prospects in the digital age. In M. Bucchi & B. Trench (Eds.), *Routledge handbook of public communication of science and technology* (pp. 27–39). London: Routledge.

Gibbs, S. (2016). US border control could start asking for your social media accounts. Retrieved January 3, 2017, from https://www.theguardian.com/technology/2016/jun/28/us-customs-border-protection-social-media-accounts-facebook-twitter

Herman, E. S., & Chomsky, N. (2010 [1984]). *Manufacturing consent: The political economy of the mass media*. London: Random House.

Keitel, C., Kotzmann, E., & Skovsmose, O. (1993). Beyond the tunnel vision: Analysing the relationship between mathematics, society and technology. In C. Keitel & K. Ruthven (Eds.), *Learning from computers: Mathematics education and technology* (pp. 243–279). New York: Springer.

Kucharski, A. (2016). Post-truth: Study epidemiology of fake news. *Nature, 540*(7634), 525–525.

Macionis, J. J. (2017). *Sociology*. London: Pearson Higher.

Maier, S. R. (2003). Numeracy in the newsroom: A case study of mathematical competence and confidence. *Journalism & Mass Communication Quarterly, 80*(4), 921–936.

Miller, J. G. (1996). *Search and destroy: African-American males in the criminal justice system*. Cambridge: Cambridge University Press.

Nguyen, A., & Lugo-Ocando, J. (2015). Introduction: The state of statistics in journalism and journalism education—Issues and debates. *Journalism, 17*(1), 3–17.

O'Neil, C. (2016). *Weapons of math destruction. How big data increases inequality and threatens democracy*. New York: Crown.

Polanyi, K. (1957 [1945]). *The great transformation* (R. M. MacIver, Trans.). Boston: Beacon Press.

Popper, K. R. (1972). *Objective knowledge: An evolutionary approach*. Oxford: Oxford University Press.

Popper, K. R. (2002). *The poverty of historicism*. Abingdon-on-Thames, OX: Psychology Press.

Ruckenstein, M., & Pantzar, M. (2015). Datafied life: Techno-anthropology as a site for exploration and experimentation. *Techné: Research in Philosophy and Technology, 19*(2), 191–210.

Sampson, R. J. (2013). The place of context: A theory and strategy for criminology's hard problems. *Criminology, 51*(1), 1–31.

Skovsmose, O. (2014). Mathematization as social process. In O. Skovsmose (Ed.), *Encyclopedia of mathematics education* (pp. 441–445). New York: Springer.

Van Dijck, J. (2014). Datafication, dataism and dataveillance: Big Data between scientific paradigm and ideology. *Surveillance & Society, 12*(2), 197–208.

Yang, X. (2016). *Analysing datafied life*. Ph.D. in Computing, Imperial College London, London. Retrieved from https://spiral.imperial.ac.uk/handle/10044/1/33722

References

Abraham, L., & Appiah, O. (2006). Framing news stories: The role of visual imagery in priming racial stereotypes. *The Howard Journal of Communications, 17*(3), 183–203.

Agerholm, H. (2016). Brexit: Wave of hate crime and racial abuse reported following EU referendum. Retrieved September 10, 2016, from http://www.independent.co.uk/news/uk/home-news/brexit-eu-referendum-racial-racism-abuse-hate-crime-reported-latest-leave-immigration-a7104191.html

Allan, S. (2004). *News culture*. Cambridge: Cambridge University Press.

Allcott, H., & Gentzkow, M. (2017). *Social media and fake news in the 2016 election*. Cambridge, MA: National Bureau of Economic Research.

Althaus, S. L., & Tewksbury, D. (2002). Agenda setting and the "new" news patterns of issue importance among readers of the paper and online versions of the New York Times. *Communication Research, 29*(2), 180–207.

Anderson, A. (2015). Reflections on environmental communication and the challenges. *Science, 1*(2), 199–230.

Anderson, D. C. (1997). The mystery of the falling crime rate. *American Prospect, 32*, 49–55.

Anselin, L., Cohen, J., Cook, D., Gorr, W., & Tita, G. (2000). Spatial analyses of crime. *Criminal Justice, 4*(2), 213–262.

© The Author(s) 2017
J. Lugo-Ocando, *Crime Statistics in the News*,
DOI 10.1057/978-1-137-39841-3

181

Asp, K. (1986). *Mäktiga massmedier: Studier i politisk opinionsbildning* [Powerful mass media: Studies in political opinion-formation]. Stockholm: Akademilitteratur.

Asthana, A. (2016). Vote Leave releases list of serious crimes by EU citizens in Britain. Retrieved September 2, 2016, from https://www.theguardian.com/politics/2016/mar/28/vote-leave-releases-list-of-serious-crimes-by-eu-citizens-in-britain

Austin, L., & Jin, Y. (2015). Approaching ethical crisis communication with accuracy and sensitivity: Exploring common ground and gaps between journalism and public relations. *Public Relations Journal, 9*(1), 2.

Bailey, O. G., & Harindranath, R. (2005). Racialized 'othering'. In S. Allan (Ed.), *Journalism: Critical issues* (pp. 274–286). Meidenhead: Open University Press and McGraw-Hill Education.

Bailey, V. (1997). English prisons, penal culture, and the abatement of imprisonment, 1895–1922. *The Journal of British Studies, 36*(03), 285–324.

Banks, M. (2005). Spaces of (in) security: Media and fear of crime in a local context. *Crime, Media, Culture, 1*(2), 169–187.

Barber, M. (2007). *Instruction to deliver: Tony Blair, public services and the challenge of achieving targets.* London: Politico.

Bardin, L. (1977). *Análise de Conteúdo.* Lisbon: Edicoes 70.

Barlow, M., Barlow, D., & Chiricos, T. (1995). Economic conditions and ideologies of crime in the media: A content analysis of crime news. *Crime & Delinquency, 41*(1), 3–19.

Barnhurst, K. G., & Mutz, D. (1997). American journalism and the decline in event-centered reporting. *Journal of Communication, 47*(4), 27–53.

Battersby, M. (2010). *Is that a Fact?* Peterborough, ON: Broadview Press.

Baumgartner, F. R., Berry, J. M., Hojnacki, M., Leech, B. L., & Kimball, D. C. (2009). *Lobbying and policy change: Who wins, who loses, and why.* Chicago: University of Chicago Press.

Baxendale, A. S. (2010). *Winston Leonard Spencer-Churchill: Penal reformer.* Oxford: Peter Lang.

BBC. (2007). Giuliani's warning over UK's NHS. Retrieved March 2, 2017, from http://news.bbc.co.uk/1/hi/uk_politics/7003286.stm

BBC. (2017). Homicide and knife crime rates 'up in England and Wales'. Retrieved March 28, 2017, from http://www.bbc.co.uk/news/uk-39729601

Beck, U. (1992). *Risk society: Towards a new modernity.* London: Sage.

Beck, U. (2010 [1998]). *La Sociedad del Riesgo. Hacia una nueva modernidad.* Madrid: Paidos Surcos.

Beckett, K. (1999). *Making crime pay: Law and order in contemporary American politics.* Oxford: Oxford University Press.

Bennett, A. (2016). Did Britain really vote Brexit to cut immigration? Retrieved October 10, 2016, from http://www.telegraph.co.uk/news/2016/06/29/did-britain-really-vote-brexit-to-cut-immigration/

Bennett, J. (2006). Modernity and its critics. In J. S. Dryzek, B. Honig, & A. Phillips (Eds.), *The Oxford Handbook of political theory* (pp. 211–224). Oxford: Oxford University Press.

Berger, P. L., & Luckmann, T. (1991). *The social construction of reality: A treatise in the sociology of knowledge*. London: Penguin.

Berkowitz, D., & TerKeurst, J. V. (1999). Community as interpretive community: Rethinking the journalist-source relationship. *Journal of Communication, 49*(3), 125–136.

Bernstein, P. L. (1996). *Against the Gods. The remarkable history of risk*. New York: John Wiley and Sons, Inc.

Best, J. (2004). *More damned lies and statistics: How numbers confuse public issues*. Berkeley: University of California Press.

Best, J. (2012). *Damned lies and statistics: Untangling numbers from the media, politicians, and activists*. Berkeley: University of California Press.

Biderman, A. D., & Lynch, J. P. (2012). *Understanding crime incidence statistics: Why the UCR diverges from the NCS*. Berlin: Springer Science & Business Media.

Bindel, J. (2012). Sexual abuse of children is widespread—Let's confront the difficult truth. *The Guardian*. Retrieved from https://www.theguardian.com/commentisfree/2012/jun/13/sexual-abuse-children-difficult-truth

Black, S. (2013). *Practice of public relations*. Abingdon, OX: Routledge.

Blastland, M., & Dilnot, A. (2008). *The Tiger that isn't—Seeing through a world of numbers*. London: Profile Books.

Board, E. (2017). Editorial: What's behind Chicago's surge in violence? *The Chicago Tribune*. Retrieved March 26, 20017, from http://www.chicagotribune.com/news/opinion/editorials/ct-chicago-crime-increase-causes-edit-0118-md-20170117-story.html

Borges-Rey, E. (2016). Unravelling Data Journalism: A study of data journalism practice in British newsrooms. *Journalism Practice, 10*(7), 833–843.

Borges-Rey, E. (2017). Towards an epistemology of data journalism in the devolved nations of the United Kingdom: Changes and continuities in materiality, performativity and reflexivity. *Journalism*. doi:10.1177/1464884917693864.

Bosshoff, A. (2013). Inside Nigella's toxic marriage: She was haunted by depression. He was a terrible bully driven mad by jealousy of her children. The bitter truth behind Nigella and Saatchi's marital breakdown. *The Daily Mail*.

Retrieved from http://www.dailymail.co.uk/news/article-2527397/Inside-Nigellas-toxic-marriage-She-haunted-depression-He-terrible-bully-driven-mad-jealousy-children-The-bitter-truth-Nigella-Saatchis-marital-break-down.html#ixzz4TeaLb6EI

Bottomley, A. K., & Coleman, C. (1981). *Understanding crime rates: Police and public roles in the production of official statistics*. Farnborough, Hampshire: Gower.

Bourdieu, P. (1998). *On television and journalism*. London: Pluto.

Bourdieu, P. (2000). For a scholarship with commitment. *Profession*, 40–45.

Bourke, J. (2005). *Fear: A cultural history*. Berkeley, CA: Counterpoint Press.

Bowling, B. (1999). The rise and fall of New York murder: Zero tolerance or crack's decline? *British Journal of Criminology, 39*(4), 531–554.

Boyd-Barrett, O. (1980). *The international news agencies* (Vol. 13). London: Constable Limited.

Boyd-Barrett, O. (1995). The political economy approach. In O. Boyd-Barrett & C. Newbold (Eds.), *Approaches to media: A reader* (pp. 186–192). London: Arnold.

Boyle, D. (2000). *The Tyranny of numbers*. London: HarperCollins Publishers.

Brandao, R. F. (2017). The uses of science statistics in the news media and on daily life. In M.-S. Ramírez-Montoya (Ed.), *Handbook of research on driving STEM learning with educational technologies* (pp. 506–523). Hershey, PA: IGI Global.

Breen, M. J., Devereux, E., & Haynes, A. (2006). Fear, framing and foreigners: The othering of immigrants in the Irish print media. *International Journal of Critical Psychology, 16*, 100–121.

Briggs, A., & Burke, P. (2009). *A social history of the media: From Gutenberg to the Internet*. Cambridge: Polity.

Brockway, K., & Beshkin, A. (2000). Winners of Pulitzer prizes in journalism, letters, drama and music, announced April 10th at the journalism school. Retrieved February 2, 2017, from http://www.columbia.edu/cu/news/00/04/pulitzer/pulitzer.html

Broersma, M. (2010). The unbearable limitations of journalism on press critique and journalism's claim to truth. *International Communication Gazette, 72*(1), 21–33.

Brown, J. D., Bybee, C. R., Wearden, S. T., & Straughan, D. M. (1987). Invisible power: Newspaper news sources and the limits of diversity. *Journalism Quarterly, 64*(1), 45–54.

Brownlee, I. (1998). New labour—New penology? Punitive rhetoric and the limits of managerialism in criminal justice policy. *Journal of Law and Society, 25*(3), 313–335.

Brownlees, N. (2011). *The language of periodical news in seventeenth-century England*. Newcastle upon Tyne: Cambridge Scholars Publishing.

Brummett, B. (2010). *Techniques of close reading*. London: Sage.

Bugeja, M. (2007). Making whole: The ethics of correction. *Journal of Mass Media Ethics, 22*(1), 49–65.

Burn-Murdoch, J. (2013). 69,000 female, 9,000 male rape victims per year: Get the full data. Retrieved March 21, 2017, from https://www.theguardian. com/news/datablog/2013/jan/11/male-female-rape-statistics-graphic

Buzan, B., Wæver, O., & De Wilde, J. (1998). *Security: A new framework for analysis*. Boulder, CO: Lynne Rienner Publishers.

Carrabine, E. (2008). *Crime, culture and the media*. Cambridge: Polity.

Carvalho, A. (2008). Media(ted) discourse and society. *Journalism Studies, 9*(2), 161–177.

Cater, D. (1964). *Power in Washington: A critical look at today's struggle to govern in the nation's capital* (Vol. 290). London: Collins.

Cavender, G., & Miller, K. W. (2013). Corporate crime as trouble: Reporting on the corporate scandals of 2002. *Deviant Behavior, 34*(11), 916–931.

Celona, L., Moore, T., & Cohen, S. (2016). Man charged in murder of imam, assistant felt 'hatred' toward Muslims. Retrieved August 17, 2016, from http://nypost. com/2016/08/15/man-charged-with-murder-for-executing-imam-assistant/

Ceyhan, A., & Tsoukala, A. (2002). The securitization of migration in Western societies: Ambivalent discourses and policies. *Alternatives: Global, Local, Political, 27*(1), S21–S21.

CFCA. (2014). Who abuses children? Retrieved February 2, 2017, from https:// aifs.gov.au/cfca/publications/who-abuses-children

Chan, A. K. P., & Chan, V. M. S. (2012). *Public perception of crime and attitudes toward police: Examining the effects of media news*. Run Run Shaw Library, City University of Hong Kong.

Chan, J., & Bennett Moses, L. (2016). Is big data challenging criminology? *Theoretical Criminology, 20*(1), 21–39.

Chan, J., To, H.-P., & Chan, E. (2006). Reconsidering social cohesion: Developing a definition and analytical framework for empirical research. *Social Indicators Research, 75*(2), 273–302.

Chandler, C. R., & Tsai, Y.-M. (2001). Social factors influencing immigration attitudes: An analysis of data from the General Social Survey. *The Social Science Journal, 38*(2), 177–188.

Cheong, P. H., Edwards, R., Goulbourne, H., & Solomos, J. (2007). Immigration, social cohesion and social capital: A critical review. *Critical social policy, 27*(1), 24–49.

Chermak, S. (1995). Image control: How police affect the presentation of crime news. *American journal of police, 14*(2), 21–43.

Chibnall, S. (1977). *Law-and-order news. An analysis of crime reporting in the British press.* London: Tavistock Publications.

Chin, G. (2002). Race, the war on drugs, and the collateral consequences of criminal conviction. *Journal of Gender, Race & Justice, 6*(1), 255–278.

Chiricos, T., Eschholz, S., & Gertz, M. (1997). Crime, news and fear of crime: Toward an identification of audience effects. *Social Problems, 44*(3), 342–357.

Chung, D. S., & Yoo, C. Y. (2008). Audience motivations for using interactive features: Distinguishing use of different types of interactivity on an online newspaper. *Mass Communication and Society, 11*(4), 375–397.

CIPR. (2016). Using statistics in public relations. Retrieved February 12, 2017, from https://www.cipr.co.uk/content/cpd/summer-cpd/using-statistics-public-relations

Clement, S., & Tankersley, J. (2016). Even if Trump loses, this poll shows why hard-line immigration positions are here to stay. Retrieved October 10, 2016, from https://www.washingtonpost.com/news/wonk/wp/2016/10/06/even-if-trump-loses-this-poll-shows-why-hard-line-immigration-positions-are-here-to-stay/

Cohen, B. (1967 [1963]). *The press and foreign policy.* Princeton, NJ: Princeton University Press.

Cohen, S. (1972 [2002]). *Folk devils and moral panics: The creation of the mods and rockers.* New York: Psychology Press.

Conboy, M. (2001). *The press and popular culture.* London: Sage.

Conboy, M. (2004). *Journalism: A critical history.* London: Sage.

Connolly, E. S. (2014). Crime journalism: Barriers in Ireland. *Journal of Applied Journalism & Media Studies, 3*(1), 59–69.

Conrad, P. (1999). Uses of expertise: Sources, quotes, and voice in the reporting of genetics in the news. *Public Understanding of Science, 8*(4), 285–302.

Cornwell, E. E. (1965). *Presidential leadership of public opinion.* Bloomington: Indiana University Press.

Cottle, S. (2006a). *Mediatized conflict: Understanding media and conflicts in the contemporary world.* London: McGraw-Hill Education.

Cottle, S. (2006b). Mediatized rituals: Beyond manufacturing consent. *Media, Culture & Society, 28*(3), 411–432.

Couldry, N., Hepp, A., & Krotz, F. (2009). *Media events in a global age.* London: Routledge.

Cozens, C. (2003). Tabloids 'stoke fear of crime'. Retrieved March 11, 2016, from https://www.theguardian.com/media/2003/jul/17/pressandpublishing.politics

Crawford, K., & Schultz, J. (2014). Big data and due process: Toward a framework to redress predictive privacy harms. *BCL Review, 55*, 93–128.

CRCVC. (2015). Understanding how the media reports crime. Retrieved August 11, 2016, from https://crcvc.ca/publications/media-guide/understanding/#fn3

Crick, E. (2012). Drugs as an existential threat: An analysis of the international securitization of drugs. *International Journal of Drug Policy, 23*(5), 407–414.

Crozier, M. (2007). Recursive governance: Contemporary political communication and public policy. *Political Communication, 24*(1), 1–18.

Curran, J., Salovaara-Moring, I., Coen, S., & Iyengar, S. (2010). Crime, foreigners and hard news: A cross-national comparison of reporting and public perception. *Journalism, 11*(1), 3–19.

Cutler, T., & Waine, B. (2000). Managerialism reformed? New Labour and public sector management. *Social Policy & Administration, 34*(3), 318–332.

Cutlip, S. M. (2013). *The unseen power: Public relations—A history*. London: Routledge.

Daniel, A., & Flew, T. (2010). *The Guardian reportage of the UK MP expenses scandal: A case study of computational journalism*. Paper presented at the Record of the Communications Policy and Research Forum 2010.

Davidson, S. (2015). Everywhere and nowhere: Theorising and researching public affairs and lobbying within public relations scholarship. *Public Relations Review, 41*(5), 615–627.

Davies, A. (2007). The Scottish Chicago? From 'hooligans' to 'gangsters' in inter-war Glasgow. *Cultural and Social History, 4*(4), 511–527.

Davies, N. (2008). *Flat earth news: An award-winning reporter exposes falsehood, distortion and propaganda in the global media*. London: Random House.

Davis, A. (2000). Public relations, news production and changing patterns of source access in the British national media. *Media, Culture & Society, 22*(1), 39–59.

Davis, P. J., & Hersh, R. (1986). *Descartes' dream: The world according to mathematics*. London: Penguin Books.

Davis, R., & Taras, D. (2017). *Justices and journalists: The global perspective*. Cambridge: Cambridge University Press.

Dayan, D., & Katz, E. (1994). *Media events*. Cambridge, MA: Harvard University Press.

De Figueiredo, J. M., & Richter, B. K. (2014). Advancing the empirical research on lobbying. *Annual Review of Political Science, 17*, 163–185.

Debreu, G. (1991). The mathematization of economic theory. *The American Economic Review, 81*(1), 1–7.

Dentzer, S. (2009). Communicating medical news—Pitfalls of health care journalism. *New England Journal of Medicine, 360*(1), 1–3.

Desrosieres, A. (1993). *The politics of large numbers: A history of statistical reasoning*. London: Harvard University Press.

Deuze, M. (2002). National news cultures: A comparison of Dutch, German, British, Australian, and US journalists. *Journalism & Mass Communication Quarterly, 79*(1), 134–149.

Devlin, K. (1998). *The language of mathematics: Making invisible visible*. New York: W. H. Freeman and Company.

Diamond, J. (2017). Trump falsely claims US murder rate is 'highest' in 47 years. *CNN Online*. Retrieved March 12, 2017, from http://edition.cnn.com/2017/02/07/politics/donald-trump-murder-rate-fact-check/index.html.

Ditton, J., & Duffy, J. (1983). Bias in the newspaper reporting of crime news. *The British Journal of Criminology: An International Review of Crime and Society, 23*(2), 159–165.

Dorling, D., & Simpson, S. (1999). *Statistics in society: The arithmetic of politics*. London: Arnold.

Dowden, A. R., Ethridge, G., & Brooks, M. (2016). The impact criminal history has on the employability of African American and Latino populations with disabilities receiving state vocational rehabilitation services: Implications for adding a criminal history variable to the RSA-911 data. *Journal of Vocational Rehabilitation, 45*(2), 213–224.

Dowler, K. (2003). Media consumption and public attitudes toward crime and justice: The relationship between fear of crime, punitive attitudes, and perceived police effectiveness. *Journal of Criminal Justice and Popular Culture, 10*(2), 109–126.

Dowler, K., Fleming, T., & Muzzatti, S. L. (2006). Constructing crime: Media, crime, and popular culture. *Canadian Journal of Criminology and Criminal Justice, 48*(6), 837–850.

Dowler, K., & Zawilski, V. (2007). Public perceptions of police misconduct and discrimination: Examining the impact of media consumption. *Journal of Criminal Justice, 35*(2), 193–203.

Doyle, G. (2013). *Understanding media economics*. London: SAGE Publications Limited.

Doyle, J., & Wright, S. (2012). 'Immigrant crimewave' warning: Foreign nationals were accused of a QUARTER of all crimes in London. Retrieved August 1, 2016, from http://www.dailymail.co.uk/news/article-2102895/Immigrant-crimewave-warning-Foreign-nationals-accused-QUARTER-crimes-London.html

Dunwoody, S. (2014). Science journalism: Prospects in the digital age. In M. Bucchi & B. Trench (Eds.), *Routledge handbook of public communication of science and technology* (pp. 27–39). London: Routledge.

Durham, M. G. (1998). On the relevance of standpoint epistemology to the practice of journalism: The case for "strong objectivity". *Communication Theory, 8*(2), 117–140.

Eberstadt, N. (1995). *The Tyranny of numbers: Mismeasurement and misrule.* Washington, DC: AEI Press.

Edwards, L., & Hodges, C. E. (2011). Introduction: Implications of (a radical) socio-cultural 'turn' in public relations scholarship. In L. Edwards & C. E. Hodges (Eds.), *Public relations, society & culture: Theoretical and empirical explorations* (pp. 1–15). Abingdon, OX: Taylor & Francis.

Eldridge, S. A. (2014). Boundary maintenance and interloper media reaction: Differentiating between journalism's discursive enforcement processes. *Journalism Studies, 15*(1), 1–16.

Emmers, R. (2002). *The securitization of transnational crime in ASEAN.* Singapore: Institute of Defence and Strategic Studies, Nanyang Technological University.

Ericson, R., Baranek, O., & Chan, J. (1987). *Visualising deviance.* Buckingham: Open University Press.

Ernest, P. (1997). *Social constructivism as a philosophy of mathematics.* New York: State University of New York Press.

Esrock, S. L., & Leichty, G. B. (1998). Social responsibility and corporate web pages: Self-presentation or agenda-setting? *Public Relations Review, 24*(3), 305–319.

Esser, F. (1999). Tabloidization' of news a comparative analysis of Anglo-American and German Press Journalism. *European Journal of Communication, 14*(3), 291–324.

Esser, F. (2013). Mediatization as a challenge: Media logic versus political logic. In H. Kriesi (Ed.), *Democracy in the age of globalization and mediatization* (pp. 155–176). Basingstoke: Palgrave Macmillan.

Esser, F., & Strömbäck, J. (2014). *Mediatization of politics.* Basingstoke: Palgrave Macmillan.

Eterno, J. A., & Silverman, E. B. (2006). The New York City police department's Compstat: Dream or nightmare? *International Journal of Police Science & Management, 8*(3), 218–231.

Ettema, J., & Glasser, T. (1998). *Custodians of conscience: Investigative journalism and public virtue.* New York: Columbia University Press.

Evans, H. (1973). *Newspaper design.* London: Holt, Rinehart & Winston.

Evans, H. (2013). The media has a duty to scrutinise the use of power. Retrieved June 10, 2016, from https://www.theguardian.com/commentisfree/2013/oct/20/media-duty-scrutinise-use-of-power

Fagan, J., & Davies, G. (2000). Street stops and broken windows: Terry, race and disorder in New York City. *Fordham Urban Law Journal, 28,* 457–504.

Fairclough, N. (2000). *New labour, new language?* London: Routledge.

Feilzer, M. (2007). Criminologists making news? Providing factual information on crime and criminal justice through a weekly newspaper column. *Crime, Media, Culture, 3*(3), 285–304.

Fetzer, J. S. (2000). *Public attitudes toward immigration in the United States, France, and Germany.* Cambridge: Cambridge University Press.

Fields, I. W. (2004). Family values and feudal codes: The social politics of America's twenty-first century gangster. *The Journal of Popular Culture, 37*(4), 611–633.

Fioramonti, L. (2014). *How numbers role the world. The use and abuse of statistics in global politics.* London: Zed Books.

Fisher, N. (1996). *Statistical analysis of circular data.* Cambridge: Cambridge University Press.

Fitzgerald, J., Curtis, K. A., & Corliss, C. L. (2012). Anxious publics worries about crime and immigration. *Comparative Political Studies, 45*(4), 477–506.

Formicola, J. R. (2011). Catholic clerical sexual abuse: Effects on Vatican sovereignty and papal power. *Journal of Church and State, 53*(4), 523–544.

Foucault, M. (1979 [1977]). *Discipline and punish.* New York: Vintage.

Frankin, B. (2011). Sources, credibility and the continuing crisis of UK journalism. In B. Franklin & M. Carlson (Eds.), *Journalists, sources, and credibility* (pp. 90–106). London: Routledge.

Franklin, B., & Carlson, M. (2011). Sources, credibility and the continuing crisis of UK journalism. *Journalists, Sources and Credibility: New Perspectives,* 90–106.

Friedman, M., Grawert, A., & Cullen, J. (2016). *Crime in 2016: A preliminary analysis.* New York: NYU School of Law.

Fuchs, C. (2013). *Social media: A critical introduction.* Thousand Oaks, CA: Sage.

Furedi, F. (2015). The media's first moral panic. *History Today, 65.*

Gagne, T. S. (2015). *Eliot Ness.* Newark, DE: Mitchell Lane Publishers, Inc.

Gallagher, C. (1986). The body versus the social body in the works of Thomas Malthus and Henry Mayhew. *Representations, 14,* 83–106.

Galtung, J., & Ruge, M. H. (1965). The structure of foreign news the presentation of the Congo, Cuba and Cyprus Crises in four Norwegian newspapers. *Journal of Peace Research, 2*(1), 64–90.

Gamson, W. A., Croteau, D., Hoynes, W., & Sasson, T. (1992). Media images and the social construction of reality. *Annual Review of Sociology, 18*(1), 373–393.

Gans, H. J. (1980). *Deciding what's news NBC. A study of CBS Evening News Nightly News, Newsweek, and Time.* New York: Vintage Books.

Garcia, F. (2016). Rudy Giuliani says black people have a 99% chance of killing each other. Retrieved August 22, 2016, from http://www.independent.co.uk/news/world/americas/rudy-giuliani-black-people-kill-each-other-99-percent-nyc-mayor-black-lives-matter-a7129926.html

Garland, D. (1985). *Punishment and welfare: A history of penal strategies.* Farnham, Surrey: Gower Aldershot.

Gee, J. P. (2014). *An introduction to discourse analysis: Theory and method.* Abingdon-on-Thames, OX: Routledge.

Gest, T. (2001). *Crime & politics: Big government's erratic campaign for law and order.* New York: Oxford University Press.

Gibbs, S. (2016). US border control could start asking for your social media accounts. Retrieved January 3, 2017, from https://www.theguardian.com/technology/2016/jun/28/us-customs-border-protection-social-media-accounts-facebook-twitter

Gigerenzer, G., Gaissmaier, W., Kurz-Milcke, E., Schwartz, L. M., & Woloshin, S. (2007). Helping doctors and patients make sense of health statistics. *Psychological Science in the Public Interest, 8*(2), 53–96.

GlasgowMediaGroup. (1976). *Bad news.* London: Routledge.

Godwin, R. K., Godwin, K., Ainsworth, S., & Godwin, E. K. (2012). *Lobbying and policymaking.* London: Sage.

Goethe, J. (1787). *The sorrows of young werther.* Leipzig: Weygand'sche Buchhandlung.

Goffman, E. (1986). *Frame analysis. An essay on the organization of expierence.* Boston: Northeastern University Press.

Goldacre, B. (2009). *Bad science.* London: Fourth State.

Goldsmith, R. E., Lafferty, B. A., & Newell, S. J. (2000). The impact of corporate credibility and celebrity credibility on consumer reaction to advertisements and brands. *Journal of Advertising, 29*(3), 43–54.

Gomes de Melo, C. (2010). Mídia e Crime: liberdade de informacao jornalística e presuncao de inocencia. *Revista do Direito Público, 5*(2), 106–122.

Goode, E., & Ben-Yehuda, N. (2010). *Moral panics: The social construction of deviance.* New York: John Wiley & Sons.

Gray, J., Chambers, L., & Bounegru, L. (2012). *The data journalism handbook: How journalists can use data to improve the news*. Newton, MA: O'Reilly Media, Inc.

Greene, J. (1999). Zero tolerance: A case study of police policies and practices in New York City. *Crime & Delinquency, 45*(2), 171–187.

Greer, C., & McLaughlin, E. (2011). Trial by media': Policing, the 24-7 news mediasphere and the 'politics of outrage. *Theoretical Criminology, 15*(1), 23–46.

Greer, C., & McLaughlin, E. (2013). La giustizia mediatica nel Regno Unito: il caso Madeleine McCann. *Sicurezza e scienze sociali, 2*(1), 151–164. doi:10.3280/SISS2013-002012.

Griffiths, D. (1992). *The Encyclopedia of the British press, 1422–1992*. London: Macmillan.

Hackett, R. A. (1984). Decline of a paradigm? Bias and objectivity in news media studies. *Critical Studies in Media Communication, 1*(3), 229–259.

Hagan, J., Levi, R., & Dinovitzer, R. (2008). The symbolic violence of the crime-immigration nexus: Migrant mythologies in the americas. *Criminology & Public Policy, 7*(1), 95–112.

Hainmueller, J., & Hopkins, D. J. (2014). Public attitudes toward immigration. *Annual Review of Political Science, 17*, 225–249. doi:10.1146/annurev-polisci-102512-194818.

Hall, S. (1975). *Newsmaking and crime*. Birmingham: Centre for Contemporary Cultural Studies.

Hall, S., Critcher, C., Jefferson, T., Clarke, J., & Roberts, B. (1978). The social production of news. In S. Hall (Ed.), *Policing the crisis; Mugging, the state and law and order* (pp. 53–60). London: Macmillan.

Hampton, M. (2008). The "objectivity" ideal and its limitations in 20th-century British journalism. *Journalism Studies, 9*(4), 477–493.

Hampton, M. (2010). The Fourth Estate ideal in journalism history. In S. Allan (Ed.), *The Routledge companion to news and journalism* (pp. 3–12). London: Routledge.

Harcourt, B. (1998). Reflecting on the subject: A critique of the social influence conception of deterrence, the broken windows theory, and order-maintenance policing New York style. *Michigan Law Review, 97*(2), 291–389.

Harcup, T., & O'Neill, D. (2001). What is news? Galtung and Ruge revisited. *Journalism Studies, 2*(2), 261–280.

Harper, S. (2014). Framing the Philpotts: Anti-Welfarism and the British newspaper reporting of the Derby house fire verdict. *International Journal of Media & Cultural Politics, 10*(1), 83–98.

Harrison, J. (2006). *News*. Abingdon, OX: Routledge.

Hartley, S. (2014). Do local newspapers still report important court and council decisions? Retrieved July 20, 2016, from http://www.prolificnorth.co.uk/2014/04/do-local-newspapers-still-report-important-court-and-council-decisions/

Haug, M., & Koppang, H. (1997). Lobbying and public relations in a European context. *Public Relations Review, 23*(3), 233–247.

Helpman, E., & Persson, T. (2001). Lobbying and legislative bargaining. *Advances in Economic Analysis & Policy, 1*(1). doi:10.2202/1538-0637.1008

Herman, E. S., & Chomsky, N. (2010 [1984]). *Manufacturing consent: The political economy of the mass media*. London: Random House.

Hickey, W. (2013). The worst chart in the world. Retrieved March 23, 2017, from http://www.businessinsider.com/pie-charts-are-the-worst-2013-6?IR=T

Hier, S. P. (2011). *Moral panic and the politics of anxiety*. Abingdon, OX: Routledge.

Higgs, M. D. (2013). Do we really need the S-word? *American Scientist, 101*, 6–9.

Hind, K. (2014). Nigella Lawson uses high public profile to back domestic violence charity after split from Charles Saatchi. *The Mirror*. Retrieved from http://www.mirror.co.uk/tv/tv-news/nigella-lawson-domestic-abuse-campaign-3222401

Hjarvard, S. (2008). The mediatization of society. *Nordicom Review, 29*(2), 105–134.

Hjarvard, S. (2013). *The mediatization of culture and society*. London: Routledge.

Hohl, K., Stanko, B., & Newburn, T. (2012). The effect of the 2011 London disorder on public opinion of police and attitudes towards crime, disorder, and sentencing. *Policing, 7*(1), 12–20.

Hollway, W. (1981). I just wanted to kill a woman.' Why? The ripper and male sexuality. *Feminist Review, 9*, 33–40.

Holtzhausen, D. R. (2000). Postmodern values in public relations. *Journal of Public Relations Research, 12*(1), 93–114.

Home Office. (2013). The government responses to the second report from the Home Affairs Committee Sesssion 2013–14 HC68. Childe sexual exploitation and the responses to localised grooming. Home Office, London.

Hope, T. (2004). Pretend it works evidence and governance in the evaluation of the reducing burglary initiative. *Criminal Justice, 4*(3), 287–308.

Hope, T. (2008a). Dodgy evidence—Fallacies and facts of crime reduction, Part 2. *Safer Communities, 7*(4), 46–51.

Hope, T. (2008b). The first casualty: Evidence and governance in a war against crime. In P. Carlen (Ed.), *Imaginary Penalities* (pp. 45–63). London: Routledge.

Hough, M., & Roberts, J. (2005). *Understanding public attitudes to criminal justice*. New York: McGraw-Hill Education.

Humpherys, A. (1977). *Travels into the poor man's country: The work of Henry Mayhew*. Atlanta: University of Georgia Press.

Hunt, A. (1997). 'Moral panic' and moral language in the media. *British Journal of Sociology*, 629–648.

Huysmans, J. (2000). The European Union and the securitization of migration. *JCMS: Journal of Common Market Studies, 38*(5), 751–777.

Ipsos MORI. (2013). Ipsos MORI public understanding of statistics. Retrieved February 2, 2016, from https://www.ipsos-mori.com/Assets/Docs/Polls/rss-kings-ipsos-mori-trust-in-statistics-topline.pdf

Iyengar, S., & Simon, A. (1993). News coverage of the Gulf crisis and public opinion: A study of agenda-setting, priming, and framing. *Communication Research, 20*(3), 365–383.

Jaffe, A., & Spirer, H. (1987). *Misused statistics: Straight talk for twisted numbers*. New York: Marcel Dekker, Inc.

Jenkin, B. (2014). Why we can't rely on police recorded crime statistics. Retrieved March 2, 2017, from http://www.parliament.uk/business/committees/committees-a-z/commons-select/public-administration-select-committee/news/crime-stats-substantive/

Jensen, K. B. (1987). News as ideology: Economic statistics and political ritual in television network news. *Journal of Communication, 37*(1), 8–27.

Jewkes, Y. (2004). The construction of crime news. In Y. Jewkes (Ed.), *Media and crime* (pp. 35–62). Los Angeles: Sage.

Jewkes, Y. (2015). *Media and crime*. London: Sage.

Jewkes, Y., & Yar, M. (2010). Introduction: The Internet, cybercrime and the challenges of the twenty-first century. In Y. Jewkes & M. Yar (Eds.), *Handbook of internet crime* (pp. 1–8). Devon: Willan Publishing.

Jinfeng, D. (1997). Police-public relations—A Chinese view. *Australian & New Zealand Journal of Criminology, 30*(1), 87–94.

Joachim, J. M. (2007). *Agenda setting, the UN, and NGOs: Gender violence and reproductive rights*. Washington, DC: Georgetown University Press.

Johnson, J. (2003). Horror stories and the construction of child abuse. In D. Loseke & J. Best (Eds.), *Social problems: Constructionist readings* (pp. 267–279). New York: Aldine de Gruyter.

Jones, N. (1999). *Sultans of spin*. London: Gollancz.

Jordan, L., & Van Tuijl, P. (2000). Political responsibility in transnational NGO advocacy. *World Development, 28*(12), 2051–2065.

Josselson, R. (2013). *Interviewing for qualitative inquiry. A relational approach.* New York: The Guildford Press.

Kamisar, Y. (1972). How to use, abuse -and fight back with- crime statistics. *Oklahoma Law Review, 25,* 239–258.

Kane, M. (2014). Eliot Ness' revolutionary police work goes far beyond Al Capone. Retrieved February 2, 2016, from http://nypost.com/2014/02/22/eliot-ness-didnt-take-down-al-capone-but-what-he-did-is-better/

Kaplan, R. (2009). The origins of objectivity in american journalism. In S. Allan (Ed.), *The Routledge companion to news and journalism studies.* New York: Routledge.

Kapuscinski, R. (2002). *Los cinicos no sirven para este oficio.* Barcelona: Editorial Anagrama.

Karabell, Z. (2014). *The leading Indicators. A short hitory of the numbers that rule our world.* New York: Simon & Schuster.

Katz, E., & Dayan, D. (1992). *Media events: The live broadcasting of history.* Cambridge, MA: Harvard University Press.

Kawai, Y. (2005). Stereotyping Asian Americans: The dialectic of the model minority and the yellow peril. *The Howard Journal of Communications, 16*(2), 109–130.

Keim, D. A. (2002). Information visualization and visual data mining. *IEEE Transactions on Visualization and Computer Graphics, 8*(1), 1–8.

Keitel, C., Kotzmann, E., & Skovsmose, O. (1993). Beyond the tunnel vision: Analysing the relationship between mathematics, society and technology. In C. Keitel & K. Ruthven (Eds.), *Learning from computers: Mathematics education and technology* (pp. 243–279). New York: Springer.

Kelling, G. L., & Bratton, W. J. (1998). Declining crime rates: Insiders' views of the New York City story. *The Journal of Criminal Law and Criminology (1973–), 88*(4), 1217–1232.

Kidd-Hewitt, D., & Osborne, R. (1995). *Crime and the media: The post-modern spectacle.* London: Pluto Press.

Kirschbaum, E., & Shalal, A. (2016). German anti-immigrant party beats Merkel in her home district. Retrieved September 4, 2016, from http://www.reuters.com/article/us-germany-election-idUSKCN1190XG

Koch, T. (1990). *The news as a myth: Fact and context in journalism.* Westport, CT: Greenwood Press.

Korteweg, A., & Yurdakul, G. (2009). Islam, gender, and immigrant integration: Boundary drawing in discourses on honour killing in the Netherlands and Germany. *Ethnic and Racial Studies, 32*(2), 218–238.

Krippendorff, K. (2013). *Content analysis. An introduction to its methods.* London: Sage.

Krum, R. (2013). *Cool infographics: Effective communication with data visualization and design.* Indianapolis, IN: John Wiley & Sons.

Kruvand, M. (2012). "Dr. Soundbite" the making of an expert source in science and medical stories. *Science Communication, 34*(5), 566–591.

Kucharski, A. (2016). Post-truth: Study epidemiology of fake news. *Nature, 540*(7634), 525–525.

Kuhn, T. S., & Hawkins, D. (1963). The structure of scientific revolutions. *American Journal of Physics, 31*(7), 554–555.

Kunh, T. (1962). *The structure of scientific revolutions.* Chicago: The University of Chicago Press.

L'Etang, J. (1994). Public relations and corporate social responsibility: Some issues arising. *Journal of Business Ethics, 13*(2), 111–123.

L'Etang, J. (2004). *Public relations in Britain: A history of professional practice in the twentieth century.* Abingdon-on-Thames, OX: Routledge.

L'Etang, J. (2008). *Public relations.* Hoboken, NJ: Wiley Online Library.

Landau, T. C. (2014). *Challenging notions: Critical victimology in Canada.* Toronto: Canadian Scholars' Press.

Langer, J. (1998). *Tabloid television: Popular journalism and the "other news".* New York: Psychology Press.

Larsson, A. O. (2011). Interactive to me—Interactive to you? A study of use and appreciation of interactivity on Swedish newspaper websites. *New Media & Society, 13*(7), 1180–1197.

Laville, S. (2016). Violent crimes against women in England and Wales reach record high. Retrieved November 9, 2016, from https://www.theguardian.com/society/2016/sep/05/violent-crimes-against-women-in-england-and-wales-reach-record-high

Lee, A. M. (2013a). News audiences revisited: Theorizing the link between audience motivations and news consumption. *Journal of Broadcasting & Electronic Media, 57*(3), 300–317.

Lee, E. (2007). The "Yellow Peril" and Asian exclusion in the Americas. *Pacific Historical Review, 76*(4), 537–562.

Lee, M. (2013b). *Inventing fear of crime.* London: Routledge.

Léonard, S., & Kaunert, C. (2010). Reconceptualizing the audience in securitization theory. In T. Balzacq (Ed.), *Securitization theory: How security problems emerge and dissolve* (pp. 57–76). Abingdon, OX: Routledge.

Levenson, J. S., & Cotter, L. P. (2005). The effect of Megan's Law on sex offender reintegration. *Journal of Contemporary Criminal Justice, 21*(1), 49–66.

Levi, M. (2006). The media construction of financial white-collar crimes. *British Journal of Criminology, 46*(6), 1037–1057.

Levi, M., & Jones, S. (1985). Public and police perceptions of crime seriousness in England and Wales. *British Journal of Criminology, 25*(3), 234–250.

Lewis, J., Williams, A., & Franklin, B. (2008). A compromised fourth estate? UK news journalism, public relations and news sources. *Journalism Studies, 9*(1), 1–20.

Liberman, M. (2007). The pirahã and us. Retrieved April 21, 2016, from http://itre.cis.upenn.edu/~myl/languagelog/archives/004992.html

Lindgren, S. (2008). Crime, media, coding: Developing a methodological framework for computer-aided analysis. *Crime, Media, Culture, 4*(1), 95–100.

Lippmann, W. (1922). Public opinion. New York: Hartcourt Brace.

Lipschultz, J. H., & Hilt, M. L. (2014). *Crime and local television news: Dramatic, breaking, and live from the scene.* Abingdon, OX: Routledge.

Livingstone, S., & Lunt, P. (2014). Mediatization: An emerging paradigm for media and communication studies. In K. Lundby (Ed.), *Mediatization of communication. Handbooks of communication science* (Vol. 21, pp. 703–724). Berlin: De Gruyter Mouton.

Lloyd, J., & Toogood, L. (2014). *Journalism and PR: News media and public relations in the digital age.* London: IB Tauris.

Lowry, D. T., Nio, T. C. J., & Leitner, D. W. (2003). Setting the public fear agenda: A longitudinal analysis of network TV crime reporting, public perceptions of crime, and FBI crime statistics. *Journal of Communication, 53*(1), 61–73.

Lugo, J. (2007). A tale of donkeys, swans and racism: London tabloids, Scottish independence and refugees. *Communication and Social Change, 1*(1), 22–37.

Lugo-Ocando, J. (2011). Media campaigns and asylum seekers in Scotland. In M. Alleyne (Ed.), *Anti-racism & Multi-culturalism: Studies in international communication* (pp. 95–128). New Brunswick, NJ: Transaction Publishers.

Lugo-Ocando, J. (2014). *Blaming the victim: How global journalism fails those in poverty.* London: Pluto Press.

Lugo-Ocando, J., & Brandão, R. F. (2016). Stabbing news: Articulating crime statistics in the newsroom. *Journalism Practice, 10*(6), 715–729.

Lugo-Ocando, J., & Faria Brandão, R. (2015). STABBING NEWS: Articulating crime statistics in the newsroom. *Journalism Practice, 10*(6), 715–729. doi:1 0.1080/17512786.2015.1058179.

Lugo-Ocando, J., & Lawson, B. (2017). Poor numbers, poor news: The ideology of poverty statistics in the media. In A. Nguyen (Ed.), *News, numbers and public opinion in a data-driven world*. London: Bloomsbury.

Luhmann, N. (1993). *Communication and social order: Risk: A sociological theory*. Piscataway, NJ: Transaction Publishers.

Lynch, J. P., & Addington, L. A. (2006). *Understanding crime statistics: Revisiting the divergence of the NCVS and the UCR*. Cambridge: Cambridge University Press.

Lynch, T. (2000). Population bomb behind bars. Retrieved March 21, 2017, from https://www.cato.org/publications/commentary/population-bomb-behind-bars

MacDonald, Z. (2002). Official crime statistics: Their use and interpretation. *The Economic Journal, 112*(477), 85–106.

Macionis, J. J. (2017). *Sociology*. London: Pearson Higher.

Maguire, M. (2012). Criminal statistics and the construction of crime. In M. Maguire & R. Morgan (Eds.), *The Oxford handbook of criminology* (Vol. 5, pp. 206–244). Oxford: Oxford University Press.

Maier, S. R. (2003). Numeracy in the newsroom: A case study of mathematical competence and confidence. *Journalism & Mass Communication Quarterly, 80*(4), 921–936.

Maier, S. R. (2005). Accuracy matters: A cross-market assessment of newspaper error and credibility. *Journalism & Mass Communication Quarterly, 82*(3), 533–551.

Mair, G., & Burke, L. (2013). *Redemption, rehabilitation and risk management: A history of probation*. London: Routledge.

Mallows, C. (2006). Tukey's paper after 40 years. *Technometrics, 48*(3), 319–325.

Manheim, J. B., & Albritton, R. B. (1983). Changing national images: International public relations and media agenda setting. *American Political Science Review, 78*(03), 641–657.

Manning, P. (2001). *News and news sources: A critical introduction*. London: Sage.

Manning, P. (2006). There's no glamour in glue: News and the symbolic framing of substance misuse. *Crime, Media, Culture, 2*(1), 49–66.

Maras, S. (2013). *Objectivity in journalism*. Hoboken, NJ: John Wiley & Sons.

Marcinkowski, F., & Steiner, A. (2014). Mediatization and political autonomy: A systems approach. In H. Kriesi (Ed.), *Mediatization of politics: Understanding the transformation of western democracies* (pp. 74–89). Basingstoke: Palgrave Macmillan.

Marion, N. E. (1997). Symbolic policies in Clinton's crime control agenda. *Buffalo Criminal Law Review, 1*(1), 67–108.

Marsh, I., & Melville, G. (2011). Moral panics and the British media—A look at some contemporary 'folk devils'. *Internet Journal of Criminology, 1*(1), 1–21.

Martin, J. D. (Producer). (2010). Journalists need to do the math—CJR. Retrieved from http://www.cjr.org/behind_the_news/journalists_need_to_do_the_math.php

Martinisi, A. (2017). Understanding quality of statistics in news stories: A theoretical approach from the audience's perspective. In *Handbook of research on driving STEM learning with educational technologies* (pp. 485–505). Hershey, PA: IGI Global.

Martinisi, A., & Lugo-Ocando, J. (2015a). Overcoming the objectivity of the senses: Enhancing journalism practice through Eastern philosophies. *International Communication Gazette, 77*(5), 409–412.

Martinisi, A., & Lugo-Ocando, J. (2015b). Overcoming the objectivity of the senses: Enhancing journalism practice through Eastern philosophies. *International Communication Gazette, 77*(5), 439–455.

Matheson, J. (2011). *National statistician's review of crime statistics: England and Wales.* London: Government Statistical Service.

Mauer, M. (1999). Why are tough on crime policies so popular. *Stanford Law & Policy Review, 11*(1), 9.

Mawby, R. C. (2012). Crisis? What crisis? Some research-based reflections on police–press relations. *Policing, 6*(3), 272–280.

Mawby, R. C. (2010). Police corporate communications, crime reporting and the shaping of policing news. *Policing & Society, 20*(1), 124–139.

Mawby, R. C. (2014). The presentation of police in everyday life: Police–press relations, impression management and the Leveson Inquiry. *Crime, Media, Culture, 10*(3), 239–257.

Mawby, R. C., & Worthington, S. (2002). Marketing the police—From a force to a service. *Journal of Marketing Management, 18*(9-10), 857–876.

Mayhew, H. (2009 [1851]). *London labour and the London poor: A cyclopædia of the condition and earnings of those that will work, those that cannot work, and those that will not.* Lodnon: Cosimo, Inc..

Mayhew, H., & Binny, J. (1862). *The criminal prisons of London: And scenes of prison life.* London: Griffin, Bohn, and Company.

Mazzoleni, G., & Schulz, W. (1999). "Mediatization" of politics: A challenge for democracy? *Political Communication, 16*(3), 247–261.

McCombs, M. (2013). *Setting the agenda: The mass media and public opinion.* Oxford: John Wiley & Sons.

McCombs, M. E., & Shaw, D. L. (1972). The agenda-setting function of mass media. *Public Opinion Quarterly, 36*(2), 176–187.

McGibney, M., Roberts, G., Celona, L., & Pagones, S. (2016). Queens imam and his assistant executed in broad daylight. Retrieved August 17, 2016, from http://nypost.com/2016/08/13/2-wounded-in-queens-shooting/

McKenzie, R. (2008). Crime interest. Retrieved August 13, 2016, from http://www.bbc.co.uk/blogs/theeditors/2008/06/crime_interest.html

McLachlan, S., & Golding, P. (2000). Tabloidization in the British press: A quantitative investigation into changes in. In C. Sparks & J. Tulloch (Eds.), *Tabloid tales: Global debates over media standards* (pp. 75–90). Oxford: Rowman and Littlefield.

McManus, J. H. (1992). What kind of commodity is news. *Communication Research, 19*(6), 787–805.

McNair, B. (2004). PR must die: Spin, anti-spin and political public relations in the UK, 1997–2004. *Journalism Studies, 5*(3), 325–338.

McNair, B. (2009). *News and journalism in the UK.* London: Routledge.

Mears, D. P. (2007). Towards rational and evidence-based crime policy. *Journal of Criminal Justice, 35*(6), 667–682.

Miller, D., & Dinan, W. (2007). *A century of spin: How public relations became the cutting edge of corporate power.* London: Pluto Press.

Miller, J. D. (2004). Public understanding of, and attitudes toward, scientific research: What we know and what we need to know. *Public Understanding of Science, 13*(3), 273–294.

Miller, J. G. (1996). *Search and destroy: African-American males in the criminal justice system.* Cambridge: Cambridge University Press.

Mindich, D. T. Z. (1998). *Just facts: How objectivity came to define American journalism.* New York: University Press.

Moore, M. (2014). Conservatives, liberals unite to cut prison population. Retrieved August 29, 2016, from http://www.usatoday.com/story/news/politics/2014/03/16/conservatives-sentencing-reform/6396537/

Motschall, M., & Cao, L. (2002). An analysis of the public relations role of the police public information officer. *Police Quarterly, 5*(2), 152–180.

Mountz, A., & Curran, W. (2009). Policing in drag: Giuliani goes global with the illusion of control. *Geoforum, 40*(6), 1033–1040.

Murphy, P. (1991). The limits of symmetry: A game theory approach to symmetric and asymmetric public relations. *Journal of Public Relations Research, 3*(1-4), 115–131.

Murray, R. K. (1955). *Red scare: A study in National Hysteria, 1919–1920.* Minneapolis: University of Minnesota Press.

Napoli, P. M. (2011). *Audience evolution: New technologies and the transformation of media audiences*. New York: Columbia University Press.

Napoli, P. M. (2012). *Audience economics: Media institutions and the audience marketplace*. New York: Columbia University Press.

Neavling, S. (2014). Stabbings? Shootings? Detroit police stop reporting violent crimes to media, public. Retrieved February 1, 2016, from http://motorcity-muckraker.com/2014/04/03/stabbings-shootings-detroit-police-stop-reporting-violent-crimes-to-media-public/

Newburn, T., & Jones, T. (2007). Symbolizing crime control: Reflections on zero tolerance. *Theoretical Criminology, 11*(2), 221–243.

Nguyen, A., & Lugo-Ocando, J. (2015). Introduction: The state of statistics in journalism and journalism education—Issues and debates. *Journalism, 17*(1), 3–17.

Nicholls, M., & Katz, L. (2004). Michael Howard: A life in quotes. Retrieved July 2, 2016, from http://www.theguardian.com/politics/2004/aug/26/conservatives.uk

Nielsen, K. E. (2001). *Un-American womanhood: Antiradicalism, Antifeminism, and the first red scare*. Columbus: Ohio State University Press.

Noack, R. (2017). Why are European kids are committing fewer crimes? They're too busy on their phones. Retrieved February 23, 2017, from https://www.washingtonpost.com/news/worldviews/wp/2017/02/22/why-are-european-kids-are-committing-fewer-crimes-theyre-too-busy-on-their-phones/?utm_term=.f4ee7c070405

O'Keefe, G., & Reid-Nash, K. (1987). Crime news and real-world blues the effects of the media on social reality. *Communication Research, 14*(2), 147–163.

O'Neil, C. (2016). *Weapons of math destruction. How big data increases inequality and threatens democracy*. New York: Crown.

O'Neill, D., & O'Connor, C. (2008). The passive journalist: How sources dominate local news. *Journalism Practice, 2*(3), 487–500.

ONS. (2017). Crime in England and Wales: Year ending Mar 2017. *Office for National Statistics*. Retrieved June 12, 2017, from https://www.ons.gov.uk/peoplepopulationandcommunity/crimeandjustice/bulletins/crimeinenglandandwales/yearendingmar2017

Oreskes, N., & Conway, E. M. (2011). *Merchants of doubt: How a handful of scientists obscured the truth on issues from tobacco smoke to global warming*. London: Bloomsbury Publishing.

Pahre, R. (1995). Positivist discourse and social scientific communities: Towards an epistemological sociology of science. *Social Epistemology, 9*(3), 233–255.

Pahre, R. (1996). Mathematical discourse and cross-disciplinary communities: The case of political economy. *Social Epistemology, 10*(1), 55–73.

Parker, I. (1999). Qualitative data and the subjectivity of 'objective' facts. Research fails unless it engages with subjectivity. In D. Dorling & L. Simpson (Eds.), *Statistics in society. The arithmetic of politics* (pp. 83–88). London: Arnold.

Parvez, N. (2011). Visual representations of poverty: The case of Kroo Bay, Freetown. *City, 15*(6), 686–695.

Patterson, T. E. (2013). *Informing the news.* New York: Vintage.

Paulos, J. A. (1996). *A mathematician reads the newspaper.* London: Penguin Books.

Paulos, J. A. (2013 [1995]). *A mathematician reads the newspaper.* New York: Basic Books.

Perry, D. (2014). *Eliot Ness: The rise and fall of an American hero.* London: Penguin.

Pettegree, A. (2014). *The invention of news: How the world came to know about itself.* New Heaven, CT: Yale University Press.

Pfeiffer, C., Windzio, M., & Kleimann, M. (2005). Media use and its impacts on crime perception, sentencing attitudes and crime policy. *European Journal of Criminology, 2*(3), 259–285.

Philo, G., Briant, E., & Donald, P. (2013). *Bad news for refugees.* London: Pluto.

Pieczka, M., & L'Etang, J. (2006). Public relations and the question of professionalism. In J. L'Etang (Ed.), *Public relations: Critical debates and contemporary practice* (pp. 265–278). Mahwah, NJ: Lawrence Erlbaum Associates, Inc.

Plamper, J., & Lazier, B. (2010). Introduction: The phobic regimes of modernity. *Representations, 110*(1), 58–65. doi:10.1525/rep.2010.110.1.58.

Polanyi, K. (1957 [1945]). *The great transformation* (R. M. MacIver, Trans.). Boston: Beacon Press.

Popper, K. R. (1972). *Objective knowledge: An evolutionary approach.* Oxford: Oxford University Press.

Popper, K. R. (2002). *The poverty of historicism.* Abingdon-on-Thames, OX: Psychology Press.

Porter, T. (1996). *Trust in numbers: The pursuit of objectivity in science and public life.* Princeton, NJ: Princeton University Press.

Porter, T. (1997). The triumph of numbers: Civic implications of quantitative literacy. In L. Steen (Ed.), *Why numbers count: Quantitative literacy for tomorrow's America.* New York: College Board.

Potters, J., & Winden, F. (1992). Lobbying and asymmetric information. *Public Choice, 74*(3), 269–292.

Poveda, T. G. (1994). Clinton, Crime, and the Justice Department. *Social Justice, 21*(57), 73–84.

Pratt, J. (2002). *Punishment and civilization: Penal tolerance and intolerance in modern society*. London: Sage.

Prescott, J. J., & Rockoff, J. E. (2008). *Do sex offender registration and notification laws affect criminal behavior?* NBER Working Paper No. 13803. Retrieved December 13, 2016, from http://www.nber.org/papers/w13803

Preston, P. (2008). *Making the news: Journalism and news cultures in Europe*. Abingdon-on-Thames, OX: Routledge.

Protess, D., & McCombs, M. E. (2016). *Agenda setting: Readings on media, public opinion, and policymaking*. Abingdon, OX: Routledge.

Quinney, R. (1970). *The social reality of crime*. Piscataway, NJ: Transaction Publishers.

Randall, D. (2000). *The universal journalism*. London: Pluto Press.

Read, D. (1999). *The power of news: The history of reuters*. Oxford: Oxford University Press.

Reinemann, C., Stanyer, J., Scherr, S., & Legnante, G. (2012). Hard and soft news: A review of concepts, operationalizations and key findings. *Journalism, 13*(2), 221–239.

Reiner, R., Livingstone, S., & Allen, J. (2003). From law and order to lynch mobs: Crime news since the Second World War. In P. Mason (Ed.), *Criminal visions* (pp. 13–32). London: Routledge.

Robert, P., & Zauberman, R. (2009). Introduction. In P. Robert (Ed.), *Comparing crime data in Europe: Official crime statistics and survey based data*. Brussels: Brussels University Press.

Robertson, G. (2010). *The case of the Pope: Vatican accountability for human rights abuse*. London: Penguin.

Robin, C. (2004). *Fear: The history of a political idea*. Oxford: Oxford University Press.

Romer, D., Jamieson, K. H., & Aday, S. (2003). Television news and the cultivation of fear of crime. *Journal of Communication, 53*(1), 88–104.

Rosanvallon, P. (2012). *La Sociedad de los Iguales*. Barcelona: RBA Libros.

Rowbotham, J., Stevenson, K., & Pegg, S. (2013). *Crime news in modern Britain: Press reporting and responsibility, 1820–2010*. New York: Springer.

RSS. (2014). PASC sets out criticism of police-recorded crime statistics. Retrieved March 28, 2017, from https://www.statslife.org.uk/news/1352-pasc-sets-out-criticism-of-police-recorded-crime-stats

Rubin, D. M. (1987). How the news media reported on Three Mile Island and Chernobyl. *Journal of communication, 37*(3), 42–57.

Ruckenstein, M., & Pantzar, M. (2015). Datafied life: Techno-anthropology as a site for exploration and experimentation. *Techné: Research in Philosophy and Technology, 19*(2), 191–210.

Rudin, R., & Ibbotson, T. (2002). *An introduction to journalism: Essential techniques and background knowlegde.* Oxford: Focal Press.

Sacco, V. (1995). Media constructions of crime. *The Annals of the American Academy of Political and Social Science,* 141–154.

Sampson, R. J. (2013). The place of context: A theory and strategy for criminology's hard problems. *Criminology, 51*(1), 1–31.

Schechter, H. (2003). *The serial killer files: The who, what, where, how, and why of the world's most terrifying murderers.* New York: Ballantine Books.

Scheurer, V. (2009). Convicted on statistics? Retrieved March 2, 2017, from https://understandinguncertainty.org/node/545#notes

Schiller, D. (1981). *Objectivity and the news: The public and the rise of commercial journalism.* Philadelphia: University of Pennsylvania Press.

Schlesinger, P., & Tumber, H. (1994). *Reporting crime. The media politics of criminal justice.* Oxford: Oxford University Press.

Schlesinger, P., Tumber, H., & Murdock, G. (1991). The media politics of crime and criminal justice. *British Journal of Sociology, 42*(3), 397–420.

Schlueter, E., Meuleman, B., & Davidov, E. (2013). Immigrant integration policies and perceived group threat: A multilevel study of 27 Western and Eastern European countries. *Social Science Research, 42*(3), 670–682.

Schrott, A. (2009). Dimensions: Catch-all label or technical term. In K. Lundby (Ed.), *Mediatization: Concept, changes, consequences* (pp. 41–61). Bern: Peter Lang Publishing Inc..

Schudson, M. (2001). The objectivity norm in American journalism. *Journalism, 2*(2), 149–170.

Schuilenburg, M. (2015). *The securitization of society: Crime, risk, and social order.* New York: NYU Press.

Schultz, J. (1998). *Reviving the fourth estate: Democracy, accountability and the media.* Cambridge: Cambridge University Press.

Schulz, W. (2004). Reconstructing mediatization as an analytical concept. *European journal of communication, 19*(1), 87–101.

Scowcroft, H. (2009). We need to be careful when comparing US and UK cancer care. Retrieved March 21, 2017, from http://scienceblog.cancerresearchuk.org/2009/08/17/we-need-to-be-careful-when-comparing-us-and-uk-cancer-care/

Searle, J. R. (1995). *The construction of social reality*. New York: Simon and Schuster.

Sharman, D. (2016). 'What is the point of local newspapers?' Says court news agency chief. Retrieved July 20, 2016, from http://www.holdthefrontpage.co.uk/2016/news/court-news-chief-questions-point-of-local-papers-which-dont-cover-case/

Silverman, J. (2010). Addicted to getting drugs wrong. *British Journalism Review, 21*(4), 31–36.

Simon, R. J., & Sikich, K. W. (2007). Public attitudes toward immigrants and immigration policies across seven nations. *International Migration Review, 41*(4), 956–962.

Sklansky, D. A. (2012). Crime, immigration, and ad hoc instrumentalism. *New Criminal Law Review: In International and Interdisciplinary Journal, 15*(2), 157–223.

Skovsmose, O. (2014). Mathematization as social process. In O. Skovsmose (Ed.), *Encyclopedia of mathematics education* (pp. 441–445). New York: Springer.

Slovic, P. (1986). Informing and educating the public about risk. *Risk analysis, 6*(4), 403–415.

Soothill, K., Peelo, M., Pearson, J., & Francis, B. (2004). The reporting trajectories of top homicide cases in the media: A case study of The Times. *Howard Journal of Criminal Justice, 43*(1), 1–14.

Soroka, S. N. (2002). Issue attributes and agenda-setting by media, the public, and policymakers in Canada. *International Journal of Public Opinion Research, 14*(3), 264–285.

Sparks, R. (1992). *Television and the Drama of Crime*. Buckingham: Open University Press.

Spivak, G. (1988). Can the subaltern speak? In C. Nelson & L. Grossberg (Eds.), *Marxism and the Interpretation of Culture* (pp. 271–313). Urbana; Chicago: University of Illinois Press.

Stillman, S. (2007). 'The missing white girl syndrome': Disappeared women and media activism. *Gender & Development, 15*(3), 491–502.

Stocking, S. H., & Gross, P. H. (1989a). *How do journalists think? A proposal for the study of cognitive bias in newsmaking*. Bloomington: ERIC Clearinghouse on Reading and Communication Skills, Smith Research Center, Indiana University.

Stocking, S. H., & Gross, P. H. (1989b). Understanding errors, biases that can affect journalists. *The Journalism Educator, 44*(1), 4–11.

Strömbäck, J. (2008). Four phases of mediatization: An analysis of the mediatization of politics. *The International Journal of Press/Politics, 13*(3), 228–246.

Strömbäck, J., & Esser, F. (2014). Mediatization of politics: Towards a theoretical framework. In *Mediatization of politics: Understanding the transformation of western democracies* (pp. 3–27). London: Palgrave Macmillan.

Sumner, P., Vivian-Griffiths, S., Boivin, J., Williams, A., Venetis, C. A., Davies, A., … Dalton, B. (2014). The association between exaggeration in health related science news and academic press releases: Retrospective observational study. *BMJ, 349*(g7015), 1–8.

Surette, R. (1998). *Media, Crime and Criminal Justice: Images and Realities.* Belmont, CA: West/Wadsworth.

Taibbi, M. (2014). *The divide: American injustice in the age of the wealth gap.* New York: Spiegel & Grau.

Talwar, D., & Ahmad, A. (2015). 'Honour crime': 11,000 UK cases recorded in five years. Retrieved December 2, 2016, from http://www.bbc.com/news/uk-33424644

Tarde, G. (2005 [1890]). *The laws of imitation.* New York: Holt.

Taylor, J. (2011, June 1). Force writes off a third of crimes. *Metro,* p. 12.

Taylor, P. M. (1999). *British propaganda in the 20th century: Selling democracy.* Edinburgh: Edinburgh University Press.

Thomas, G., & Durant, J. (1987). Why should we promote the public understanding of science. *Scientific Literacy Papers, 1,* 1–14.

Thompson, J. B. (1995). *The media and modernity: A social theory of the media.* Cambridge: Polity Press.

Thompson, K. (2013). *Moral panics.* London: Routledge.

Thussu, D. K. (2008). *News as entertainment: The rise of global infotainment.* London: Sage.

Tiegreen, S., & Newman, E. (2008). How News is "Framed". Retrieved March 27, 2017, from https://dartcenter.org/content/how-news-is-framed

Tilley, N. (2001). Evaluation and evidence-led crime reduction policy and practice. In *Crime, disorder and community safety* (pp. 81–97). London: Routledge.

Tuchman, G. (1972). Objectivity as strategic ritual: An examination of newsmen's notions of objectivity. *American Journal of sociology, 77*(4), 660–679.

Tuchman, G. (1978). *Making news: A study in the construction of reality.* New York: Free Press.

Tuchman, G. (1980). *Making news.* New York: Free Press.

Tucker, K. (2000). *Eliot Ness and the untouchables: The Historical reality and the film and television depictions.* London: McFarland.

Tufail, W. (2015). Rotherham, Rochdale, and the racialised threat of the' Muslim Grooming Gang'. *International Journal for Crime, Justice and Social Democracy, 4*(3), 30–43.

Tufte, E. (2001). *The visual display of quantitative information.* Chesire, CT: The Graphic Press.

Underwood, D. (1993). *When MBAs rule the newsroom: How markets and managers are shaping today's media.* New York: Columbia University Press.

Ungar, S. (2001). Moral panic versus the risk society: The implications of the changing sites of social anxiety. *The British Journal of Sociology, 52*(2), 271–291.

Utts, J. (2003). What educated citizens should know about statistics and probability. *The American Statistician, 57*(2), 74–79.

Utts, J. (Producer). (2010). Unintentional lies in the media: Don't blame journalists for what we don't teach. Retrieved from http://citeseerx.ist.psu.edu/viewdoc/summary?doi=10.1.1.205.227

Valentino, N. A., Brader, T., & Jardina, A. E. (2013). Immigration opposition among US Whites: General ethnocentrism or media priming of attitudes about Latinos? *Political Psychology, 34*(2), 149–166.

Van Dijck, J. (2014). Datafication, dataism and dataveillance: Big Data between scientific paradigm and ideology. *Surveillance & Society, 12*(2), 197–208.

Van Dijk, J. (2009). Approximating the truth about crime: Comparing crime data based on general population surveys with police figures of recorded crime. In P. Robert (Ed.), *Comparing crime data in Europe: Official crime statistics and survey based data.* Brussels: Brussels University Press.

Vanlandingham, G. R., & Drake, E. K. (2012). Results first: Using evidence-based policy models in state policymaking. *Public Performance & Management Review, 35*(3), 550–563.

Vásquez, B. E., Maddan, S., & Walker, J. T. (2008). The influence of sex offender registration and notification laws in the United States: A time-series analysis. *Crime & Delinquency.* doi:10.1177/0011128707311641.

Von Roten, F. C. (2006). Do we need a public understanding of statistics? *Public Understanding of Science, 15*(2), 243–249.

Wacquant, L. (2011). From 'public criminology' to the reflexive sociology of criminological production and consumption a review of public criminology? by Ian Loader and Richard Sparks (London: Routledge, 2010). *British Journal of Criminology, 51*(2), 438–448.

Waddington, P. (1986). Mugging as a moral panic: A question of proportion. *British Journal of Sociology, 37,* 245–259.

Weitzer, R., & Kubrin, C. E. (2004). Breaking news: How local TV news and real-world conditions affect fear of crime. *Justice Quarterly, 21*(3), 497–520.

Welch, M., Fenwick, M., & Roberts, M. (1997). Primary definitions of crime and moral panic: A content analysis of experts' quotes in feature newspaper articles on crime. *Journal of Research in Crime and Delinquency, 34*(4), 474–494.

Welsh, B. C., & Farrington, D. P. (2004). Surveillance for crime prevention in public space: Results and policy choices in Britain and America. *Criminology & Public Policy, 3*(3), 497–526.

Wien, C. (2005). Defining objectivity within journalism. *Nordicom Review, 26*(2), 3–15.

Wilby, P. (Producer). (2007). Damn journalists and statistics. *The Guardian.* Retrieved from http://www.theguardian.com/media/2007/nov/05/monday-mediasection.pressandpublishing

Williams, A., Wardle, C., & Wahl-Jorgensen, K. (2011). "Have they got news for us?" Audience revolution or business as usual at the BBC? *Journalism Practice, 5*(1), 85–99.

Williams, M. C. (2003). Words, images, enemies: Securitization and international politics. *International studies quarterly, 47*(4), 511–531.

Williams, P., & Dickinson, J. (1993a). Fear of crime: Read all about it? The relationship between newspaper crime reporting and fear of crime. *British journal of criminology, 33*(1), 33–56.

Williams, P., & Dickinson, J. (1993b). Mass media, drugs and deviance. In P. Rock & M. McIntosh (Eds.), *Deviance and social control* (pp. 33–56). London: Tavistock.

Winston, B. (2002). Towards tabloidization? Glasgow revisited, 1975–2001. *Journalism Studies, 3*(1), 5–20.

Wood, J. C. (2016). Crime news and the press. In P. Knepper & A. Johansen (Eds.), *The Oxford Handbook of the history of crime and criminal justice* (pp. 301–319). Oxford: Oxford University Press.

Worley, W. (2016). Normandy church attack: France fears religious war after symbolic killing of Catholic priest. Retrieved August 17, 2016, from http://www.independent.co.uk/news/world/europe/france-cchurch-attack-normandy-latest-news-religion-jacques-hamel-adel-kermiche-isis-a7157556.html

Xu, J., & Chen, H. (2005). Criminal network analysis and visualization. *Communications of the ACM, 48*(6), 100–107.

Yang, X. (2016). *Analysing datafied life*. Ph.D. in Computing, Imperial College London, London. Retrieved from https://spiral.imperial.ac.uk/handle/10044/1/33722

Yau, N. (2011). *Visualize this. The flowing data guide to design, visualisation and statistics*. Indianapolis, IN: Wiley Piblishing, Inc.

Yau, N. (2013). *Data points: Visualization that means something*. Hoboken, NJ: John Wiley & Sons.

Young, R. K., & Veldman, D. J. (1972). *Introductory statistics for the behavioral sciences* (2nd ed.). New York: Holt, Rinehart, Winston.

Zelizer, B. (1993a). Has communication explained journalism? *Journal of Communication, 43*(4), 80–88.

Zelizer, B. (1993b). Journalists as interpretive communities. *Critical Studies in Media Communication, 10*(3), 219–237.

Zelizer, B. (2004). *Taking journalism seriously: News and the academy*. London: Sage.

Zimring, F. (2006). *The great American crime decline*. Oxford: Oxford University Press.

Zuberi, T. (2001). *Thicker than blood: How racial statistics lie*. Minneapolis: Minnesota Press.

Index[1]

[1] Note: Page numbers followed by "n" refers to note.

© The Author(s) 2017
J. Lugo-Ocando, *Crime Statistics in the News*,
DOI 10.1057/978-1-137-39841-3

Printed in the United States
By Bookmasters